OSGi and Apache Felix 3.0
Beginner's Guide

Build your very own OSGi applications using the flexible and powerful Felix Framework

Walid Gédéon

[PACKT] open source
PUBLISHING   community experience distilled

BIRMINGHAM - MUMBAI

OSGi and Apache Felix 3.0

Beginner's Guide

First published: November 2010

Production Reference: 1291010

Published by Packt Publishing Ltd.
32 Lincoln Road
Olton
Birmingham, B27 6PA, UK.

ISBN 978-1-849511-38-4

www.packtpub.com

Cover Image by John M. Quick (john.m.quick@gmail.com)

Credits

Author

Walid Gédéon

Reviewers

Thorsten Harbig

Jettro Coenradie

Acquisition Editor

Chaitanya Apte

Development Editor

Chaitanya Apte

Technical Editor

Prashant Macha

Copy Editor

Leonard D'Silva

Indexers

Hemangini Bari

Rekha Nair

Editorial Team Leader

Mithun Sehgal

Project Team Leader

Priya Mukherji

Project Coordinator

Jovita Pinto

Proofreader

Lynda Silwoski

Graphics

Nilesh Mohite

Production Coordinator

Aparna Bhagat

Cover Work

Aparna Bhagat

About the Author

Walid Gédéon is a telecommunications network and OSS expert. His experience over the past decade has been focused on distributed software architecture and development, including the re-architecture, integration of systems, and data transformation, in the context of mergers of telecommunications companies and the improvement of their processes, operations, and support.

This book would not have been possible without the extensive and generous contributions from the online open source community: We are the change we want to see in this world.

About the Reviewers

Thorsten Harbig was born on August 30, 1977. He grew up at Lake Constance in the Southern part of Germany. After high school, he started studying physics at the University of Constance. While there, his interest in programming and software development drove him towards studying computer sciences instead. Working on his Diploma thesis, he spent seven months abroad at the University in Ghent (Belgium). Two years later, he finished his Master's degree about energy savings on mobile phones at the Aalborg University in Denmark. In 2006, Thorsten started working for LogicLine, a software consulting company in Sindelfingen near Stuttgart (Germany). In his daily work, he is a Java specialist for an internationally-active corporation in the automotive industry. From time to time, he teaches JEE courses and is eager to use new technologies. At the moment, he is fond of Groovy and its frameworks.

Thorsten Harbig was married on December 27, 2007 and has a son. He enjoys martial arts, role playing games, and geocaching.

Jettro Coenradie is a software architect and developer for 12 years now. He has gained a lot of experience in enterprise Java while working for large organizations in finance, transport, and government. Jettro is always looking for new technologies to help him meet the challenges of customers. This is how he got involved with Spring framework, OSGi, Flex, Grails, and the Axon framework. A big part of his enthusiasm for new technologies is reflected by sharing his knowledge through presentations at conferences, writing articles, and maintaining a blog together along with a few others.

Jettro is currently the Chief Architect at JTeam B.V, a Java software house situated in the Netherlands.

Table of Contents

Preface

The OSGi specification is a module system and service platform that implements a complete and dynamic component model. Wasn't that a complicated definition! So how would you really use it to practical modular applications? Let this book break down the seemingly overwhelming OSGi standards for you by explaining Apache Felix's powerful architecture in a simple and easy-to-understand manner using Apache Felix framework to get you up and running sooner than you expect.

The OSGi standards have found a wide range of applications in the context of the Enterprise, Telecommunications, Telematics, Smart Home, E-Health, and Mobile, to name just a few. Apache Felix is one of the most famous implementations of the OSGi framework specification. This book introduces OSGi on the simple and extensible Felix framework and guides the reader from the development environment setup to the troubleshooting of potential issues, walking them through the development of an OSGi-based application and explaining relevant software design concepts.

This book starts with an introduction to the OSGi Service Platform, its parts and its bundle structure. It then walks the reader through the Felix framework's setup and their development environment. It describes the Felix Framework and how to operate it using Gogo. This book will teach you everything possible about the practical implementation of OSGi using the Felix Framework as a launch pad.

The book then kicks off the Bookshelf project, a case study that will be used to progressively explain the important concepts around OSGi using the Felix framework. The Bookshelf project feature trail will set the context to explain OSGi headers, the bundle activator, the bundle context and so on.

As the reader implements the bookshelf step by step, they learn about OBR repositories, dependency management, and bundle version management with Felix.

Moving ahead, a few more advanced topics are covered, such as using iPOJO for dependency injection and service registration; then carries onto the implementation of a web-based graphical interface, first using a simple Servlet, and then building a JSP-based Web Application Bundle.

OSGi service specifications such as the Log Service, Http Service, and Web Container are explained. Finally, the book describes some of the common pitfalls during bundle development and hints on troubleshooting them in Felix.

What this book covers

Chapter 1, Quick intro to OSGi and Felix gives an overview of OSGi and introduces Felix

Chapter 2, Setting up the Environment walks the reader through the pre-requisites needed for developing as they read.

Chapter 3, Felix Gogo covers the Felix Gogo command-line shell and syntax.

Chapter 4, Let's Get Started: The Bookshelf Project sets the scope of work for the case study and describes the chapter-by-chapter learning process to achieve it.

Chapter 5, The Book Inventory Bundle starts the case study inventory layer implementation and covers the basics of integrating with an OSGi framework.

Chapter 6, Using the OSGi Bundle Repository covers OBRs and shows how to use them to install the bundles developed in Chapter 5.

Chapter 7, The Bookshelf: First Stab continues the case study by laying the business logic middle tier on top of the inventory layer showing how to get access to and interact with services from other bundles on the framework.

Chapter 8, Adding a Command-Line Interface adds a first presentation layer to the case study showing how to extend the Gogo shell with custom commands.

Chapter 9, Improving the Bookshelf Service with iPOJO covers Felix iPOJO and shows how to use it for registering and injecting services. It also explains some of the major design patterns used in this context.

Chapter 10, Improving the Logging explains the importance of logging in an application, and shows how to send logs to an OSGi Log Service implementation.

Chapter 11, How about a Graphical Interface? continues the case study by implementing a simple servlet-based presentation in an OSGi framework, using the Http Service.

Chapter 12, The Web Management Console provides an overview of the Felix Web Management Console and takes the reader through the steps to install it.

Chapter 13, *Improving the Graphics* completes the case study by implementing a JSP Web Application Bundle and explaining Web Containers in the context of OSGi.

Chapter 14, *Pitfalls and Troubleshooting* includes a few tips on common issues faced when writing a bundle and describes a few means to troubleshoot them.

Appendix A, Eclipse, Maven, and Felix is an introduction to some of the productivity tools available for a Java developer in general and to an OSGi developer in specific. It covers the combined use of Eclipse as an **Integrated Development Environment (IDE)** along with plugins useful in the context of the development of OSGi bundles and Maven 2 as a build and dependency management system.

Appendix B, Where to Go from Here? provides a few leads on topics that can be investigated after having mastered the book contents, as well as a few reference sites to get more information.

What you need for this book

Armed with your background in Java programming, you're expected to develop the case study as you read the book.

You'll need a computer with access to the Internet to download the (free) software components that are installed throughout the book which include a Java Development Kit, the Felix Framework Distribution, Maven 2, and Eclipse Helios.

Many of the additional components will be retrieved and installed by the environment that will be set up in *Chapter 2, Setting up the Environment*.

Who this book is for

If you are a Java developer new to OSGi and don't really know where to start from to actually begin developing applications just pick up this book and discover the ease with which you can start developing powerful, modular and extensible applications. This book uses the Felix framework 3.0 as an OSGi service platform implementation, and covers its usage to a level where it makes you comfortable enough to write your own enterprise-level applications. This book is aimed at Java developers looking to learn about writing reusable and network distributable software following the OSGi standards using the famous Felix framework. If you are a developer who wants to focus on the business logic, and abstract away from the details of how to integrate with specific systems, then this book is meant for you.

Conventions

In this book, you will find a number of styles of text that distinguish between different kinds of information. Here are some examples of these styles, and an explanation of their meaning.

Code words in text are shown as follows: "We can include other contexts through the use of the include directive."

A block of code is set as follows:

```
public class MyClass {
    public static void main(String[] args) {
    }
}
```

When we wish to draw your attention to a particular part of a code block, the relevant lines or items are set in bold:

```
public class MyClass {
    public static void main(String[] args) {
        // this line was just added
    }
}
```

Any command-line input or output is written as follows:

```
g! frameworklevel
Level is 1
```

In some instances, the command-line input or output may be reformatted to show clearly on the book page.

New terms and **important words** are shown in bold. Words that you see on the screen, in menus or dialog boxes for example, appear in the text like this: "clicking the **Next** button moves you to the next screen".

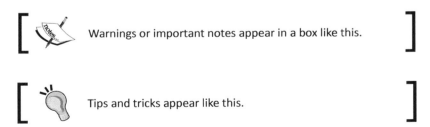

Warnings or important notes appear in a box like this.

Tips and tricks appear like this.

Reader feedback

Feedback from our readers is always welcome. Let us know what you think about this book—what you liked or may have disliked. Reader feedback is important for us to develop titles that you really get the most out of.

To send us general feedback, simply send an e-mail to feedback@packtpub.com, and mention the book title via the subject of your message.

If there is a book that you need and would like to see us publish, please send us a note in the **SUGGEST A TITLE** form on www.packtpub.com or e-mail suggest@packtpub.com.

If there is a topic that you have expertise in and you are interested in either writing or contributing to a book, see our author guide on www.packtpub.com/authors.

Customer support

Now that you are the proud owner of a Packt book, we have a number of things to help you to get the most from your purchase.

> **Downloading the example code for this book**
>
> You can download the example code files for all Packt books you have purchased from your account at http://www.PacktPub.com. If you purchased this book elsewhere, you can visit http://www.PacktPub.com/support and register to have the files e-mailed directly to you.

Errata

Although we have taken every care to ensure the accuracy of our content, mistakes do happen. If you find a mistake in one of our books—maybe a mistake in the text or the code—we would be grateful if you would report this to us. By doing so, you can save other readers from frustration and help us improve subsequent versions of this book. If you find any errata, please report them by visiting http://www.packtpub.com/support, selecting your book, clicking on the **errata submission form** link, and entering the details of your errata. Once your errata are verified, your submission will be accepted and the errata will be uploaded on our website, or added to any list of existing errata, under the Errata section of that title. Any existing errata can be viewed by selecting your title from http://www.packtpub.com/support.

Piracy

Piracy of copyright material on the Internet is an ongoing problem across all media. At Packt, we take the protection of our copyright and licenses very seriously. If you come across any illegal copies of our works, in any form, on the Internet, please provide us with the location address or website name immediately so that we can pursue a remedy.

Please contact us at copyright@packtpub.com with a link to the suspected pirated material.

We appreciate your help in protecting our authors, and our ability to bring you valuable content.

Questions

You can contact us at questions@packtpub.com if you are having a problem with any aspect of the book, and we will do our best to address it.

1
Quick Intro to Felix and OSGi

In the current fast evolving market, service providers need a way to quickly deploy new services over their networks in a managed manner. The challenge is to deliver new and updated services to devices over the network, with little or no disruption to other services provided by those devices.

Furthermore, services may be required to run on a multitude of potential targets such as embedded systems, home electronics, cable modems, set-top boxes, media gateways, and so on. A different delivery of this service per target environment constitutes an expensive overhead that is not necessary.

A universal platform with a common framework and a minimal execution environment would allow a faster time to market, reducing the component development and testing time, and thus allowing providers to quickly react to changes in the market needs.

The OSGi service platform specification aims to address this need by providing a universal platform on which applications (or bundles) can be downloaded and plugged into its base framework.

In this book, we will focus on OSGi in the context of the enterprise. Although all of the concepts introduced also apply to the other environments where OSGi is used, some of the additional discussions will be more appropriate for an enterprise service platform.

In this chapter, we will take a quick overview of the OSGi service platform and how it addresses the current market needs. We will also have a first look at the Apache Felix implementation and how it fits into the OSGi world.

You will:

◆ Take a quick overview of OSGi

◆ Understand the OSGi service platform, its functional layers, and their interaction

◆ Take a deep dive into OSGi bundles, their manifest headers

◆ Understand how bundles are activated on an OSGi platform

◆ Learn about bundle start levels and how they can be used in start-up schema

◆ Get an introduction to the Felix framework

What is OSGi?

Started in 1999 as the Open Services Gateway initiative, the OSGi alliance initially targeted embedding Java technology for networked home gateways. It has grown into a cross-market framework for the delivery of services onto a wide variety of devices ranging from customer premise equipments to cars and mobile phones, and from backend servers to home PCs.

With a widespread adoption by the Open Source community and constant improvement brought by the big market players that make up the alliance, the applications of this flexible framework has gained a fast momentum and was greatly improved in the last few releases of its specifications.

The main benefits of the OSGi framework is the standardized means of deploying and maintaining its modular system over the network; a modular system that is based on a non-intrusive, yet powerful set of specifications.

Among the many adopters of OSGi as an application framework in the Open Source community are Knopflerfish, Equinox (Eclipse), and Felix. We will be working with the Apache Felix OSGi service platform implementation.

The OSGi Service Platform's Core Specification documents the framework's expected behavior and also specifies the way its different parts interact, and react to external requests in order to offer its managed services.

This Core Specification is augmented with a set of service specifications, grouped by target market, and includes the definition of service interfaces for the common services in that market, along with specifications on how those services are to behave. Those include:

- ◆ The Service Compendium, which contains the specifications of OSGi services such as:
    - ❏ The Preferences service, which holds bundles' preferences in a persistent manner
    - ❏ The Event Admin service, which helps bundles communicate through the exchange of events

- ◆ The Enterprise Specification focuses on the enterprise side of things such as distribution, scalability, and so on. The Enterprise expert group is supported by many of the major players in the Java enterprise market such as IBM, Oracle, and SAP, to name a few. For more on this, please refer to `http://www.osgi.org/Markets/Enterprise`.

We will look more closely at the Log Service and HTTP Service from the Service Compendium in *Chapter 10, Improve the Logging* and *Chapter 11, How about a Graphical Interface?* respectively.

Moreover, the applications of OSGi extend into other market segments in addition to the enterprise with the following expert groups:

- ◆ The Mobile market, which focuses on building a robust and secure platform for mobile phones, with implementations available for the major mobile operating systems (such as Android, Windows Mobile, Symbian, Brew, and Linux). For more on this, please refer to `http://www.osgi.org/Markets/Mobile`

- ◆ The Telematics market, which focuses on automotive, railway systems, shipment tracking, and so on. For more on this, please refer to `http://www.osgi.org/Markets/Telematics`

- ◆ The Smart Home market, which focuses on the adaptation and uses of this universal platform in the residential context. Applications range from the streaming of audio and video for entertainment and education, to the monitoring and management of energy consumption. For more on this, please refer to `http://www.osgi.org/Markets/SmartHome`

- ◆ The E-Health market, which focuses on applications in the field of health services, with applications in areas such as hospitalization, personal training programs, or assisted living. For more on this, please refer to `http://www.osgi.org/Markets/EHealth`

In short, the applications of OSGi are limitless and with a wide involvement from many disparate parties. Do you think you can contributing? If yes, you can consider following one of the previous groups and contribute your experience!

Let's take a look at the layout of an OSGi service platform and understand the way it works.

The framework layout

The modular entity in an OSGi framework is referred to as a **bundle**. A bundle is a collection of code, resources, and configuration files that are packaged as a **Java ARchive (JAR)**.

A bundle can be compared to a **Web ARchive (WAR)** in the context of a web container, or to an **Enterprise ARchive (EAR)** in the context of a Java Enterprise Platform. For example, a web container would inspect the contents of a WAR for configuration, resources, and code that it needs to publish the web application and manage its lifecycle.

In the OSGi world, the framework focuses on the functionality that's required to operate the bundle as an entity with a lifecycle and provides code and services. It then communicates changes to the other components in the framework and the installed bundles.

For example, as we will see in *Chapter 13*, *Improving the Graphics*, a web container installed as a bundle listens to bundles that are installed and grabs those that are identified as web applications for registration. The web container would be a service published by a bundle on the framework. In this case, both the web container and the web application are bundles installed on the framework—one bundle using the other to provide a service.

Such a split of responsibilities (for example, web application publishing and lifecycle management) offers a greater flexibility in the design of a service platform. It is also applied within the framework in the organization of its components.

The functional layers

The components in the OSGi framework are grouped into distinct functional layers. Each layer is responsible for a specific set of tasks related to the integration of the bundle with the framework. Those layers are explained as follows:

- The **execution environment layer**, which is the bottom layer on which the bundles live, is selected to fit the underlying hardware or operating system. Two examples of the common execution environments are CDC-1.1/Foundation-1.1 and JavaSE-1.6. Others can be found in Table 3.2 of the OSGi Core specification.

- The **module layer**, which is the bundle space, holds the bundles that are installed on the framework and are managed through the lifecycle layer.

- The **lifecycle layer** manages and keeps track of the frameworks and bundles lifecycle state. It is used to install or uninstall framework objects and start or stop them.

◆ The **service layer**, which holds the service-side of the framework, keeps the service registry and manages it.

◆ The **security layer**, which extends the Java 2 security architecture, is optional. When active, it validates bundle signatures, and controls component access rights.

Although we're only going to use the service layer to register our services during this case study, it is interesting to understand the functional breakdown of the framework.

The clear definition of the interfaces of the components in each layer allows for a better flexibility in the implementation of a framework, as well as a well-defined means for bundles to communicate with the service platform.

For example, a different execution environment layer would be selected depending on the target system on which the framework will run. This will happen without affecting the other layers or the bundles that are installed on the platform.

The following diagram depicts this layering and shows some of the interaction between the layers of the framework:

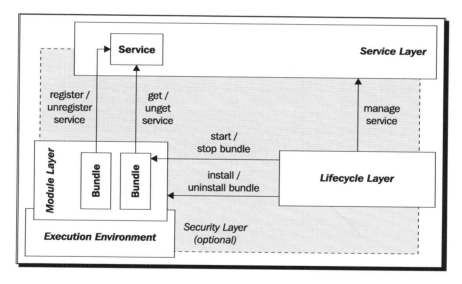

The bundles are kept in a sort of a sandbox and wired together, based on their declared requirements. This not only allows you to enforce a tight control over class visibility, but it also keeps track of which packages a bundle is using from other bundles. This control helps manage bundles better, resulting in the possibility to decide when a bundle can be updated without resetting the bundles that depend on it, allowing runtime update of bundles.

The bundle lifecycle states

The lifecycle of a bundle within a framework starts with its install. A bundle can be installed either by another bundle in the framework, using the framework API, or via the framework implementation.

For example, as we will see in *Chapter 5, The Book Inventory Bundle*, the Felix framework provides a shell command (the `install` command) that is used to install bundles. The shell service is installed as a bundle and exposes the command for use as part of the console.

Before a bundle is active on the framework, it must go through the resolution process, in which the module layer reads its manifest headers, performs required checks, and identifies the bundle's dependencies.

When a bundle is successfully resolved, it can be started and the lifecycle layer takes over the process. If a bundle activator is provided with the bundle (using the `Bundle-Activator` header), then the framework will use it to activate the bundle for initialization. The framework gives control to the bundle activator through the `start()` method. We'll look more closely at bundle activation in *Chapter 5*.

The activation can be eager or `lazy`, as defined by the `Bundle-ActivationPolicy` header we introduced a bit earlier.

With the eager activation policy, the bundle is activated as soon as it is done starting. When the activation policy is set to `lazy`, then the bundle is only activated when the first class from that bundle is loaded.

The following state machine describes the states that a bundle can go through during its lifecycle. It also shows the actions that are performed on the bundle to shift its state.

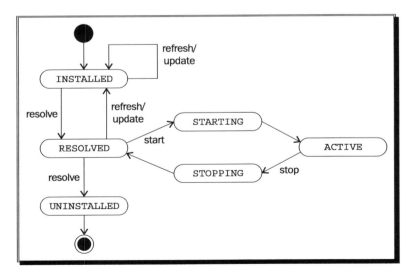

Those states are as follows:

- **INSTALLED**: The bundle has been successfully installed. The framework knows enough about this bundle to attempt to load it.
- **RESOLVED**: All resources needed for this bundle have been loaded successfully and the bundle is ready to be started. This is also the state the bundle would be in, once successfully stopped.
- **STARTING**: The bundle is being started, but has not finished starting.
- **ACTIVE**: The bundle has been successfully activated and is running, ready to be used.
- **STOPPING**: The bundle is being stopped, but has not finished stopping.
- **UNINSTALLED**: The bundle has been uninstalled. Once uninstalled, nothing can be done with the module.

As we'll see in *Chapter 5*, by defining a bundle activator, the framework will temporarily give the bundle control of the execution flow when it is in the starting and stopping states by calling the bundle activator's `start()` and `stop()` methods.

Unless instructed otherwise (that is, by requesting start or stop in transient mode), the framework will keep track of whether a bundle is active and attempt to restore that state at the next startup. When the bundle is started, it is persistently marked for start.

Bundle wiring

Without going into the details of the class loading and visibility constraints, it's worth knowing that the framework keeps separate codebases for the different bundles, controlling how each bundle's classes are loaded and which classes a bundle can "see". The process of linking a bundle to provide its access to another bundle's content is called **wiring**.

When the framework resolves a bundle for installation, it reads the bundle manifest looking for its capabilities (the packages it provides or exports) and its requirements (those that it imports). It uses this information to wire the bundles together in a mesh of dependencies, thus constructing the class space visible to each bundle.

This mechanism allows each bundle to clearly define which of its packages (and classes) are hidden from other bundles and which are shared.

For example, if Bundle B exports package `b` and Bundle C exports package `c`, then those packages are made available for bundles that require them on the framework.

Here, Bundle A imports packages b and c. Those bundle capabilities and requirements are expressed in the form of the `Import-Package` and `Export-Package` OSGi headers that we'll see in a bit.

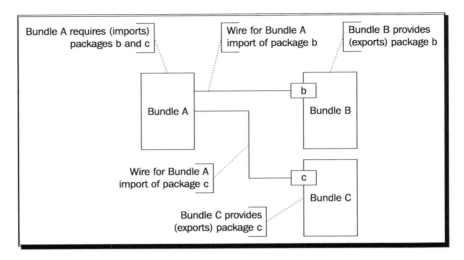

The preceding diagram is a simple view of this wiring. The wires are actually a bit more complex and keep track of constraints such as dependency version ranges, optional dependencies, and so on.

If Bundle C were not installed and package c is not provided by another bundle, then Bundle A cannot be resolved successfully because of its missing dependency.

The shared service registry

As part of the activation process, a bundle may register services with the framework's service layer registry. Services are meant to be shared among bundles in the framework.

When a bundle needs to publish a service for use by other bundles, it instantiates that service. Then using the service interface, which will identify the service within the framework, the bundle registers the service with the framework-shared service registry.

From this point, until the bundle unregisters the service, other bundles can then find and get the service, using the service interface to look it up without knowing which bundle has provided it.

Services and their interfaces can be defined and implemented by any provider (or vendor). However, there are a standard set of interfaces for some of the commonly used services defined by the OSGi specifications. This standard definition allows vendors to provide their own implementations of a service, without binding the service consumer to their proprietary interface.

As we will see in *Chapter 9, Improving the Bookshelf Service with iPOJO*, there are also a few ways to abstract away from the service registration and lookup process by using a configuration-based service definition and injection.

Working with bundles

A bundle is very much like a regular JAR, archived in a standard ZIP format.

The main difference between an OSGi bundle and a regular JAR is the additional headers in the manifest file that describe the bundle, providing the framework bundle information such as identity, version, and so on; as well as instructions relating to what this bundle provides as functionality and what it requires from the other bundles on the framework.

Anatomy of a bundle

A bundle holds the resources that are needed for it to provide functionality such as Java classes, HTML files, images, embedded JARs, and so on. It also holds its OSGi header entries in the JAR manifest file. The manifest file is found under META-INF/MANIFEST.MF.

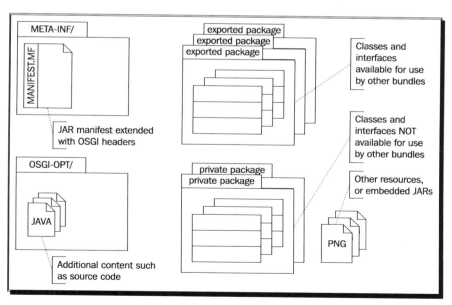

The optional OSGI-OPT/ directory can be used to store additional resources that are not needed for the proper functioning of the bundle: resources such as source code and additional documentation. The framework may choose to throw this content away, if it needs to save storage space.

Another standard OSGi directory that can also be present in a bundle archive is the OSGI-INF/ directory. This is typically used to hold bundle-related configuration and properties, used by other framework bundles when processing this bundle's registration. For example, declarative services' configurations may be placed in this directory.

As we'll see in a bit, among the OSGi manifest header entries are directives for which packages are to be exported and made available to other bundles. The other packages are private and can only be seen and used within the bundle.

The OSGi headers

The bundle uses its manifest meta-data to provide the framework with identity information, description of its content, and directives on how the framework should use this content.

When an OSGi framework attempts to resolve a bundle, it will read and process its header entries. Headers follow strict naming and format rules, the framework will ignore headers that are unknown.

The remainder of this section quickly covers the OSGi headers, stopping on a few for a more detailed description. Many of the headers described in the following sections allow optional parameters, or directives, in their syntax. Those directives are mentioned in some situations, but may have been omitted for simplicity. It is recommended that you refer to the OSGi Core Specifications documentation to get the complete syntax description.

Mandatory headers

The minimal set of headers required by an OSGi framework to correctly register a bundle is the Bundle-ManifestVersion and the Bundle-SymbolicName.

The Bundle-ManifestVersion specifies the version of the manifest header syntax. For the scope of this book, we're following version 4 of the Core Specifications. This header will have the value 2:

```
Bundle-ManifestVersion: 2
```

Combined with the bundle version, the Bundle-SymbolicName uniquely identifies the bundle within a framework.

Although not required, it is recommended that the symbolic name be based on the reverse domain name of the bundle provider. For example, the Felix Shell Service bundle, a Felix sub-project which is a project of the Apache Foundation (`apache.org`), has the symbolic name `org.apache.felix.shell`.

The `Bundle-SymbolicName` may also include optional parameters, or directives, such as `singleton` and `fragment-attachment`, which we won't describe here.

Functional headers

Some headers define the bundle requirement from the service platform, for example, the `Bundle-RequiredExecutionEnvironment` declares the list of execution environments this bundle requires to be present on the platform.

During the wiring process, information provided by headers such as `Import-Package` and `Export-Package` is used to know the capabilities and requirements of the bundle.

For example, the `Import-Package` header declares the packages that the bundle imports, that is, the packages that it needs from other bundles. The `Require-Bundle` header is used to declare that this bundle imports all packages exported by the specified, comma-separated, and bundle symbolic names.

The lifecycle layer allows the bundle to take part in the activation process. By providing a class as a `Bundle-Activator`. The bundle activator is given the execution control when (the bundle) is starting. The `Bundle-ActivationPolicy` specifies whether the framework should activate the bundle in a `lazy` manner once started or in an eager manner. Eager activation is signified by omitting the header.

The `Bundle-Version` header specifies the version of this bundle. A version is composed of a major part, optionally followed by a minor, micro, and qualifier parts. Those parts are dot separated. When not specified, the version of a bundle is set to `0.0.0`.

We'll talk a little more about versions in *Chapters 4, Let's Get Started: The Bookshelf Project*, and *Chapter 5, The Book Inventory bundle*.

Fragments are bundles that attach to other bundles, called hosts, to extend their host with manifest headers and bundle content. They are typically used to add resources such as localization files, graphical themes, and so on. Fragments declare the host that they wish to attach with the `Fragment-Host` header.

Information headers

Other headers are given for information purposes. They provide additional information to the bundle consumer.

For example, the `Bundle-Name` and `Bundle-Description` headers provide a human-readable name and a short description for the bundle. The `Bundle-Category` header tags this bundle with a set of category names. It is a comma-separated list of category names.

The `Bundle-ContactAddress` header provides the contact address of the vendor, and the `Bundle-Copyright` header contains the copyright specification for the bundle.

Many other information headers have not been listed here. The core specification is a good place to get a full listing along with a description of their usage.

Start levels

Although this is not necessary with well designed and implemented bundles, there is value in being able to define a sequence in which bundles are started when starting a service platform. This is to control the start and stop of groups of installed bundles, stepwise.

The Start Level Service

The Start Level Service on the OSGi framework allows just that—the idea is to assign a "bundle start level" to each bundle, a non-negative number, and to be able to change the "active start level" in a stepwise manner in order to control which group of bundles are active at that time.

The Start Level Service also allows setting an initial bundle start level to be assigned to newly installed bundles. The default bundle start level is 1. This level can be changed by either issuing a command to change it (we'll cover this command in *Chapter 3, Felix Gogo*) or by changing it in the framework configuration. In Felix, the configuration property to set the initial bundle start level is:

```
felix.startlevel.bundle=1
```

Change this property in `conf/config.properties` of the installed distribution.

The active start level

For example, in the following diagram, we have a Felix instance with an additional three bundles installed (bundles A, B, and C). In this example, the installed bundles are given start level 2 and Bundle C is not started.

The start level 0 is assigned to the System Bundle, no other bundle is allowed on that start level, and the bundles provided with the Felix distribution are on start level 1.

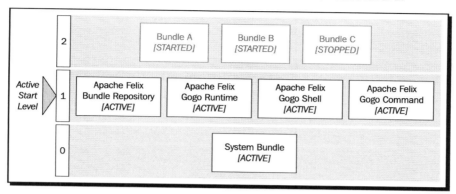

When the framework is starting up, it will first have an active start level of 0, at which point the System Bundle is starting. Once this is done, it will go onto start level 1 and start all the bundles that were persistently marked for start. All bundles on a start level are started before going onto the next.

In the *Chapter 3*, we'll look at some of the Felix shell commands and learn how to check and change the active and bundle start levels.

In this example, if we change the framework's active start level, it will attempt to start Bundle A and Bundle B, and then set the active start level to 3.

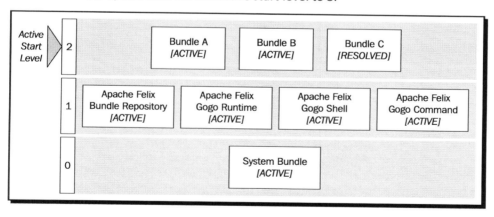

Since Bundle C was not persistently marked as started (it's stopped), it will only be resolved.

By default, Felix will start up until active start level 1. To make it set a different active start level on startup, change the configuration entry that sets the beginning start level; for example, to set it to 3, you would add a property in `conf/config.properties` as such:

```
org.osgi.framework.startlevel.beginning=3
```

ing start levels

nentioned previously, there are cases where grouping the start of bundles into distinct
ɔs can be useful.

For example, in development scenarios, one may want to split the bundles into "Validated"
and "Under Test" and assign those the start levels of 2 and 3 respectively. This would allow
separating bundles that may cause issues from the others and control their startup
more closely.

In other situations, when the start-up time is lengthy, a splash screen bundle may be placed
on start level 1 and would only be removed when all bundles are started.

In our case, we will separate the bundles from a functional point of view. Those bundles are
assigned start levels that simplify the operational and support activities needed to maintain
the application:

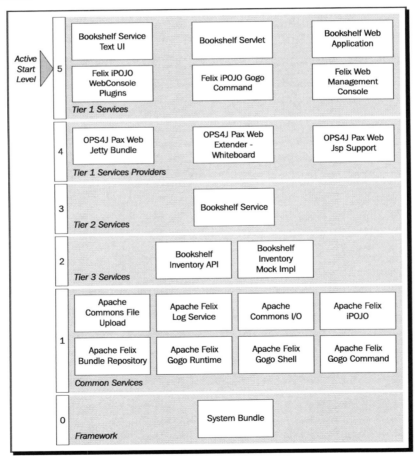

This diagram does not contain all the bundles that will be used for this case study: some of them have been hidden to reduce clutter.

The start levels that we'll use to organize the bundles in our study are as follows:

- ◆ Common Services (level 1), to which are assigned validated common services and libraries, in addition to the bundles provided as part of the distribution.

- ◆ Tier 3 Services (level 2), to which are assigned the data access related bundles. In our case, those will be the Bookshelf Inventory API and the Bookshelf Inventory Mock Impl bundles.

- ◆ Tier 2 Services (level 3), to which are assigned application business logic bundles; in our case, the Bookshelf Service bundle.

- ◆ Tier 1 Service Providers (level 4), to which are assigned bundles that provide user interaction services. For example, the Http Service (which we will look at in details in *Chapter 11*) is given the start level 4.

- ◆ Tier 1 Services (level 5), to which are assigned bundles that plug into user interface providers. For example, a bundle that implements the text UI commands (in *Chapter 8, Adding a command-line interface*) is assigned start level 5.

For example, when going through a data migration or cleansing activity; the active start level is set to 2, which keeps only the inventory bundles active and stops the ones on higher start levels.

In the case where web-server maintenance is required, going down to active start level 3 is enough.

Apache Felix and sub-projects

Apache Felix is an open-source community effort to implement the OSGi Service Platform Release 4 Core specification under the Apache license.

Started as an initial codebase donation from the Oscar project (on ObjectWeb), it graduated from incubation and became a top-level project in 2007. The result is a performant and small footprint piece of software.

In addition to the framework implementation sub-project, the Felix project provides many services specified in the OSGi Service Compendium specification such as:

- Log Service specification implementation (section 101) for message logging by bundles in the context of the framework. We will work with the Log service implementation in *Chapter 10, Improving the Logging*.

- Http Service specification implementation (section 102) for providing an http interface to bundles and allowing them to interact with users on a network using standard technologies such as XML or HTML. We will work with the Felix Http Service implementation in *Chapter 11*.

- Configuration Admin Service specification implementation (section 104), which is used to manage a bundle's configuration data.

- Metatype service implementation (section 105), which allows us to describe attribute types that bundle services can use as arguments in a machine-readable format.

- Preferences service implementation (section 106), which can be used by bundles to store settings and preferences such as user profiles or application data.

- Service Component Runtime, which is an implementation of the OSGi Declarative Services specification (section 112) providing a service-oriented component model to simplify OSGi-based development, as well as the runtime activities of service registration and handling of dependencies.

- Event Admin Service specification implementation (section 113), which facilitates the exchange of events as a means of communication between bundles using a publish and subscribe model.

- UPnP Device service implementation (section 111), which helps the integration of UPnP devices on a peer-to-peer network using XML over HTTP.

 UPnP™ is a trademark of the UPnP Implementers Corporation.

In addition to these services, the Felix project provides useful services that improve the developer's experience as well as simplify the framework administration tasks like:

- **Dependency Manager**, which uses a declarative approach to simplify dependency management.

- **File Install**, which is a service that provides a simple, directory-based, bundle deployment management.

- **Gogo**, which is an advanced shell for interacting with the OSGi frameworks (implementation of OSGi RFC 147). We will introduce Gogo in *Chapter 3*, and learn how to create new commands that hook into it in *Chapter 8*.

◆ **iPOJO**, which (provides) a sophisticated service-oriented component (environment that simplifies) the development of OSGi bundles by assisting with property injection and service registration. We will work with iPOJO in *Chapter 9*.

◆ **Maven Bundle Plugin**, which improves the bundle developer's experience by providing automation in the process of bundle creation, thus reducing the error-prone manual intervention. We will work with the Maven Bundle Plugin throughout our case study in *Chapter 5*.

◆ **Maven SCR Plugin**, which assists the developer's use of declarative services by automating the creation of metatype descriptors.

◆ **OSGi Bundle Repository Service**, which simplifies the framework administrator's task by enabling the connection to remote bundle repositories, the listing of deployed bundles and their installation onto the framework, also handling the deployment of their dependencies. We will learn more about the OSGi Bundle Repository Service and start using it in *Chapter 6*.

◆ **Shell Service**, **Remote Shell Service**, and **Shell TUI** provide means to interact with bundles on the framework, locally and remotely, using a simple command-line console.

◆ **Web Console Service** provides an extensible, browser-based, graphical administration console to the framework. We will look closely at the Web Console in *Chapter 12*.

Those services, combined with the wide variety of bundles made available by other parties, constitute a rich selection for the construction of an enterprise application.

Pop Quiz

Let's quickly check what you've learned so far:

1 Which of the following best describes an OSGi bundle?
   a. It is an XML file, with headers and properties that describe the bundle
   b. It is a service that is registered using the Service layer components
   c. It is a Java archive, containing additional headers in its manifest file

2 How would you register an OSGi bundle with the framework?
   a. I implement registration code in the `main()` method
   b. I provide properties in the bundle manifest
   c. It is detected automatically by the framework

3   What happens if, the active start level being at 4, you set it to 3?

    a.   All the bundles in level 3 are started

    b.   All the bundles in level 4 are stopped

    c.   All the bundles are stopped and those on level 3 are started.

Summary

In this chapter, we have taken a beginner's overview of the OSGi world, skimmed through some background and history. We have also covered the OSGi Service Platform, its functional layout, the framework's modular entities, and the structure of bundles and their life-cycle on the framework.

We've also introduced the Apache Felix project and quickly covered the services it provides.

By now, you should know:

*   What OSGi is and the market needs it addresses
*   How the OSGi Service Platform is laid out and the function of its layers
*   Understand OSGi bundles, how they are structured, and the way the OSGi Service Platform recognizes and handles them
*   Know about the Apache Felix project and its sub-projects
*   Understand the bundle start levels and the ways you can use them

You have also probably read some more documentation online and have deepened your understanding of those topics.

2
Setting Up the Environment

In the previous chapter we covered enough theory. Let's prepare to start our Bookshelf case study. We will also cover more on the background as we go along.

But first things first, we need to start by setting up the Felix environment and the tools that will assist in the development.

In this chapter, we will cover the installation of the Felix Framework and quickly cover its contents. Then we'll give it a try to make sure it's well installed.

In this chapter, you will:

◆ Prepare the Java development environment

◆ Download the latest Felix distribution and install it

◆ Inspect its contents and understand their purpose

◆ Have a quick introduction to Maven by covering its basic concepts

◆ Learn about the Maven plugins provided by the Felix project

So let's start by downloading and installing the Felix Framework.

Setting up the Felix framework

In this section, we will start by checking whether a compatible Java environment is installed on your machine. You will then download and set up a Felix framework, which will be our playground for the coming chapters.

Checking that a JDK is installed

The Felix Framework requires Java 2 or later versions to run. If you haven't done so yet, it's time to have your **Java™ Development Toolkit (JDK)** environment set up.

We do not cover the JDK's install in here; however, it is easy to find it online. For downloading and installing a copy of JDK, visit: `http://www.oracle.com/technetwork/java/javase/downloads/index.html` (you'll find the installation instructions on that page).

Double-check that the following items are well configured after installation:

- The `JAVA_HOME` environment variable should be set to your Java installation path
- The `PATH` environment variable should include the Java installation bin directory: `%JAVA_HOME%\bin` (on Unix systems, it would include `${JAVA_HOME}/bin`)

 The directory paths on Windows and Unix systems are slightly different. In this book, I'll be showing the examples for a Windows operating system.

To quickly check that your `JAVA_HOME` environment variable is set, open a command prompt and type the following:

```
C:\>echo %JAVA_HOME%
C:\jdk1.5.0_16
```

Here, I have Java 5 installed, but your Java home and version may be different. It depends on the version you have and where you've installed it.

Also, check that the `bin` directory of the Java installation is on the system `PATH`:

```
C:\>echo %PATH%
C:\jdk1.5.0_16\bin;.;C:\Programs\DEVELO~1\APACHE~1.0\bin;C:\WINDOWS\
system32;C:\WINDOWS
```

If you can't find your Java `bin` directory in the `PATH` environment variable, then you can add it by editing the entry and setting it to: `%JAVA_HOME%\bin;%PATH%`.

 Changing environment variables depends on the operating system you're running on. For example, under Microsoft Windows XP, this is done by adding or editing user variables in the Environment Variables (`Start -> Control Panel -> System -> Advanced`).

Finally, to check that the Java installation is working on a command line shell, execute the following:

```
C:\>java -version
java version "1.5.0_16"
Java(TM) 2 Runtime Environment, Standard Edition (build 1.5.0_16-b02)
Java HotSpot(TM) Client VM (build 1.5.0_16-b02, mixed mode, sharing)
```

If this command returns error message, then you need to update the PATH and JAVA_HOME environment variables.

Download and unpack the Felix distribution

The starting point is the Felix Framework Distribution. It is a ZIP archive released containing the system bundle, or main framework harness, along with a default selection of bundles, which is suitable for a quick start.

As we advance in the construction of our project, we will download and install more bundles and enrich its functionality; but that's for later.

The latest stable distribution of the Felix Framework can be downloaded from the **downloads** section of the Apache Felix website (http://felix.apache.org/).

 The archive you're looking for is 'Felix Framework Distribution'.

Time for action – downloading and installing Felix

Let's download the latest Felix Framework distribution from the Felix project site and install it.

Here's what you need to do:

1. Go to the **downloads** section of the Apache Felix website: http://felix.apache.org/site/downloads.cgi.

 At the time of writing, the distribution version was 3.0.1. However, be sure to check for a newer release!

2. Download the **Felix Framework Distribution** (here org.apache.felix.main.distribution-3.0.1.zip) to a temporary location.

3. Unzip the downloaded archive to a location of your choice. In my case, I've chosen: `C:\felix\`. From this point on, we will refer to this location as the Felix distribution base directory.

This concludes the installation process! The Felix distribution typically does not require any additional configuration to run. You can start using it as soon as you've unzipped it. We will touch on some configuration properties when they may be of interest.

What's in the box?

Let's quickly go through the contents of this distribution and get acquainted with its directory structure.

Under the Felix home directory, you should have the following:

◆ `bin`: Contains the main application JAR (`felix.jar`). This is actually the `org.apache.felix.main` bundle renamed to `felix.jar` for convenience. We will be starting the framework through this JAR.

◆ `bundle`: The auto-deploy directory; bundles in this directory are automatically installed and started at framework startup.

◆ `conf`: Contains the configuration files. The default configuration is very suitable for most beginners. As you start looking for more ways to customize your Felix installation, you may come back to the files in this directory for a fine-tuning of the configuration.

◆ `doc`: Contains useful documentation on the install and configuration of the framework, as well as on the bundles included by default in the distribution's bundle directory.

After the application is started for the first time, an additional folder will appear:

◆ `felix-cache`: Contains the framework's local cache of installed bundles and their information. This folder can be deleted to reset the framework. Doing this will remove all bundles that have been installed.

We will now start Felix and check its default text user interface.

Time for action – starting Felix

As mentioned a bit earlier, the Felix framework start-up Java class resides in the main bundle, located in the `bin` directory of the distribution.

To launch Felix from the distribution base directory, in a command-line shell, run:

```
C:\felix>java -jar bin/felix.jar
```

When Felix launches, it displays a welcome message followed by a command prompt:

```
Welcome to Apache Felix Gogo
```

```
g!
```

This means that the Felix user Interface is now ready to accept user commands. Felix Gogo is the default shell environment for the Felix framework. We'll look at it in greater detail in *Chapter 3*.

 You'll need to type this command every time you start Felix, it may be a good idea to create a start-up script. Under Windows, a batch file (for example, `run.bat`) containing the preceding command will do the trick.

What just happened?

Behind the scenes, the launch of the Felix application had started the system bundle and all the bundles that were placed for auto-deploy.

Felix has performed the following operations:

1 It has started System Bundle (which is `felix.jar`).

2 Installed and then started the auto-deploy bundles (from the `bundle` directory):

❑ Apache Felix Bundle Repository (`org.apache.felix.bundlerepository`), which provides tools to find, download, install, and manage installed bundles. You will learn about the commands provided by this service in a bit. Later, in Chapter 6, *Using the OSGi Bundle Repository*, you will also learn some more on bundle repositories

❑ Apache Felix Gogo Runtime (`org.apache.felix.gogo.runtime`), which provides the core command processing functionality

❑ Apache Felix Gogo Shell (`org.apache.felix.gogo.shell`), which provides the text user interface for interaction with the command processing service

❑ Apache Felix Gogo Command (`org.apache.felix.gogo.command`), which provides a set of basic commands for the operation of the framework

3 When the Gogo Shell bundle is active, it accepts input from the user on the command shell, parses it, and passes it onto the Gogo Runtime service which attempts to map it to a registered command.

The start of the Gogo text user Interface displays the command-line prompt (g!). It is now ready to accept commands.

 As new bundles are started on the framework, their information is kept in the felix-cache directory and they will also be automatically started when the framework is started.

In the next chapter, we will take a closer look at Gogo and understand some of the commands provided by the Gogo Command bundle.

Maven2 and Felix

Another useful tool to have installed as well is the build management application Maven 2 from Apache. Using Maven will greatly simplify the dependency management and the building, packaging, and deployment of developed bundles.

 Maven is not required for building OSGi bundles, since bundles are packaged as regular JARs with a customized manifest. However, using Maven does make the process much simpler and straightforward—there are Maven plugins provided as Felix sub-projects that help with this task.

The code examples and instructions to build them, shown in this book, will make use of Maven as a build environment.

A more detailed set of examples will be shown there. For now, we will cover a quick introduction to some of the main Maven concepts. You will learn how to actually configure a project to use it later, in Chapter 5, *The Book Inventory Bundle*.

Installing Maven2

If you haven't used Maven before, don't worry: we'll cover some of its usage as part of this case study.

The Maven website has a good and simple install and configuration guide. Just download Maven 2 (http://maven.apache.org/) and install it.

Life-cycles and phases

Maven is a tool for automating project development activities such as building and packaging of artifacts (for example, JARs), managing a project's dependencies, generating documentation and reports, and so on.

Its basic principle consists of a set of project 'life-cycles', processes which define the 'phases' that a project goes through to achieve a final result. For example, building an application or constructing a documentation website for it are the purposes of two of the life-cycles built into Maven. Additional life-cycles can also be defined by the user, but this is beyond the scope of this introduction.

The life-cycle clearly defines the phases that are followed to achieve its purpose. Automating those steps, executing them without human intervention, limits the human error factor in the build process, as well as provides confidence in the reproducibility of the final result of the life-cycle.

The atomic action is the 'goal', which represents a specific task to be performed. A phase is made of a sequence of goals to be achieved for that phase. The goals that are bound to a phase are decided based on factors such as the project packaging type or its configured plugins.

There's a wide range of documentation on the Maven site (`http://maven.apache.org/`). Here's a good guide on life-cycles and phases: `http://maven.apache.org/guides/introduction/introduction-to-the-lifecycle.html`.

The life-cycles built into Maven are:

◆ The default build life-cycle, which takes the project through the build phases, (we'll see this in a while)

◆ The `clean` life-cycle, which takes the project through a cleaning process to remove items such as temporary files or generated content

◆ The `site` life-cycle, which steps through the documentation and reporting phases and generates a project site

For example, some of the main phases defined in the default build life-cycles are:

◆ `validate` that the project is well defined and all required information is provided

◆ `compile` the project source code

◆ `test` the compiled code, using an automated test suite (such as JUnit). Those are unit code tests that don't require the code to be packaged or deployed

◆ `package` the code and resources into an artifact, the main deliverable for the project (a JAR, for example)

◆ `integration-test` the package, potentially deploying it to a test environment

◆ `verify` that the package fulfills additional quality checks

◆ `install` the package locally, making it available to other projects on this system

◆ `deploy` the package to an integration or release location

Each phase is dependent on the phase before it; for example, in the default build life-cycle, requesting the `deploy` phase will take the project through `validate`, `compile`, `test`, and so on.

Regularly, we will be using the `clean` and `deploy` life-cycles to produce a release of our bundles from a clean start.

Maven plugins

The build life-cycles can be customized using plugins, which are provided by Maven or third-parties. Plugins can attach to goals or extend them to provide build goals with functionality. For example, we will be using some of the plugins provided by the Felix project to help with the OSGi bundle creation process later.

Maven provides a simple way to get the required plugins. When you install it, it comes with the minimal set of libraries required for it to function. It will then download the additional JARs it needs from online repositories, based on library identification and classification information (namely, the group and artifact IDs).

The POM

The description of a project, its identification, and the way it is to be built are defined in its **Project Object Model (POM)**, an XML file that is the main source of information for Maven. It contains information such as the group and artifact IDs of the project and the dependencies it requires. It also contains information such as the developers of the project, its software configuration management system, where its packaged artifacts are deployed, and so on.

As part of the project identification, the POM holds the project packaging type which determines which goals are bound to the life-cycle phases. The default packaging type is `jar` and there are a few packaging types built-in such as `war`, `ear`, and so on. For example, the package phase will be different for a JAR and for a WAR.

The packaging we will use for our projects is a bundle, which is a custom packaging type provided by the Bundle Plugin (described in the next section). This will be used by the plugins that we will configure to generate the manifest headers and package the bundle. You will learn how to create and configure the POMs for the projects of this case study in *Chapter 5*.

The Felix Maven Plugins

Felix provides quite a few useful plugins to assist in the build and packaging process:

◆ **Bundle Plugin**: Based on the BND tool from Peter Kriens, this Maven 2 plugin will assist in the packaging of bundles based on a few build directives (configuration). It will also manage a local OSGi Bundle Repository (OBR) and provide distribution to OBRs (covered in *Chapter 6, Using the OSGi Bundle Repository*.)

- ◆ **iPOJO Plugin**: Used in conjunction with the Bundle plugin. Given an XML metafile, it will automate the iPOJO-related actions as part of the build process.

- ◆ **junit4osgi Plugin**: Integrates the jUnit test framework with the bundle build process.

- ◆ **SCR Plugin**: It simplifies the development of bundles by generating necessary descriptors based on annotations.

We will use the Bundle plugin throughout the case study and start using the iPOJO plugin in Chapter 9, *Improving the Bookshelf service with iPOJO*.

Pop quiz

1. What is a life-cycle in Maven terms?

   a. It manages the state of bundles in an OSGi framework

   b. It defines the phases that contents of a project go through to achieve a purpose in an automated fashion, such as building the project

   c. It is a check-list for developers to follow to remember the steps that are required for a build

2. What is a POM primarily used for in the build process?

   a. It is included with the produced archive as bundle configuration

   b. It is included with the produced archive as information on the project

   c. It provides Maven with project identification and build instructions

Summary

In this chapter, we've set up our environment for Felix development. Then we started up the Felix framework to ensure it works. We will cover the commands in *Chapter 3*. We've also looked at Maven and the Maven plugins made available by the Felix project.

By now, you should:

- ◆ Have your development environment ready for use. If you haven't picked an Integrated Development Environment, check out Appendix A: *Eclipse, Maven, and Felix* for a good option

- ◆ Understand Maven life-cycles, phases and goals, and how plugins play a role in those life-cycles

- ◆ Be aware of the Maven plugins provided by the Felix project

3
Felix Gogo

A request for comments (RFC 147) by Peter Kriens, an attachment to the OSGi 4.2 specifications document early draft, describes a proposed interface for the processing and launching of commands for the OSGi framework. It defines the blueprint for a shell service and its language.

The goal behind such an endeavor is to attempt to standardize the way humans and external systems interact with an OSGi framework using a text command-based interface. For example, such an interface would be used for launching, configuring, and controlling the framework using a local or remote console or scripting without locking an enterprise platform to a specific OSGi framework implementation.

Felix Gogo, a sub-project of Apache Felix, is an implementation of this early draft specification. The Gogo shell is included with the Felix Framework Distribution since version 3.0.

It is worth noting that this specification is not yet part of the official OSGi specifications, and therefore, may change in the future.

In this chapter, you will:

◆ Learn about the Tiny Shell Language and its syntax
◆ Cover some of the commands provided by Gogo

So let's start with a quick overview of the language.

The Tiny Shell Language

The command syntax for the shell interface is based on the **Tiny Shell Language** (**TSL**). It is simple enough to allow a lightweight implementation, yet provides features such as pipes, closures, variable setting and referencing, collection types such as lists and maps, and so on.

The TSL syntax allows the creation of scripts that can be executed by the shell runtime service. The introduction you will get here does not cover the complete syntax; instead, you will see the basic parts of it.

For a review of the proposal in its initial state, please refer to the OSGi 4.2 early draft appendix (`http://www.osgi.org/download/osgi-4.2-early-draft.pdf`). You may also refer to the RFC 147 Overview on the Felix documentation pages (`http://felix.apache.org/site/rfc-147-overview.html`) for potential differences with the initial draft.

Chained execution

A program is a set of chained execution blocks. Blocks are executed in parallel, and the output of a block is streamed as input to the next. Blocks are separated by the pipe character (|). Each block is made up of a sequence of statements, separated by a semicolon (;).

For example, as we'll see in the next section, the `bundles` command lists the currently installed bundles and the `grep` command takes a parameter that it uses to filter the input. The program below:

```
bundles | grep gogo
```

is made of two statement blocks, namely, `bundles` and grep gogo. The output of the `bundles` statement will be connected to the input of the grep gogo statement (here each the statement block contains one statement).

Running this program on your Felix installation, in the state it is now, will produce:

```
g! bundles | grep gogo
    2|Active      |    1|org.apache.felix.gogo.command (0.6.0)
    3|Active      |    1|org.apache.felix.gogo.runtime (0.6.0)
    4|Active      |    1|org.apache.felix.gogo.shell (0.6.0)
true
```

The `grep` statement has filtered the output of the `bundles` statement for lines containing the filter string `gogo`. In this case, the `grep` statement outputs the results of its execution to the shell which prints it.

Executing the statement grep gogo on its own, without a piped block that feeds it input, will connect its input to the user command line. In that case, use *Ctrl-Z* to terminate your input:

```
g! grep gogo
line 1
line 2 gogo
line 2 gogo
line 3
^z
true
```

Notice that `line 2 gogo` is repeated right after you have entered it, showing that the `grep` statement is running in parallel. It receives the input and processes it right after you enter it.

Variable assignment and referencing

A session variable is assigned a value using the equal character (=) and referenced using its name preceded with a dollar character ($). For example:

```
g! var1 = 'this is a string'
this is a string
g! echo $var1
this is a string
```

The assignment operation returns the assigned value.

Value types

We've seen the string type previously, which is indicated by surrounding text with single quotes (').

A list is a sequence of terms separated by whitespace characters and is delimited by an opening and a closing square bracket.

For example:

```
g! days = [ mon tue wed thu fri sat sun ]
mon
tue
wed
thu
fri
sat
sun
```

Here the variable, days, was created, assigned the list as a value, and stored in the session.

A map is a list of assignments, the value is assigned to the key using the equal character (=).

For example:

```
g! sounds = [ dog=bark cat=meow lion=roar ]
dog                bark
cat                meow
lion               roar
```

Here, the variable sounds is assigned a map with the preceding key value pairs.

Object properties and operations

The shell uses a mapping process that involves reflection to find the best operation to perform for a request. We're not going to go into the details of how this happens; instead, we'll give a few examples of the operations that can be performed. We'll see a few others as we go along.

In the same session, days and sounds are defined previously to retrieve an entry in the $days list:

```
g! $days get 1
tue
```

To retrieve an entry in the sounds map:

```
g! $sounds get dog
bark
```

An example we've seen earlier is the bundles command used when illustrating the piping. Bundles was mapped to the method getBundles() from the Gogo Runtime bundle BundleContext instance. Another property of this object that we'll use in the next section is bundle <id> to get a bundle object instance using getBundle(long).

Execution quotes

Similar to the UNIX back-quote syntax, but providing one that's simpler for a lightweight parser, the execution quotes are used to return the output of an executed program.

For example:

```
g!(bundle 1) location
file:/C:/felix/bundle/org.apache.felix.bundlerepository-1.6.2.jar
```

Here, (bundle 1) has returned the bundle with ID 1, which we've re-used to retrieve the property location making use of Gogo's reflexion on beans (location is mapped to getLocation() on the Bundle object).

Commands and scopes

The Gogo Runtime command processor is extensible and allows any bundle to register the commands it needs to expose to the user. Then, when the user types a command, the processor will attempt to find the method that's best fit to be executed, based on the command name and passed arguments.

However, there are potential cases where two bundles would need to register the same command name. To avoid this clash, commands are registered with an optional scope. When there is no ambiguity as to which scope the command belongs to, the command can be used without a scope; otherwise, the scope must be included.

The scope of a command is specified by pre-pending it to the command, separated from the command with a colon (:). In the previous examples, we've used the grep command, which is in the gogo scope. In this case, grep and gogo:grep achieve the same result.

We will look closer at the command registration mechanism in *Chapter 8, Adding a Command-Line Interface*, when we define our own for the Bookshelf case study.

Let's take a tour of some of the commands available in the Felix distribution.

At the time of writing of this book, the Gogo bundles are at version 0.6.0, which means that they are not yet finalized and may change by the time they are released with version 1.0.

felix scope commands

One of the many powerful features of Felix (and OSGi-compliant applications in general) is that many actions can be applied on bundles without needing to restart the framework. Bundles can be installed, updated, uninstalled, and so on while the remaining functionality of the framework is active.

The following are some of the available commands and a description of their usage. We will get to use many of those as we go along, so you need not worry much about learning them by heart. Just know they exist.

Listing installed bundles: lb

One of the most frequently used shell commands is the list bundles command (lb), which gives a listing of the currently installed bundles, showing some information on each of them.

Let's check what's running on our newly installed framework:

```
g! lb
START LEVEL 1
   ID|State      |Level|Name
    0|Active     |    0|System Bundle (3.0.1)
    1|Active     |    1|Apache Felix Bundle Repository (1.6.2)
    2|Active     |    1|Apache Felix Gogo Command (0.6.0)
    3|Active     |    1|Apache Felix Gogo Runtime (0.6.0)
    4|Active     |    1|Apache Felix Gogo Shell (0.6.0)
```

The listing provides the following useful information about each bundle:

- Each bundle is given a unique id on install—this ID is used by commands such as update or uninstall to apply actions on that bundle
- The bundle's lifecycle state, which we've introduced in Chapter 1, *Quick intro to Felix and OSGi*
- The bundle's start level
- The bundle's name and version

This command also takes a parameter for filtering the bundles list. For example, to include only bundles that have 'bundle' in their name:

```
g! lb bundle
START LEVEL 1
   ID|State      |Level|Name
    0|Active     |    0|System Bundle (3.0.1)
    1|Active     |    1|Apache Felix Bundle Repository (1.6.2)
```

help

The help command provides hints on the usage of commands.

When called without any parameters, the help command gives a listing of the available commands:

```
g! help
felix:bundlelevel
felix:cd
```

```
felix:frameworklevel
felix:headers
felix:help
felix:inspect
felix:install
felix:lb
felix:log
felix:ls
felix:refresh
felix:resolve
felix:start
felix:stop
felix:uninstall
felix:update
felix:which
gogo:cat
gogo:each
gogo:echo
gogo:format
gogo:getopt
gogo:gosh
gogo:grep
gogo:not
gogo:set
gogo:sh
gogo:source
gogo:tac
gogo:telnetd
gogo:type
gogo:until
obr:deploy
obr:info
obr:javadoc
obr:list
obr:repos
obr:source
```

We'll cover the `felix` scope commands here and some of the `gogo` scope commands in the next section. The `obr` scope commands will be covered later, in *Chapter 6, Using the OSGi Bundle Repository*.

More help on the syntax of each command can be requested by typing `help <command-name>`.

For example, for more help on the `repos` command:

```
g! help repos


repos - manage repositories
   scope: obr
   parameters:
      String    ( add | list | refresh | remove )
      String[]    space-delimited list of repository URLs
```

When the command is available with multiple signatures, a help block per signature is provided, for example:

```
g! help help


help - displays information about a specific command
   scope: felix
   parameters:
      String    target command


help - displays available commands
   scope: felix
```

Here, the `help` command has 2 syntaxes: one that takes a parameter (the target command), and another that takes no parameters. We've used the first one to get help on help.

> Some commands may have not registered help content with the shell service. Those will show minimal information using `help <command>`. In most cases, they expose a separate help listing—usually `<command> -?` or `<command> --help`.

install

The `install` command is used to instruct Felix to install an external bundle. The syntax is as follows:

```
g! help install

install - install bundle using URLs
    scope: felix
    parameters:
        String[]    target URLs
```

Each bundle is located using the URL and is downloaded to the local cache for installation.

Once a bundle is installed, it is given a unique `id`. This ID is used to refer to this bundle when using commands such as `update` or `uninstall`. For example:

```
g! install http://www.mysite.com/testbundle-1.0.0.jar
Bundle ID: 7
```

Here, the bundle I've just installed has the ID `7`.

```
g! lb
START LEVEL 1
    ID|State        |Level|Name
    0|Active        |    0|System Bundle (3.0.1)
    1|Active        |    1|Apache Felix Bundle Repository (1.6.2)
    2|Active        |    1|Apache Felix Gogo Command (0.6.0)
    3|Active        |    1|Apache Felix Gogo Runtime (0.6.0)
    4|Active        |    1|Apache Felix Gogo Shell (0.6.0)
    7|Installed     |    1|Test Bundle (1.0.0)
```

In cases where many bundles are to be installed from the same base URL, you may want to set a session variable with the common base URL to simplify the task.

For example, instead of executing:

```
g! install http://site.com/bundle1.jar http://site.com/bundle2.jar
```

You would write:

```
g! b = http://site.com
g! install $b/bundle1.jar $b/bundle2.jar
```

update

As newer versions of bundles are released, it is easy to update the installed bundle with a newer version by using the `update` command.

The `update` command takes a bundle ID and an optional source URL as parameters. Its syntax is:

```
g! help update

update - update bundle
   scope: felix
   parameters:
      Bundle    target bundle

update - update bundle from URL
   scope: felix
   parameters:
      Bundle    target bundle
      String    URL from where to retrieve bundle
```

For example:

```
g! update 7 http://www.mysite.com/testbundle-1.0.1.jar
g!
g! lb
START LEVEL 1
   ID|State        |Level|Name
    0|Active        |    0|System Bundle (3.0.1)
    1|Active        |    1|Apache Felix Bundle Repository (1.6.2)
    2|Active        |    1|Apache Felix Gogo Command (0.6.0)
    3|Active        |    1|Apache Felix Gogo Runtime (0.6.0)
    4|Active        |    1|Apache Felix Gogo Shell (0.6.0)
    7|Installed     |    1|Test Bundle (1.0.1)
```

Notice that the bundle ID remains unchanged.

When a source URL is not provided, the bundle is updated from the same location it was installed from.

resolve

The `resolve` command requests that the framework undergo the resolution process for the given bundle. Refer to *Chapter 1* for a review of the bundle life-cycle stages.

The syntax of this command is as follows:

```
g! help resolve


resolve - resolve bundles
   scope: felix
   parameters:
      Bundle[]   target bundles (can be null or empty)
```

If no parameter is provided, then the framework will resolve all unresolved bundles. To resolve specific bundles, the list `ids` of the bundles to be resolved are passed as parameters.

stop and start

The `stop` and `start` commands take a space-separated sequence of bundle IDs to stop or to start (refer to *Chapter 1* for more on the lifecycle of a bundle).

The `stop` command syntax is as follows:

```
g! help stop


stop - stop bundles
   scope: felix
   flags:
      -t, --transient   stop bundle transiently
   parameters:
      Bundle[]   target bundles
```

Use the `-t` (or `--transient`) flag to stop the bundle in transient mode, that is, not saving its state to the persisted auto-start state. The framework will not remember this bundle as having been stopped the next time it is restarted.

The `start` command syntax is similar to the `stop` command:

```
g! help start


start - start bundles
   scope: felix
```

```
flags:
    -p, --policy    use declared activation policy
    -t, --transient    start bundle transiently
parameters:
    String[]    target bundle identifiers or URLs
```

It uses the -t flag in the same way as the stop command.

Use the -p (of --policy) flag to use the activation policy declared in the Bundle-ActivationPolicy header.

 To exit the framework, use stop 0 which stops the System Bundle, thus launching the stop process for the other bundles before shutting down.

uninstall

The uninstall command is used to remove one or more bundles from the framework. The bundles are first stopped and then uninstalled.

The usage of this command is as follows:

```
g! help uninstall

uninstall - uninstall bundles
    scope: felix
    parameters:
        Bundle[]    target bundles
```

The list of IDs of bundles to be uninstalled is passed as a parameter.

refresh

The refresh command forces the update of the packages exported by the refreshed bundles. The refresh is performed to the provided bundles and the bundles that depend on them. It is typically used after an update or after an uninstall of a bundle, to update the packages exported by an updated bundle and to completely remove those of an uninstalled one.

The syntax of the `refresh` command is as follows:

```
g! help refresh

refresh - refresh bundles
   scope: felix
   parameters:
      Bundle[]   target bundles (can be null or empty)
```

To refresh specific bundles, the `ids` of those bundles are passed as parameters. Otherwise, calling `refresh` with no parameters refreshes all bundles that were updated or uninstalled.

headers and inspect

The `headers` and `inspect` commands provide valuable information on how a bundle is perceived by the framework. The `headers` command lists the bundle headers in the main section of the bundle's manifest. Its usage is as follows:

```
g! help headers

headers - display bundle headers
   scope: felix
   parameters:
      Bundle[]   target bundles
```

For example, to display the headers of the bundle `Apache Felix Bundle Repository`, use:

```
g! headers 1

Apache Felix Bundle Repository (1)
----------------------------------
Bnd-LastModified = 1272565441581
Build-Jdk = 1.6.0_17
Built-By = gnodet
Bundle-Activator = org.apache.felix.bundlerepository.impl.Activator
Bundle-Description = Bundle repository service.
Bundle-DocURL = http://felix.apache.org/site/apache-felix-osgi-bundle-
repository.html
```

```
Bundle-License = http://www.apache.org/licenses/LICENSE-2.0.txt
Bundle-ManifestVersion = 2
Bundle-Name = Apache Felix Bundle Repository
Bundle-Source = http://felix.apache.org/site/downloads.cgi
Bundle-SymbolicName = org.apache.felix.bundlerepository
Bundle-Url = http://felix.apache.org/site/downloads.cgi
Bundle-Vendor = The Apache Software Foundation
Bundle-Version = 1.6.2
Created-By = Apache Maven Bundle Plugin
...
```

The `inspect` command displays various information on a bundle's dependencies, requirements, packages it exports, and so on. Its usage is as follows:

```
g! help inspect

inspect - inspects bundle dependency information
   scope: felix
   parameters:
      String    (package | bundle | fragment | service)
      String    (capability | requirement)
      Bundle[]    target bundles
```

The first parameter is the inspection `type`:

♦ `package` to inspect package-related information, for example, which packages the specified bundles import from or export to other bundles

♦ `bundle` to inspect the requirements or capabilities of the given bundles

♦ `fragment` to inspect fragment-related information, such as a fragment's host or the list of hosted fragments

♦ `service` to inspect the bundles service related information, such as the list of imported or exported services

The second parameter is the direction of the inspection, with respect to the bundle:

♦ `capability` to inspect what the specified bundles can give to the platform

♦ `requirement` to inspect what the specified bundles need from the platform

The remaining parameters are one or more bundles to be inspected.

For example, the package capability of the bundle Apache Felix Bundle Repository are as follows:

```
g! inspect package capability 1
org.apache.felix.bundlerepository [1] exports packages:
------------------------------------------------------
org.apache.felix.bundlerepository; version=2.0.0 imported by:
   org.apache.felix.gogo.command [2]
```

This says that the bundle exports a package (org.apache.felix.bundlerepository), which is imported by bundle 2, Apache Felix Gogo Command.

 Inspect also accepts shorthand first letters for the inspection type and direction. For example, the command inspect p c 1 can be used instead of the longer one seen previously.

which

The which command will provide information on where a given bundle loads a given class. This command is useful when investigating problems related to conflicts between classes or issues with their visibility.

Its syntax is as follows:

```
g! help which

which - determines from where a bundle loads a class
   scope: felix
   parameters:
      Bundle    target bundle
      String    target class name
```

The first parameter is the bundle to use as the context for the class loading and the second is the name of the class to load.

For example, to know where the bundle Apache Felix Gogo Command loads its
`org.apache.felix.bundlerepository.Repository` class, use:

```
g! which 2 org.apache.felix.bundlerepository.Repository
Loaded from: org.apache.felix.bundlerepository [1]
```

The answer is bundle 1: Apache Felix Bundle Repository. The result shows the bundle
symbolic name and the bundle ID.

log

The `log` command allows us to peek into the list of the last few log entries. Its usage is
as follows:

```
g! help log

log - display some matching log entries
   scope: felix
   parameters:
      int    maximum number of entries
      String    minimum log level [ debug | info | warn | error ]

log - display all matching log entries
   scope: felix
   parameters:
      String    minimum log level [ debug | info | warn | error ]
```

The default Felix distribution doesn't come with a log service installed, so running this
command at this point will issue a warning:

```
g! log debug
Log reader service is unavailable.
```

We will install one in *Chapter 10, Improving the Logging*, when we add proper logging to our
case study and also cover its usage in more details at that point.

cd and ls

Some of the commands that are available through this console may read from or write to
files. For example, the `grep` command can read a file and display the lines that match a given
pattern. It will read the file relative to the shell session working directory. We will look at this
and other file manipulating commands in a short while.

The cd and ls commands are very similar to their Unix counterparts.

The cd command is used to display or change the current shell working directory. Its usage is as follows:

```
g! help cd

cd - change current directory
    scope: felix
    parameters:
        CommandSession    automatically supplied shell session
        String    target directory


cd - get current directory
    scope: felix
    parameters:
        CommandSession    automatically supplied shell session
```

When called without parameters, it will display the current working directory. To change the current directory, pass the target directory as a parameter.

The ls command is used to list the contents of a directory. Its syntax is as follows:

```
g! help ls

ls - get specified path contents
    scope: felix
    parameters:
        CommandSession    automatically supplied shell session
        String    path with optionally wild carded file name


ls - get current directory contents
    scope: felix
    parameters:
        CommandSession    automatically supplied shell session
```

The path of the directory to be listed is passed as a parameter. If no parameters are passed, then the contents of the current working directory are shown.

For example, the contents of the current directory are as follows:

```
g! ls
C:\felix\bin
C:\felix\bundle
C:\felix\conf
C:\felix\DEPENDENCIES
C:\felix\doc
C:\felix\felix-cache
C:\felix\LICENSE
C:\felix\LICENSE.kxml2
C:\felix\NOTICE
C:\felix\run.bat
```

Changing to a sub-directory:

```
g! cd bundle
Name                bundle
CanonicalPath       C:\felix\bundle
Parent              C:\felix
Path                C:\felix\bundle
AbsoluteFile        C:\felix\bundle
AbsolutePath        C:\felix\bundle
CanonicalFile       C:\felix\bundle
ParentFile          C:\felix
```

frameworklevel and bundlelevel

In *Chapter 1*, we've covered the start level of the framework and bundles. The frameworklevel and bundlelevel commands allow us to modify those start levels.

The frameworklevel command is used to get or set the framework's active start level. Its syntax is as follows:

```
g! help frameworklevel

frameworklevel - query framework active start level
   scope: felix
```

```
frameworklevel - set framework active start level
   scope: felix
   parameters:
      int   target start level
```

To get the active start level of the framework, use the command without any parameters:

```
g! frameworklevel
Level is 1
```

To change it, pass the target start level as a parameter.

The bundle level displays and manipulates the bundle's start levels. Its syntax is:

```
g! help bundlelevel
```

```
bundlelevel - set bundle start level or initial bundle start level
   scope: felix
   flags:
      -i, --setinitial   set the initial bundle start level
      -s, --setlevel    set the bundle's start level
   parameters:
      int   target level
      Bundle[]   target identifiers
```

```
bundlelevel - query bundle start level
   scope: felix
   parameters:
      Bundle   bundle to query
```

To query the start level of a bundle, use the command with one parameter—the bundle ID:

```
g! bundlelevel 2
org.apache.felix.gogo.command [2] is level 1
```

To change the framework's initial bundle start level, use the command with the option -i set:

```
g! bundlelevel -i 2
```

This has set the initial bundle start level to 2 for newly installed bundles.

To change the start level of one or more bundles, use the -s option followed by the target start level and the list of bundles to modify.

gogo scope commands

The commands in the gogo scope provide a few additional tools that are especially useful when scripting a recurrent set of operations. We will cover some of them here.

echo

The echo command will evaluate its arguments and display the result on the console. For example:

```
g! var1 = 'this is'
this is
g! var2 = ' a string'
 a string
g! echo $var1$var2
this is a string
```

grep

The grep command is used to search the input for lines that match a given pattern; it is very similar to the Unix grep tool. The input is either standard input, the output of a command piped to grep, or the contents of files.

The grep command will return false if there were no lines in the input that match the pattern. It will return true otherwise.

Its usage is as follows:

```
g! grep -?
grep -  search for PATTERN in each FILE or standard input.
Usage: grep [OPTIONS] PATTERN [FILES]
  -? --help                show help
  -i --ignore-case         ignore case distinctions
  -n --line-number         prefix each line with line number within its
input file
  -q --quiet, --silent     suppress all normal output
  -v --invert-match        select non-matching lines
true
```

The PATTERN argument is an encoded **regular expression (regex)** that defines the sequence of characters that are considered a match. It follows the regex pattern format, defined for the Java java.util.regex.Pattern class.

You can visit the following for more information on regex:

```
http://download-llnw.oracle.com/javase/1.5.0/docs/api/java/util/
regex/Pattern.html
```

For example, to grep the output of the `lb` command for lines containing the string `Apache`:

```
g! lb | grep Apache
    1|Active       |      1|Apache Felix Bundle Repository (1.6.2)
    2|Active       |      1|Apache Felix Gogo Command (0.6.0)
    3|Active       |      1|Apache Felix Gogo Runtime (0.6.0)
    4|Active       |      1|Apache Felix Gogo Shell (0.6.0)
true
```

The `-i` (short for `--ignore-case`) option makes the pattern not case sensitive, thus matching both the lowercase and uppercase for a letter.

The `-n` (or `--line-number`) option requests that the command include the line number when printing the results. For example:

```
g! lb | grep -n Apache
4:      1|Active       |      1|Apache Felix Bundle Repository (1.6.2)
5:      2|Active       |      1|Apache Felix Gogo Command (0.6.0)
6:      3|Active       |      1|Apache Felix Gogo Runtime (0.6.0)
7:      4|Active       |      1|Apache Felix Gogo Shell (0.6.0)
true
```

The `-q` option (also `--quiet` or `--silent`) is used to suppress the `grep` command output. The command will only return `true` or `false` after it is finished with the input. This is especially useful when using the command for its returned value only (as a loop guard, for example).

The `-v` (or `--invert-match`) is used to show the lines that don't match the pattern (inverse match). For example:

```
g! lb | grep -v Apache
START LEVEL 1
   ID|State       |Level|Name
    0|Active       |     0|System Bundle (3.0.1)
true
```

cat

The `cat` command is used to concatenate files and display their contents on the console. It takes one or more filenames relative to the current shell session directory (see `cd` and `ls` in the previous section) and displays them.

For example, to display the `run.bat` file we had created at the beginning of this chapter, use the following:

```
g! cat run.bat
java -jar bin/felix.jar
```

Separate the arguments with whitespace to display more than one file sequentially.

tac

The `tac` command, in a way, is the opposite of the `cat` command. Here it takes the text from the standard input and either returns it as a string or as a list for use as input for another command or writes it to a file.

The syntax is as shown here:

```
g! tac -?
tac - capture stdin as String or List and optionally write to file.
Usage: tac [-al] [FILE]
   -a --append           append to FILE
   -l --list             return List<String>
   -? --help             show help
```

The following example makes a list of the input and then gets the second item in the resulting list.

```
g! var1 = tac -l ; $var1 get 1
a1
a2
a3
^Z
a2
```

Notice the use of `Ctrl-Z` (shows as `^Z` on the console display) to terminate user input.

Passing a filename as an argument will create the file and write the input text to it. The `-a` or `--append` option can be used to append to an existing file. For example, this will create a file from the standard input and display its contents using the `cat` command:

```
g! tac test.out ; cat test.out
this is a test, line 1
last line
^Z
this is a test, line 1
last line
```

The input of the `tac` command can also be the piped output of another. For example, the next command will make a backup copy of our `test.out` file created previously:

```
g! cat test.out | tac test.out.bak
this is a test, line 1 last line
g!
g! cat test.out.bak
this is a test, line 1
last line
```

set

The `set` command is used to inspect session variable information, as well as turn session tracing `on` or `off`.

Help on the usage of the `set` command can be retrieved as follows:

```
g! set -?
set - show session variables
Usage: set [OPTIONS] [PREFIX]
  -? --help           show help
  -a --all            show all variables, including those starting with .
  -x                  set xtrace option
  +x                  unset xtrace option
If PREFIX given, then only show variable(s) starting with PREFIX
```

The `-x` option is used to turn execution traces on. For example, taking one of the samples used previously, without setting the `xtrace` option:

```
g! var = 'this is a string'
this is a string
g! echo $var
this is a string
```

When setting the `xtrace` option, the shell will output a trace message for each command it will execute and for each result of that command. In this case:

```
g! set -x
g!
g! var = 'this is a string'
+ var '=' 'this is a string'
```

```
this is a string
g! echo $var
+ echo $var
this is a string
```

Setting shell execution traces on is especially useful when working on a script (see the previous source).

Use set +x to turn traces off.

Pop Quiz

Let's test if you remember some of the basics of this chapter with a quick pop quiz.

1. How do you list the installed bundles?
   a. ls
   b. lb
   c. ps

2. How do you shutdown the framework?
   a. shutdown
   b. exit
   c. stop 0

Summary

In this chapter, you have learned about the Gogo command-line language and some of its commands. By now, you should:

- Understand the Gogo command syntax
- Know about most of the commands available in the Gogo shell
- Know how to get help on the usage of commands

4

Let's Get Started: The Bookshelf Project

Practicing while learning is the best way to get started with any technology. When you work hands-on and apply what you've learned as you go, you pay more attention to the details. These details may later make the difference between a smooth working project and one that requires long nights of debugging.

This book is based on a simple bookshelf service case study that we will construct step-by-step. The goal, of course, is for you to follow along and learn as you advance in the chapters.

The bookshelf application will touch on the important features of OSGi, completing the basics you've covered in the previous chapters, mainly in the context of the Felix framework as well as using components and services from other providers.

In this chapter, we will spend some time designing our project, setting its scope of work, and describing its components layout. By the end of this chapter, you will know what topics are covered in this book. You can also come back to this chapter to get a global view of the project plan.

We will:

- ◆ Describe the bookshelf case study and set the scope of work
- ◆ Go through a tiered layout of its bundles
- ◆ Define some of the conventions for the case study bundles

A simple Bookshelf project

The case study we will construct here is a three-tiered web-based bookshelf application. Each tier consists of a functional area of the application.

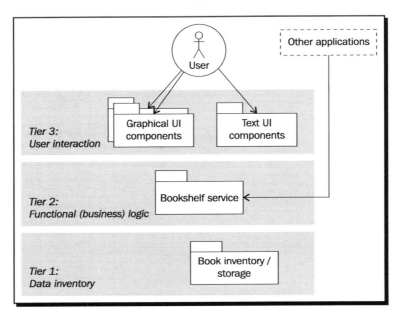

The first tier is the data inventory tier, which is responsible for storing the books as well as providing management functionality.

The second tier, the main bookshelf service, holds the business logic around the bookshelf functionality.

The third tier is the user interaction tier. It provides user access to the application through a command-line interface at first, then through a simple servlet, and later through a JSP web application.

This split between the user interface, business logic, and inventory is good practice. It adds flexibility to the design by allowing the upgrade or replacement of each of the layer implementations without impacting the others and thus reducing regression testing.

Let's look at each of those layers in more detail.

The data inventory tier

For our case study, we will need a data inventory layer for storing, searching, and retrieving books.

The Book interface defines the read-only book bean and it provides the user access to the bean attributes. This interface is used when the Book entry does not require any updates. The MutableBook interface exposes the attribute-setting methods for the book bean. It is used when the caller needs to update the bean attributes.

This separation between Book and MutableBook is especially useful when developing a multi-threaded, multi-session implementation of the data inventory repository. It allows us to keep track of changes by monitoring the beans as they change and notify components of those changes when needed. The Book and MutableBook interfaces will be defined in *Chapter 5, The Book Inventory Bundle*, as part of the implementation of the data inventory tier.

We will define a BookInventory interface that abstracts over the repository implementation specifics.

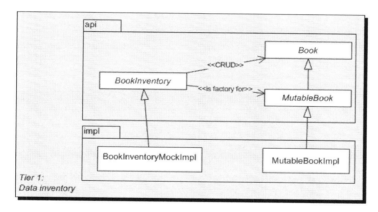

In addition to the CRUD functionality, the book inventory interface also offers a factory method for creating new book entries. This factory method gives the caller a mutable book.

What's CRUD?

CRUD is short for **Create-Retrieve-Update-Delete**. It is the typical functionality-set expected from an inventory service:

 ◆ **Create**: Add a new book to the inventory. This operation typically checks the repository for an item with the same identifier (unique reference) and throws an exception if there's an attempt to add an item that already exists

- ◆ **Retrieve**: Load a book based on its unique reference, also get a list of references of items that match a set of filter criteria

- ◆ **Update**: Modify an existing book properties, based on its unique reference

- ◆ **Delete**: Remove an existing book from the inventory based on its unique reference

We'll separate the inventory API definition from its implementation, packaging each of them in its own bundle. In *Chapter 5*, we will write a mock implementation of the inventory that will use memory for volatile storage. It is recommended that you write another implementation for those interfaces—one that's based on permanent storage, when you're more comfortable with the process.

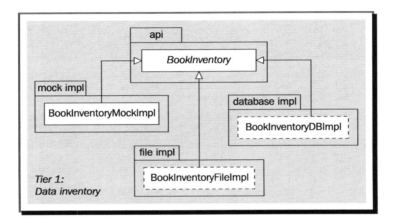

The separation between the API and implementation will allow you to swap an implementation with another one when it is ready. We will focus on the mock implementation in *Chapter 5* and leave it to you to implement other potential flavors of it (in the previous dashed boxes).

The business logic tier

The middle tier, or the business logic tier, of this application is the bookshelf service API and implementation. The bookshelf service implementation uses the inventory functionality exposed by the data tier, delegating book storage functionality. It also overlays application business logic by enriching the operation operation-set.

For example, one of the business logic functionalities, integrated into the bookshelf service, is user authentication. This is defined as an interface that the `BookshelfService` extends.

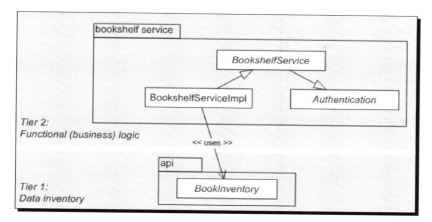

Some classes have been hidden for clarity in the preceding diagram.

During the course of our progression through the chapters, we will make changes to the implementation of the bookshelf inventory as well as to that of the bookshelf service. For the sake of making the point on API-implementation loose coupling, our case study will not separate the bookshelf service API from its implementation. This will allow you to compare the impact of changes to the bookshelf service implementation to those made to the inventory implementation.

We will look at the bookshelf service interface definition and its implementation in detail in *Chapter 7, The Bookshelf: First Stab*.

The user interaction tier

The upper-most layer in our application is the user interaction or presentation layer. The presentation layer integrates with the business logic layer and exposes a few flavors of interfaces accessible to the application user.

The user interaction layer in our case study will be composed of two flavors of interfaces:

- ◆ **Console text user interface**: Providing users access to the bookshelf application functionality through the Felix command-line shell
- ◆ **Web-based graphical interfaces**: Providing users access to the application functionality through a web browser

The console text user interface is simpler to implement and gives early access to the application operations. The web-based graphical interface is covered later on.

The following shows the bundles that will be implemented as part of the user interaction tier and their relationship with the business logic tier.

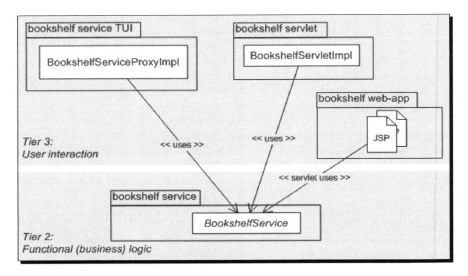

The `bookshelf-service-tui` bundle will implement text user interface commands for two of the operations defined for the bookshelf service, namely, the `book:search` and `book:add` commands. The remaining commands will be left for you to implement.

The `bookshelf-servlet` bundle will provide a servlet graphical interface to the bookshelf service. The servlet is encoded to generate HTML and respond to user requests to the following operations:

- Listing bookshelf groups
- Listing books in a group
- Searching books by author
- Adding a book

The `bookshelf-webapp` bundle will provide the same functionality as the servlet bundle, implemented using **Java Server Pages (JSP)**.

OSGi, Felix, and...

As this book is focused on OSGi and Felix, it is important to keep a clear separation between materials that are OSGi-specific and those that are Felix-specific. Recognizing and following the OSGi-specific directives allows you to develop bundles for any framework that is OSGi-compliant.

For example, in *Chapter 1, Quick Intro to Felix and OSGi*, we've looked at the OSGi core specifications which govern the way an OSGi framework must behave and the rules required to be followed by the bundles targeted for an OSGi framework.

Felix is an OSGi-compliant service platform implementation. It also provides a selection of bundles that are OSGi-compliant. The sections having to do with installing and operating Felix are Felix-specific. However, there are chapters that will discuss bundles provided by Felix, but that may be used on any other OSGi compliant framework.

For example, the chapters talking about the Log Service and Http Service implementations will cover bits from OSGi specification as well as ones specific to the Felix implementation. Understanding which sides are part of the OSGi specification and which parts are Felix-specific will help when you want to replace the implementation bundle from one provider to another.

Furthermore, additional hints and discussions around general design-related topics and tools that help with the development activities apply to a context wider than that on which this book focuses. They aim to augment the basic integration requirements with ones that may improve the development experience.

Taking it step-by-step

As mentioned earlier, we will construct this target application in small steps from the bottom up. At every step, the functionality related to OSGi and to Felix will be introduced and explained, thus constructing your knowledge base progressively.

In the previous chapters, you took a dive into the OSGi world and got your environment ready for development by installing the Felix Framework Distribution. Also, you quickly covered an introduction to the Felix Gogo shell. Your system is thus set.

Here, we've established the scope of work and defined the application blueprint. The rest of the book will take you through the implementation and testing of the application.

For the first integration with the OSGi framework, to understand how a bundle interacts with it using bundle activators and the bundle context, we start with the inventory bundles in *Chapter 5, The Book Inventory bundle*. Those require no interaction with other bundles and will be a good start.

Chapter 5 will also cover how to use the Maven build mechanism to simplify the development of OSGi bundles. It will take you through the definition of a POM for the bundle, the structure of the project contents, and the execution of the build lifecycle to deploy it.

Then, after learning about the OBR service, in *Chapter 6, Using the OSGi Bundle Repository*, you'll install and start the inventory bundles on the Felix framework and quickly test them.

By then, you would have covered a complete develop-to-test cycle; it's the long "Hello world" that covers all that you need for a fully validated environment.

As you have no interface to interact with the bundle service yet, the testing is done as part of the bundle startup in the bundle activator code. This is later removed when shell commands are implemented for the application in *Chapter 8, Adding a Command-Line Interface*.

The next step is to learn how to interact with other bundles in the framework. In *Chapter 7*, you will implement the bookshelf service, which constitutes the business layer. Then in *Chapter 8*, you will add the shell commands of the presentation layer.

The end of *Chapter 7* is a milestone in the case study. By that point, you would have covered most of the OSGi core specification material that's in scope for this book.

By the end of *Chapter 8*, you would be ready to move to more advanced concepts. In *Chapter 9*, dependency injection is introduced with iPOJO. This adds a layer of separation between our bundles and the framework.

The last part of the book goes into the graphical interface world. It deals with building a simple servlet in *Chapter 11*, while introducing the OSGi Http Service and its Felix implementation.

In *Chapter 13*, you will learn about OSGi Web Containers, which allow the deployment of **Web Application Bundles** (**WAB**s) and **Web Archives** (**WAR**s) and look at the Pax Web services to provide this functionality.

You will also cover a quick tour of the Felix Web Management Console in *Chapter 12*, which provides a graphical management interface to the Felix framework and some of its common services. We will also look at the iPOJO Web Console Plugins service.

The last chapter, *Chapter 14, Pitfalls and Troubleshooting* looks into some of the common pitfalls while developing bundles and ways to troubleshoot and resolve them.

For reference, Appendix A guides you through the use of some of the available tools that would simplify the development process. We will look at how to use Eclipse, an **Integrated Development Environment** (**IDE**), along with Maven, to develop and debug bundles on the Felix framework. We will cover how to connect to a remote Felix instance as well as how to embed a Felix instance into Eclipse.

Finally, Appendix B will give you a few leads on additional interesting topics that you may choose to follow after having completed this case study.

But before we get started, let's lay down the naming conventions that will be used for the bundle projects.

Some conventions

During this case study, we'll create a good deal of bundles for deployment. Here we will define the common conventions that will be used for identifying the bundles and organization of the Java code.

As we will see in greater detail in *Chapter 5*, a bundle is identified by a symbolic name, associated with a version sequence. It is also, usually, given a name. I have chosen a common group identifier for all the bundles `com.packtpub.felix` and a common bundle artifact base prefix `com.packtpub.felix.bookshelf-`. The common group identifier will also be used as the base package for the Java code.

For example, the Book Inventory API bundle would be given the symbolic name `com.packtpub.felix.bookshelf-inventory-api` and its Java classes would be organized under the package `com.packt.felix.bookshelf.inventory.api`. Notice the switch from dot to dash separation; this allows a quick visual split between the group and artifact IDs of the project. In this case, `com.packt.felix` is the group ID and `bookshelf-inventory-api` is the artifact ID.

In regular development contexts, an artifact's version progresses following best practices, rules that were put in place to transmit information about compatibility between different versions of a bundle. We'll look at the topic of versioning in greater detail in *Chapter 5*, but the following is a quick introduction.

This compatibility information is encoded in three parts of a version string: the major, minor, and patch level. Typically, a bundle would start with a major version of 0 until it is first released. While its major version is 0, the interfaces exposed by the bundle are still in development mode and may undergo any change found to improve them.

When the bundle is released, it is given the version 1.0.0. After this point, changes to the bundle that do not affect the exposed interfaces impact the patch level of the version. For example, a bundle with version 1.0.0 undergoes bug fixes that do not affect its interfaces. This bundle is released with version 1.0.1.

Backward compatible changes to a bundle's interfaces impact the minor version part and reset the patch level. For example, if a new getter method is added to an interface in a bundle with version 1.2.1, it would be released with version 1.3.0. In this instance, a component that had a dependency on this bundle when it had version 1.2.1 can use the one with version 1.3.0 without requiring any changes to its code.

A change in the major version of a bundle means that the changes to the functionality are not backwards compatible. This may include removal of methods, changes in the return types, or an optional bean property that becomes mandatory.

In our context, to make it easier for you to know in which chapter a bundle was last updated, we will encode the chapter number as the minor version. For example, the `bookshelf-inventory-api` bundle is released with version 1.5.0 in *Chapter 5*.

The following are the bundles we will produce as part of our case study:

- `com.packt.felix.bookshelf-inventory-api`: The Book Inventory API bundle, released in *Chapter 5* with version 1.5.0

- `com.packt.felix.bookshelf-inventory-impl-mock`: The Book Inventory Mock Implementation bundle, released in *Chapter 5* with version 1.5.0, then in *Chapter 9* with version 1.9.0, and finally in *Chapter 10* with version 1.10.0

- `com.packt.felix.bookshelf-service`: The Bookshelf Service bundle, released in *Chapter 7* with version 1.7.0, then in *Chapter 8* with version 1.8.0, and finally in *Chapter 10* with version 1.10.0

- `com.packt.felix.bookshelf-service-tui`: The Bookshelf Service Text-UI commands bundle, released in *Chapter 8* with versions 1.8.0 and 1.8.1 and then again in *Chapter 9* with version 1.9.0

- `com.packt.felix.bookshelf-servlet`: The Booshelf Servlet bundle, released in *Chapter 12* with version 1.12.0

- `com.packt.felix.bookshelf-webapp`: The Bookshelf Web application bundle, released in *Chapter 13* with version 1.13.0

Summary

One of the most important parts in the preparation of a project is the definition of the overall design and the setting of a specific scope. In this chapter, we have prepared the grounds for our bookshelf case study. We have looked at the tiered layout of the application and the mapping of the different components of the bookshelf case study to the data, business logic, and presentation tiers.

We have:

♦   Designed the bookshelf case study, describing its components and their mapping to the data inventory, business logic, and presentation tiers

♦   Set a specific scope for the work to be covered in this book as part of the case study

♦   Laid down a few naming conventions for the bundles that will be produced

Now, it's time to start with the data inventory bundles.

The Book Inventory Bundle

5

The Book Inventory interface will define the Book's storage and look-up functionality for the bookshelf. It will be the contract that a bundle providing book inventory functionality must follow.

The interface is designed to allow many possible implementations of the location where the data is persisted. The goal is to be able to quickly write an implementation that only stores the books in memory (non-persistent when the bundle is stopped); then later replaces it with one that stores the data to a file or to a database.

In this chapter, we will define the Book Inventory API and write a mock implementation. The mock implementation will store the Book items in memory. We will also start looking at how bundles are packaged for installation onto an OSGi framework.

We will:

- ◆ Create the book inventory API bundle project skeleton
- ◆ Define the Book bean
- ◆ Define the Book Inventory API
- ◆ Package and deploy the bundle

Then we will:

- ◆ Create the book inventory mock implementation (memory-based)
- ◆ Package and deploy the new bundle

So let's start with the first bundle, namely, the book inventory API bundle.

The accompanying code for this book can be downloaded from:

```
http://www.packtpub.com/files/code/1384_Code.zip
```

Set up the Book Inventory API Bundle project

By now, you should have gone through the environment setup. If you've just been reading through so far, it's a good idea to go back to *Chapter 2*, *Setting up the environment*, and set yourself up for starting the project development.

We'll set up the skeleton of our first bundle, to which we'll add the interface definitions through this chapter.

Here, we will go through the manual steps for the setup of a bundle—it's always good to know how to do things without the assistance of tools. *Appendix A*, *Eclipse, Maven, and Felix*, guides you through the steps to automate a lot of the following topics for the same outcome using Eclipse and its plugins.

Time for action – setting up the project skeleton

Choose a location in your filesystem to home your development activity. I'm working on a Windows platform and have picked `C:\projects\felixbook\sources\` to hold my projects. We'll call this the case study source directory.

For each new project, we'll create a sub-directory with the name of the bundle. This bundle is the `com.packtpub.felix.bookshelf-inventory-api`. So create the following directory structure under your common directory:

```
com.packtpub.felix.bookshelf-inventory-api
 └ src
   └ main
     ├ java
     └ resources
```

The newly created directory `com.packtpub.felix.bookshelf-inventory-api` is this project's base directory.

The `src/main/java` directory will hold our Java sources, the `src/main/resources` will contain the other files (resources) that are needed by the java code or the framework.

This file structure adheres to the default Maven settings, we'll use it to keep the project object model definition simple. If you are bound to use another file structure for your projects, take a look at the Maven references for the ways to customize the source's layout.

Time for action – creating the project POM

The next step is to create the `pom.xml` file, which tells Maven and the Felix plugins how to build this project.

The **Project Object Model (POM)** is located in the project base directory (in this case, under `com.packtpub.felix.bookshelf-inventory-api`).

Create a file named `pom.xml`. You will edit its contents as we go through their meaning in the coming sections.

```
<project
    xmlns="http://maven.apache.org/POM/4.0.0"
    xmlns:xsi="http://www.w3.org/2001/XMLSchema-instance"
    xsi:schemaLocation="http://maven.apache.org/POM/4.0.0
        http://maven.apache.org/maven-v4_0_0.xsd">

    <modelVersion>4.0.0</modelVersion>
```

The first part is common to all POMs; it's the XML schema information and the POM model version.

The Bundle identity

Next comes the project identification; this information will be used in the construction of the bundle JAR, as well as for referring to it from other projects as a dependency.

The `artifactId` will be used in the naming of the packaged JAR and will also be used in the generated manifest metadata as the `Bundle-Name`:

```
<groupId>com.packtpub.felix</groupId>
<artifactId>com.packtpub.felix.bookshelf-inventory-api
</artifactId>
<version>1.5.0</version>

<packaging>bundle</packaging>

<name>Bookshelf Inventory API</name>
<description>Defines the API for the Bookshelf inventory.
</description>
```

The previous syntax says that we're working with the `com.packtpub.felix.bookshelf-inventory-api` bundle artifact, which is in the `com.packtpub.felix` group and currently having the version `1.5.0`.

The packaging element tags this project to be treated as a bundle when packaging the artifact. This will be picked up by the Felix plugins (we'll set those up in a short while).

More on bundle versions

Versions are used to distinguish between multiple releases of the bundle. In its simplest form, a version would be a number that grows sequentially between releases of the bundle, also called *major* releases.

In the most complete form, the version is made of dot separated parts—the major, minor, micro, and qualifier parts. The major, minor, and micro parts are numbers, and the qualifier part is alpha-numeric and allows underscore (_) and dash (-). For example, `1.618.p-5` is a valid version for a bundle, and so are `1.1`, `3.4.1`, and `2`.

The idea is to be able to encode in the bundle version information about the relative differences between releases of the bundle. This information allows making decisions about whether to update to a newer release of a bundle or not.

When a new release of a bundle comes out with no changes to its API, it means that it mainly addresses bug fixes. This is reflected in an increment of the micro version. When a backwards compatible change is made to the code (that is, a component depending on the previous version can use this one without changing it), the minor version is incremented.

For example, say you have Bundle A that holds Class X and another bundle, B, that uses the method `doThat()` from Class X. Bundle A was released with version 1.3.0. However, there's a bug in method `doThat()`.

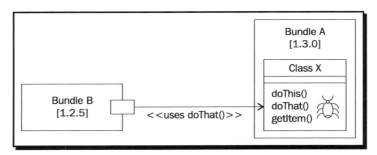

When a new version of Bundle A is released with the fix to that bug being the only change (that is, the API has not changed), it is released with version 1.3.1 (increment to the micro version part). We know that Bundle B can use this new version safely by a mere inspection of the new version.

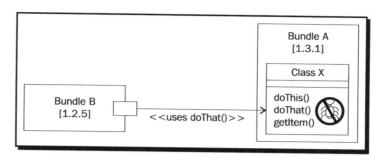

In this scenario, versions 1.3.0 and 1.3.1 are interchangeable—a bundle that depends on the bundle with version 1.3.1 can use that with version 1.3.0. In this example, this would not make sense because we know that version 1.3.0 was buggy and the bug was fixed with version 1.3.1. However, in some cases, a micro release may have introduced regression defects and the previous version would be more desirable.

In this same example, adding a method to Class X, say `addItem()`, is a backwards compatible change, that is, parties that were dependent on the previous version are not affected by upgrading to this one. All the methods that they need are still there. The result is a release of the bundle with version 1.4.0.

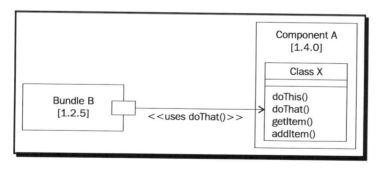

In a typical development process, the version of a bundle is important in order to follow its progress and to reflect on its backwards compatibility with previous releases. Of course, the version provides a hint of the kind of change that occurred. The release notes would contain more details on the actual changes.

There are a few factors that may impact compatibility, the main driving logic being the work required for the integration of the updated bundle. Here are a few examples:

- Changing the implementation of a method is typically both forwards and backwards compatible. The bundle requires regression testing and some validation end-to-end testing.
- Adding a method to an interface is backwards compatible when the third party uses this interface. However, it is not the case when the third-party extends it, as it will require development for the integration of the changed bundle.
- Making a bean attribute optional when it was mandatory is backwards compatible, however, the opposite is not.

The above highlights the importance of keeping a close eye on dependencies and their versions, as well as documenting the usage of each dependency.

As mentioned earlier, in our case, to make the mapping between the released bundles and the book chapters easier, we will use the chapter number as a minor version for the bundle. Therefore, the first released version of a bundle will not be 1.0.0. As the changes made through the chapters are all backwards compatible, this does not break the versioning schema. However, it provides an easy reference back to the chapter in which this bundle was released.

Let's go back to our POM now and look at its dependencies section.

Dependencies

The dependencies section of the POM lists the components that this artifact depends on. It identifies each of those dependencies by specifying their `groupId`, `artifactId`, and `version`.

The `scope` of a dependency defines whether the dependency is required at compile time (default), at `runtime`, during the unit and integration testing phase (`test`), whether the dependency is already available on the target platform (`provided`), or that the dependency JAR is explicitly provided on the filesystem (`system`).

This bundle doesn't have any dependencies yet. Therefore, its dependencies section is empty:

```
<dependencies>
</dependencies>
```

Later in this chapter, when working on the inventory implementation, we'll see an example of a `dependencies` section that's not empty.

Customizing the build

We had tagged this project with the `bundle` packaging in the identification part previously. This packaging type is a custom packaging (that does not come with the default Maven distribution). It is defined by the `maven-bundle-plugin` provided by the Felix project.

The `maven-bundle-plugin` attaches to some of the goals in the build lifecycle and assists in the creation of the bundle. For example, it will generate the manifest OSGi headers based on the analysis of the code and the directives provided in the plugin configuration part of the POM.

To instruct Maven to use this plugin during the build process, we add it to the build plugins section in the POM:

```
<build>
  <plugins>
    <plugin>
      <groupId>org.apache.felix</groupId>
      <artifactId>maven-bundle-plugin</artifactId>
      <version>2.1.0</version>
      <extensions>true</extensions>
```

The configuration section tells the plugin how to generate the bundle manifest file including OSGi-related information. Here, the `Bundle-Category` and `Bundle-SymbolicName` are set:

```
<configuration>
  <instructions>
    <Bundle-Category>sample</Bundle-Category>
    <Bundle-SymbolicName>${artifactId}
    </Bundle-SymbolicName>
```

The `${artifact}` is Maven's way of requesting the substitute with the value of the `artifactId` in this POM.

I've picked `sample` as the bundle category, but we could have categorized it as `inventory` to reflect its purpose. This attribute has no functional impact.

This bundle will provide the `com.packtpub.felix.bookshelf.inventory.api` package for export. It will be imported by the inventory implementation and the bookshelf bundles.

```
<Export-Package>
  com.packtpub.felix.bookshelf.inventory.api
</Export-Package>
  </instructions>
```

The `remoteOBR` element provides the plugin with the name of the distribution management repository (see the following section):

```
        <remoteOBR>repo-rel</remoteOBR>
        <prefixUrl>
          file:///C:/projects/felixbook/releases
        </prefixUrl>
      </configuration>
    </plugin>
```

The plugin will update a `repository.xml` file on that distribution repository and use the `prefixUrl` for references to the bundle artifacts.

We'll also keep a tight check on which Java version we're using as this is a good practice to avoid later integration and deployment issues. The plugin that Maven uses during the compile phase is the `maven-compiler-plugin`. Here we configure it to use source compatibility and to generate bytecode for Java release 1.5; this is similar to using the `-source` and `-target` options of the `javac` tool.

```
      <plugin>
        <artifactId>maven-compiler-plugin</artifactId>
        <inherited>true</inherited>
        <configuration>
          <source>1.5</source>
          <target>1.5</target>
        </configuration>
      </plugin>
    </plugins>
  </build>
```

Defining the distribution parameters

The last item we need to look at in the POM is the definition of the bundle distribution management section. The distribution management section is used during the deploy phase of a build and tells Maven where the packaged bundle is to be deployed.

```
  <distributionManagement>
    <!-- releases repo -->
    <repository>
      <id>repo-rel</id>
      <url>file:///C:/projects/felixbook/releases</url>
    </repository>
  </distributionManagement>
</project>
```

That's it for the setup of the project POM. Let's move on to the Book bean interface definition.

The Book bean interface

The Book bean is the main data item that is used in this application. It is stored by the Book Inventory and served by the Bookshelf Service for display by the web application or on the text user interface.

The Book bean attributes

We want to reference a book by its ISBN and keep the basic attributes that describe it.

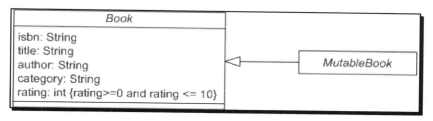

The attributes for our Book bean are:

◆ **ISBN**: The book reference number (mandatory)

◆ **Title**: The book title (optional)

◆ **Author**: The author of the book (optional)

◆ **Category**: The category of the book (optional)

◆ **Rating**: How much I liked this book (from 0 to 10, optional)

The **International Standard Book Number (ISBN)** is the primary reference to the book entry. It is used to uniquely reference a Book entry when updating or deleting. Although there's a strict convention for ISBNs, we won't be checking them—any string will be accepted.

The Category attribute is a personal grouping of books such as "Literature", "Technology", and so on. It is simply a way to organize our books into sub-sets.

The remaining attributes are pretty much self-explanatory.

Time for action – creating the Book bean interface

Let's add the `Book` and `MutableBook` interfaces, which are the beans of our bookshelf. They are placed in the package `com.packtpub.felix.bookshelf.inventory.api`.

The `Book` interface only exposes read access to the book attributes. It is usually a good practice to separate immutable parts of the interface from mutable parts. This way, we can separate between parts of the application that do read-only access to the data and others that are allowed to update it. Javadocs have been removed for clarity.

```
public interface Book
{
    String getIsbn();
    String getTitle();
    String getAuthor();
    String getCategory();
    int getRating();
}
```

We will extend this interface for the mutable type, which provides the additional write access to the Book bean:

```
public interface MutableBook extends Book
{
    void setIsbn(String isbn);
    void setTitle(String title);
    void setAuthor(String author);
    void setCategory(String category);
    void setRating(String rating);
}
```

 Did you notice that the interfaces we've just designed have no knowledge of OSGi? As we've seen in *Chapter 1, Quick Intro to Felix and OSGi*, OSGi requires very little to integrate with your application. Later in this chapter, we'll see Activators, which will be our first use of OSGi-specific API.

Have a go hero – personalize the Book Bean API

There are many other potential candidates for the book attributes. The ones we've chosen previously are minimalistic.

Here are some you may want to add to personalize this implementation:

◆ **Start date**: Date I started reading this book (optional)

◆ **Finish date**: Date I finished reading this book (optional)

◆ **Front cover**: An image of the book's front cover and so on

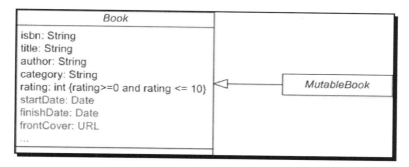

You'll have to follow those additional attributes throughout the implementation, all the way to the graphics and text user interface.

Don't forget to impact the version of the bundle according to the change!

Adding an optional attribute to the Book bean makes this attribute available to bundles that need it. However, it allows bundles that used the previous version to be able to use this one as well. It's a minor version change. If the added attribute is mandatory, then it's a major version change!

The Book Inventory interface

Now that the Book bean is defined, we can implement its inventory API as we have defined it in *Chapter 4, Let's Get Started: The Bookshelf Project*. The interface hosts the inventory methods as well as the Book factory method:

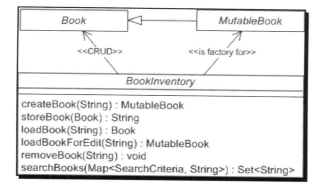

Now, let's add this interface to our project.

Time for action – writing the BookInventory interface

The inventory interface is `BookInventory`. Package declaration, imports, and Javadocs have been removed for clarity:

```
public interface BookInventory
{
    enum SearchCriteria
    {
        ISBN_LIKE,
        TITLE_LIKE,
        AUTHOR_LIKE,
        GROUP_LIKE,
        GRADE_GT,
        GRADE_LT
    }

    Set<String> getCategories();


    MutableBook createBook(String isbn)
        throws BookAlreadyExistsException;;

    MutableBook loadBookForEdit(String isbn)
        throws BookNotFoundException;

    String storeBook(MutableBook book) throws InvalidBookException;

    Book loadBook(String isbn) throws BookNotFoundException;

    void removeBook(String isbn) throws BookNotFoundException;

    Set<String> searchBooks(
        Map<SearchCriteria, String> criteria);
}
```

The method `getCategories` gives back the list of book categories.

The method `createBook` is the factory method. It is used to create a new book for a given ISBN and throws a `BookAlreadyExistsException` if a book with that ISBN is already inventoried. The `loadBookForEdit` method will retrieve a book that's already created or throw a `BookNotFoundException` if the book is not in the inventory.

Both of these methods will return a `MutableBook` as the intention is to edit the book and then store it using the `storeBook` method.

The `storeBook` method saves changes made to a book. It will check that the book has all mandatory attributes set and throw an `InvalidBookException` if it's not the case. It returns the ISBN of the book that was stored.

The `loadBook` method loads an existing book, given its ISBN reference. It returns a read-only `Book` or throws a `BookNotFoundException` if no book was previously stored with this particular ISBN reference.

The `removeBook` method removes a book from the inventory, based on its ISBN reference, or throws a `BookNotFoundException`, if no book was previously stored with this ISBN reference.

The exceptions are straightforward and are not listed here.

The `searchBooks` method finds the books in the bookshelf that match a given set of criteria. It returns the set of ISBNs for the books that match the search criteria. They are as follows:

- ◆ `ISBN_LIKE` to filter on ISBN. For example, "123-%" and "%987", would include books with ISBN starting with "123-" and ending with "987" respectively
- ◆ `TITLE_LIKE` to filter on title
- ◆ `AUTHOR_LIKE` to filter on author
- ◆ `CATEGORY_LIKE` to filter on book category
- ◆ `RATING_GT` to include books with a rating greater than that of a given value
- ◆ `RATING_LT` to include books with a rating lesser than that of a given value

For example, if we want to search for all books from "John Doe", which we assigned a grade higher than 5, we would call:

```
Map<SearchCriteria, String> criteria =
    new HashMap<SearchCriteria, String>();

crits.put(SearchCriteria.AUTHOR_LIKE, "John Doe");
crits.put(SearchCriteria.GRADE_GT, "5");

Set<String> results = impl.searchBooks(crits);
```

The Book Inventory API is now ready to be bundled.

Build and deploy the bundle

Let's go through the build process in further detail. It will not be repeated with as many details for the remaining bundles.

Time for action – building and deploying the bundle

Open up a command shell and go to the project base directory (in my case, it's
`C:\projects\felixbook\sources\com.packtpub.felixguide.bookshelf-inventory-api`).

Run the following command to first `clean` the previous build temporary file (in this case,
it's the first build, so there are none), then go through the build lifecycle up to `deploy`:

```
mvn clean deploy
```

The final outcome is the deployment of the bundle artifact to the repository under
`file:///C:/projects/felixbook/releases/com/packtpub/felix/com.packtpub.felix.bookshelf-inventory-api/1.5.0/com.packtpub.felix.bookshelf-inventory-api-1.5.0.jar` and its registration on the repository for
later use.

What just happened?

We've just used Maven to build, package, and deploy our bundle. It's that easy.

The repository it has deployed to is listed in the last parts of the build steps; look for logs
like the following:

```
...
[INFO] [bundle:deploy]
[INFO] LOCK file:///C:/projects/felixbook/releases/repository.xml
[INFO] Downloading repository.xml
[INFO] Computed bundle uri: file:/C:/projects/felixbook/releases/com/
packtpub/felix/com.packtpub.felix.bookshelf-inventory-api/1.5.0/com.
packtpub.felix.bookshelf-inventory-api-1.5.0.jar
[INFO] Writing OBR metadata
[INFO] Deploying file:/C:/projects/felixbook/releases/com/packtpub/felix/
com.packtpub.felix.bookshelf-inventory-api/1.5.0/com.packtpub.felix.
bookshelf-inventory-api-1.5.0.jar
[INFO] Writing OBR metadata
[INFO] Uploading repository.xml
[INFO] UNLOCK file:///C:/projects/felixbook/releases/repository.xml
[INFO] ------------------------------------------------------------------
----
[INFO] BUILD SUCCESSFUL
...
```

My OBR repository will be `file:///C:/projects/felixbook/releases/`
`repository.xml`. This is the repository that we'll feed into Felix's bundle repository service
as an additional source of bundles. We will cover OBRs in more details in *Chapter 6, Using
the OSGi Bundle Repository.*

For now, let's carry on and create another bundle, the one for the inventory implementation.

Let's implement those interfaces

We will start with a quick-and-dirty implementation of the `BookInventory` interface, a
mock implementation.

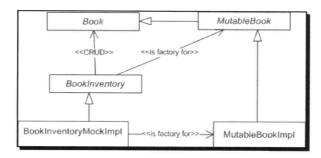

Later, you may want to replace it with one that saves the books to a file or database.

Time for action – creating the POM

This bundle will be called `com.packtpub.felix.bookshelf-inventory-impl-mock`.
We won't see the whole POM here, but only the parts that are different from the one we
saw previously. As we go through the book, I'll start hinting for those contents instead of
showing them.

The identity section of the POM for this bundle will look like the following:

```xml
<groupId>com.packtpub.felix</groupId>
<artifactId>
  com.packtpub.felix.bookshelf-inventory-impl-mock
</artifactId>
<version>1.5.0</version>

<packaging>bundle</packaging>

<name>Bookshelf Inventory Impl - Mock</name>
<description>
  Memory-based mock implementation of the Bookshelf Inventory API
</description>
```

This bundle depends on the inventory API bundle. This dependency is declared as:

```
<dependencies>
  <dependency>
    <groupId>com.packtpub.felix</groupId>
    <artifactId>
        com.packtpub.felix.bookshelf-inventory-api</artifactId>
    <version>1.5.0</version>
  </dependency>
</dependencies>
```

A dependency is declared by specifying the `groupId`, `artifactId`, and `version` of the target library.

The other part that needs to be looked at is the `Export-Package` header in the instructions section of the `maven-bundle-plugin` configuration.

This bundle exports `com.packtpub.felix.bookshelf.inventory.impl.mock`:

```
<plugin>
  <groupId>org.apache.felix</groupId>
  <artifactId>maven-bundle-plugin</artifactId>
  <version>2.1.0</version>
  <extensions>true</extensions>
    <configuration>
      <instructions>
        <Bundle-Category>sample</Bundle-Category>
        <Bundle-SymbolicName>${artifactId}
        </Bundle-SymbolicName>
        <Export-Package>
          com.packtpub.felix.bookshelf.inventory.impl.mock
        </Export-Package>
      </instructions>
      <remoteOBR>repo-rel</remoteOBR>
      <prefixUrl>
        file:///C:/projects/felixbook/releases</prefixUrl>
      <ignoreLock>true</ignoreLock>
    </configuration>
</plugin>
```

Project inheritance

As you can see, we're repeating a lot of the POM configuration for each project. In Maven, there's a possibility of declaring a parent POM that contains the common configuration and inherits it in its children, thus tremendously reducing the size of each project's POM, but also making it easier to update a configuration centrally and have it applied to all projects.

Consider taking a look at it, under project inheritance, in the Maven POM online documentation.

That's all! Let's get right to the implementation of those interfaces.

Time for action – implementing a mutable book

The MutableBook implementation is straightforward. We'll put it in the following package: com.packtpub.felix.bookshelf.inventory.impl.mock.

```java
public class MutableBookImpl implements MutableBook
{
    private String isbn;
    private String author;
    private String title;
    private String category;
    private int rating;
```

The sole constructor takes an ISBN as the parameter; it's the Book's mandatory attribute:

```java
public MutableBookImpl(String isbn)
{
    setISBN(isbn);
}
```

Then we implement the setters and getters. I'll show the first and then you can carry on with the others.

```java
public void setISBN(String isbn)
{
    this.isbn = isbn;
}

public String getISBN()
{
    return this.isbn;
}

// ...
```

The `toString()` method returns a string representation of this book for debug printing:

```
public String toString() {
  StringBuffer buf = new StringBuffer();
  buf.append(getCategory()).append(": ");
  buf.append(getTitle()).append(" from ").append(getAuthor());
  buf.append(" [").append(getRating()).append(']');
  return buf.toString();
}
}
```

Simple implementation: Let's move onto the `BookInventory` mock implementation.

Time for action – implementing the mock (memory-stored) Book Inventory

In fast development cycles, applying continuous integration, we develop mock implementations of interfaces that we need to get our system up and running as quickly as possible.

The mock implementation provides the functionality required by its interface in a minimalistic manner. The goal is to make it available to components that depend on that interface early on in the development process.

This way, the mock implementation can be replaced with a more final one at the same time as the rest of the application is developed. This development strategy speeds up time-to-market quite a bit.

Here, we will store the books in a Map, indexed by ISBN, for look-up on modify operations.

```
public class BookInventoryMockImpl implements BookInventory
{
    public static final String DEFAULT_CATEGORY = "default";

    private Map<String, MutableBook> booksByISBN =
        new HashMap<String, MutableBook>();
```

The factory method

A factory method provides the caller with a new instance of a `MutableBook`. This re-enforces the decoupling between the components—the component that uses the `Book` and `MutableBook` does not need to know the class or classes that implement the interfaces.

```
public MutableBook createBook(String isbn)
{
    return new MutableBookImpl(isbn);
}
```

Implementing a mock getGoups()

In order to have a listing of the categories (without having to go through the whole map every time), we'll keep a count of the books that are in a category and update that count as we store and remove books.

```java
private Map<String, Integer> categories =
    new HashMap<String, Integer>();

public Set<String> getCategories()
{
    return this.categories.keySet();
}
```

Storing a book

Before storing a book, we first check if its attributes are valid. In our case, the only requirement is that it has an ISBN set.

We also need to keep track of the category to which it belongs to, to update the `categories` cache. This implementation will place books that don't have a set category into the `default` category.

```java
public String storeBook(MutableBook book)
    throws InvalidBookException
{
    String isbn = book.getIsbn();
    if (isbn == null) {
        throw new InvalidBookException("ISBN is not set");
    }
    this.booksByISBN.put(isbn, book);
    String category = book.getCategory();
    if (category == null) {
        category = DEFAULT_CATEGORY;
    }
    if (this.categories.containsKey(category)) {
        int count = this.categories.get(category);
        this.categories.put(category, count + 1);
    }
    else {
        this.categories.put(category, 1);
    }
    return isbn;
}
```

Removing a stored book

Removing a stored book is the opposite operation. We remove it from the mapping and update the categories cache accordingly.

```
public void removeBook(String isbn)
    throws BookNotFoundException
{
    Book book = this.booksByISBN.remove(isbn);
    if (book == null) {
        throw new BookNotFoundException(isbn);
    }
    String category = book.getCategory();
    int count = this.categories.get(category);
    if (count == 1) {
        this.categories.remove(category);
    }
    else {
        this.categories.put(category, count - 1);
    }
}
```

Loading a stored book

Since we've carefully designed our BookInventory interface, separating operations that use a Book from those that use a MutableBook, we are safe to use the same implementation (MutableBookImpl) for either of them.

In our case, we don't pay any attention to concurrency concerns as they are beyond the scope of this book and therefore no data locking is implemented when an item is loaded for edit. When a file- or database-based implementation of this interface is written, consider adding a lock mechanism to prevent multiple parties from editing a book simultaneously.

```
public Book loadBook(String isbn)
    throws BookNotFoundException
{
    return loadBookForEdit(isbn);
}

public MutableBook loadBookForEdit(String isbn)
    throws BookNotFoundException
{
    MutableBook book = this.booksByISBN.get(isbn);
    if (book == null) {
        throw new BookNotFoundException(isbn);
    }
    return book;
}
```

Implementing the book search

We're expecting the search functionality to be slow. Remember, this is a mock implementation. In a database-based implementation, the criteria can be used in turn to specify a filter and provide a significantly better performance.

```java
public Set<String> searchBooks(
    Map<SearchCriteria, String> criteria)
{

    LinkedList<Book> books = new LinkedList<Book>();
    books.addAll(this.booksByISBN.values());

    for (Map.Entry<SearchCriteria, String> criterion
            : criteria.entrySet()) {
        Iterator<Book> it = books.iterator();
        while (it.hasNext()) {
            Book book = it.next();
            switch (criterion.getKey()) {
                case AUTHOR_LIKE:
                    if (
!checkStringMatch(book.getAuthor(), criterion.getValue()))
                    {
                        it.remove();
                        continue;
                    }
                    break;
```

The `checkStringMatch` method will attempt to match the given string attribute to the given criterion value.

The same matching mechanism is applied for the ISBN, group, and title. The rating matching uses another set of methods listed further down.

```java
                case ISBN_LIKE:
                    if (!checkStringMatch(
                      book.getISBN(), criterion.getValue()))
                    {
                        it.remove();
                        continue;
                    }
                    break;
                case CATEGORY_LIKE:
                    if (!checkStringMatch(
                      book.getCategory(), criterion.getValue()))
                    {
```

```
                it.remove();
                continue;
            }
            break;
        case TITLE_LIKE:
            if (!checkStringMatch(
              book.getTitle(), criterion.getValue()))
            {
                it.remove();
                continue;
            }
            break;
        case RATING_GT:
            if (!checkIntegerGreater(
              book.getRating(), criterion.getValue()))
            {
                it.remove();
                continue;
            }
            break;
        case RATING_LT:
            if (!checkIntegerSmaller(
              book.getRating(), criterion.getValue()))
            {
                it.remove();
                continue;
            }
            break;
        }
    }
}
```

Next, gather the books that match, extract their ISBNs, and return the result to the caller.

```
    // copy ISBNs
    HashSet<String> isbns = new HashSet<String>();
    for (Book book : books) {
        isbns.add(book.getISBN());
    }
    return isbns;
}
```

In a typical implementation, returning the references to items as a result of a search improves performance, especially when the results returned are many. It saves the time and resources required to load and transmit the results.

The method `checkIntegerGreater` for checking the rating criterion match is as follows:

```
private boolean checkIntegerGreater(int attr, String critVal)
{
    int critValInt;
    try {
        critValInt = Integer.parseInt(critVal);
    }
    catch (NumberFormatException e) {
        return false;
    }
    if (attr >= critValInt) {
        return true;
    }
    return false;
}
```

The method `checkIntegerSmaller` is similar to the previous one, the difference being the presence of the compare operator (not listed).

The last missing method is the `checkStringMatch` method for comparing strings having a wildcard:

```
private boolean checkStringMatch(String attr, String critVal)
{
    if (attr == null) {
        return false;
    }
    attr = attr.toLowerCase();
    critVal = critVal.toLowerCase();

    boolean startsWith = critVal.startsWith("%");
    boolean endsWith = critVal.endsWith("%");

    if (startsWith && endsWith) {
        if (critVal.length()==1) {
            return true;
        }
        else {
            return attr.contains(
                critVal.substring(1, critVal.length() - 1));
        }
    }
    else if (startsWith) {
```

```
                return attr.endsWith(critVal.substring(1));
            }
            else if (endsWith) {
                return attr.startsWith(
                    critVal.substring(0, critVal.length() - 1));
            }
            else {
                return attr.equals(critVal);
            }
        }
    }
}
```

Even though we're done with the implementation of the service, we still need to hook it into the Felix framework and make it available as a service.

Writing the Bundle Activator

To increase flexibility in integrating existing services to an OSGi framework (in general), a service can be accompanied with a bundle activator, which will get temporary control of execution during the bundle start and stop, thus performing the necessary tasks such as registering services.

In this section, we will implement a small bundle activator for our inventory implementation. It will instantiate and register the service on start and then unregister it on stop.

For that, we will create an implementation of the `BundleActivator` interface (from the OSGi Core API) and declare it as our bundle activator in the POM.

Time for action – add a dependency to the OSGi Core library

To make the OSGi Core API available for our bundle, we need to add it as a dependency in the POM.

```
<dependencies>
  <!-- ... -->
  <dependency>
    <groupId>org.osgi</groupId>
    <artifactId>org.osgi.core</artifactId>
    <version>4.2.0</version>
  </dependency>
</dependencies>
```

This will ensure the library is on the classpath when compiling the bundle. We'll come back to the POM in a bit to declare the `Bundle-Activator` manifest header.

Time for action – creating the Activator

Now that the dependency has been added, we can implement the `BundleActivator` interface.

We will name our activator `BookInventoryMockImplActivator` and place it in a different package (say `com.packtpub.felix.bookshelf.inventory.impl.mock.activator`) and declared as a private package to avoid it being exported along with the other classes of the bundle.

```
package com.packtpub.felix.bookshelf.inventory.impl.mock.activator;

import org.osgi.framework.BundleActivator;
import org.osgi.framework.BundleContext;
import org.osgi.framework.ServiceRegistration;

import com.packtpub.felix.bookshelf.inventory.api.BookInventory;

public class BookInventoryMonkImplActivator
    implements BundleActivator
{
```

The bundle activator `start()` method is invoked at the start of the service and given a `BundleContext` reference. This context allows us to register and unregister services (among other operations).

We will keep the service registration reference to be used when unregistering the service.

```
    private ServiceRegistration reg = null;

    public void start(BundleContext context) throws Exception {
        System.out.println(
            "\nStarting Book Inventory Mock Impl");
        this.reg = context.registerService(
            BookInventory.class.getName(),
            new BookInventoryMockImpl(), null);
    }
```

The `registerService` method is used to make a service available for look-up by other bundles on the framework. Its parameters are as follows:

◆ `String clazz`: The class name that will be used to look up the service

◆ `Object service`: The service to be registered

◆ `Dictionary properties`: Optional dictionary of properties attached with this service registration

The second parameter in the `registerService` method can also be a `ServiceFactory` object that the framework would use to create an instance of the service.

When the bundle is stopping, the activator `stop()` method is invoked. We can use the stored service reference to unget the service.

```
public void stop(BundleContext context) throws Exception {
    System.out.println("\nStoping Book Inventory Mock Impl");
    if (this.reg!=null) {
        context.ungetService(reg.getReference());
        this.reg = null;
    }
}
}
```

Note that this is not strictly necessary, as all services from a bundle are unregistered by the framework when the bundle is stopped. However, it's good to know how this is done.

More on Bundle Contexts

The `BundleContext` can be considered as the proxy that bundles use to interact with the framework. It allows access to framework functionality such as:

- Registering a `BundleListener` to get framework events. `BundleEvents` are fired when:
  - A bundle is resolved (`BundleEvent.RESOLVED`)
  - A bundle is installed (`BundleEvent.INSTALLED`)
  - A bundle is about to start (`BundleEvent.STARTING`)
  - A bundle has started (`BundleEvent.STARTED`), among others. Have a look at the `BundleEvent` API Docs online for the other events that can be fired at: (`http://www.osgi.org/Specifications/Javadoc`).
- Registering and retrieving registered services as well as unregistering them
- Installing bundles to the framework, listing the installed bundles or a specific bundle
- Request for a location (`File`) to use as persistent storage

The `BundleContext` object is private to the bundle and can be shared within the bundle. However, it is not supposed to be shared with other bundles.

This should be enough for this class; let's declare it as the bundle activator in the POM and then deploy it. We'll try the bundles in the next chapter.

Time for action – declaring Bundle-Activator

The last thing that's left is to declare the bundle activator to be added to the bundle manifest. You also need to declare the package `com.packtpub.felix.bookshelf.inventory.impl.mock.activator` as a private package, so that it is made available for the bundle at runtime, but not visible to other bundles.

Edit the `maven-bundle-plugin` configuration instructions in the POM build plugins section and add the `Bundle-Activator` tag (in bold below). It holds the name of the bundle activator class.

```
<plugin>
    <groupId>org.apache.felix</groupId>
    <artifactId>maven-bundle-plugin</artifactId>
    <extensions>true</extensions>
    <configuration>
      <instructions>
        <Bundle-Category>sample</Bundle-Category>
        <Bundle-SymbolicName>
          ${artifactId}</Bundle-SymbolicName>
        <Bundle-Activator>
com.packtpub.felix.bookshelf.inventory.impl.mock.activator.-
BookInventoryMockImplActivator
        </Bundle-Activator>
        <Export-Package>
          com.packtpub.felix.bookshelf.inventory.impl.mock
        </Export-Package>
        <Private-Package>
com.packtpub.felix.bookshelf.inventory.impl.mock.activator
        </Private-Package>
      </instructions>
      <obrRepository>file:/P:/projects/felixbook/dev
      </obrRepository>
    </configuration>
  </plugin>
</plugins>
```

That's it!

Build and deploy the bundle

Build this bundle in the same way as we've done for the `bookshelf-inventory-api` bundle.

In the next chapter, we'll look into OBRs in greater detail. We'll then see how to install our bundles onto the Felix framework.

Pop quiz

Okay, let's see if you've been following—try answering these questions:

1. Which OSGi interface must you extend when defining a service API in an OSGi bundle?
    a. The Service interface
    b. The BundleActivator interface
    c. None, I can pick any interface I want

2. How do you deploy a bundle to the OBR repository once it's packaged?
    a. I need to fill out a form and submit my bundle
    b. Maven does it for me, using the `deploy` target
    c. I have to copy or ftp the bundle to the OBR

3. How do you register a service on an OSGi framework?
    a. I deploy it to the OBR repository
    b. I register it using a BundleContext
    c. I don't need to do anything

Summary

In this chapter, you've created the two bundles of the data inventory tier—the API bundle and a mock implementation bundle.

You have:

♦   Gone through the steps to manually set up a bundle to be built by Maven making use of the Felix Maven Bundle Plugin
♦   Created the book inventory API bundle (`bookshelf-inventory-api`), which defines the inventory and the book APIs
♦   Written a mock implementation of those APIs (`bookshelf-inventory-impl-mock`)
♦   Written a bundle activator for the mock implementation
♦   Built and deployed those bundles to the repository

We're ready to learn how to install those bundles onto Felix, which you will do in the next chapter, after an introduction to OBRs.

6
Using the OSGi Bundle Repository

So far, we have mentioned OBRs a few times without really diving into them. We're now at a point where we need to start using them, so it's time to take that dive.

In this chapter, we will first have a look at the OBR service in some level of detail, and then we'll see how we use it to install bundles from a remote location onto our Felix framework. We'll use the bundles we've created in Chapter 5, The Book Inventory Bundle, to practice what we've learned.

By the end of this chapter, you will have:

- ◆ Learned about the OSGi Bundle Repository concepts and the OBR repository XML file format
- ◆ Inspected the local releases repository
- ◆ Installed the bundles from *Chapter 5* onto Felix

OBR, the OSGi Bundle Repository

The **OSGi Bundle Repository (OBR)** is a draft specification from the OSGi alliance for a service that would allow getting access to a set of remote bundle repositories. Each remote repository, potentially a front for a federation of repositories, provides a list of bundles available for download, along with some additional information related to them.

The access to the OBR repository can be through a defined API to a remote service or as a direct connection to an XML repository file.

The bundles declared in an OBR repository can then be downloaded and installed to an OSGi framework like Felix. We will go through this install process a bit later.

 The OSGi specification for OBRs is currently in the draft state, which means that it may change before it is released.

The following diagram shows the elements related to the OBR, in the context of the OSGi framework:

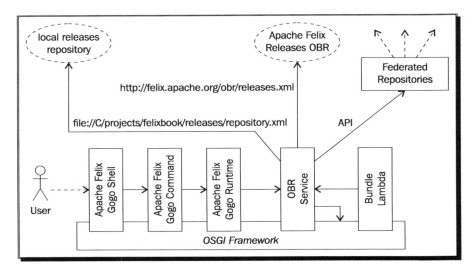

The OBR bundle exposes a service that is registered with the framework. This interface can be used by other components on the framework to inspect repositories, download bundles, and install them.

The Gogo command bundle also registers commands that interact with the OBR service to achieve the same purpose. Later in this chapter, we will cover those commands. API-based interaction with the service is not covered, as it is beyond the scope of this book.

The OBR service currently implements remote XML repositories only. However, the Repository interface defined by the OBR service can be implemented for other potential types of repositories as well as for a direct API integration.

There are a few OSGi repositories out there, here are some examples:

* **Apache Felix:** `http://felix.apache.org/obr/releases.xml`
* **Apache Sling:** `http://sling.apache.org/obr/sling.xml`

◆ **Paremus**: `http://sigil.codecauldron.org/spring-external.obr` and `http://sigil.codecauldron.org/spring-release.obr`

Those may be of use later, as a source for the dependencies of your project.

The repository XML Descriptor

We already have an OBR repository available to us, our releases repository. We have deployed the bookshelf bundles to it in the previous chapter as part of the Maven `deploy` phase (`file:///C/projects/felixbook/releases/repository.xml`).

Typically, you'll rarely need to look into the repository XML file. However, it's a good validation step when investigating issues with the deploy/install process.

Let's inspect some of its contents:

```
<repository lastmodified='20100905070524.031'>
```

Not included above in the automatically created repository file is the optional repository `name` attribute.

The repository contains a list of resources that it makes available for download. Here, we're inspecting the entry for the bundle `com.packtpub.felix.bookshelf-inventory-api`:

```
<resource
    id='com.packtpub.felix.bookshelf-inventory-api/1.4.0'
    symbolicname='com.packtpub.felix.bookshelf-inventory-api'
    presentationname='Bookshelf Inventory API'
    uri='file:/C:/projects/felixbook/releases/com/packtpub/felix/
com.packtpub.felix.bookshelf-inventory-api/1.4.0/com.packtpub.felix.
bookshelf-inventory-api-1.4.0.jar'
    version='1.4.0'>
<description>
    Defines the API for the Bookshelf inventory.</description>
<size>7781</size>
<category id='sample'/>
<capability name='bundle'>
  <p n='symbolicname'
    v='com.packtpub.felix.bookshelf-inventory-api'/>
  <p n='presentationname' v='Bookshelf Inventory API'/>
  <p n='version' t='version' v='1.4.0'/>
  <p n='manifestversion' v='2'/>
</capability>
<capability name='package'>
  <p n='package'
```

```
                v='com.packtpub.felix.bookshelf.inventory.api'/>
        <p n='version' t='version' v='0.0.0'/>
     </capability>
     <require name='package'
         filter=
 '(&amp;(package=com.packtpub.felix.bookshelf.inventory.api))'
         extend='false' multiple='false'
         optional='false'>
       Import package com.packtpub.felix.bookshelf.inventory.api
     </require>
  </resource>
```

Notice that the bundle location (attribute `uri`), which points to where the bundle can be downloaded, relative to the base repository location. The `presentationname` is used when listing the bundles and the `uri` is used to get the bundle when a request to install it is issued.

Inside the main resource entry tag are further bundle characteristics, a description of its capabilities, its requirements, and so on.

Although the same information is included in the bundle manifest, it is also included in the repository XML for quick access during validation of the environment, before the actual bundle is downloaded.

For example, the `package` capability elements describe the packages that this bundle exports:

```
        <capability name="package">
          <p n="package" v="com.packtpub.felix.bookshelf.inventory.api"/>
          <p n="version" t="version" v="0.0.0"/>
        </capability>
```

The `require` elements describe the bundle requirements from the target platform:

```
        <require extend="false"
          filter="(&amp;(package=com.packtpub.felix.bookshelf.inventory.
 api)(version&gt;=0.0.0))"
          multiple="false" name="package" optional="false">
            Import package com.packtpub.felix.bookshelf.inventory.api
        </require>
     </resource>
     <!-- ... -->
 </repository>
```

The preceding excerpts respectively correspond to the `Export-Package` and `Import-Package` manifest headers.

Each bundle may have more than one entry in the repository XML: an entry for every deployed version.

Updating the OBR repository

In *Chapter 5*, we had briefly looked at how to deploy a bundle to a remote repository using Maven. The Felix Maven Bundle Plugin attaches to the `deploy` phase to automate the bundle deployment and the update of the `repository.xml` file.

Using the OBR scope commands

The Gogo Command bundle registers a set of commands for the interaction with the OBR service. Those commands allow registering repositories, listing their bundles, and requesting their download and installation.

Let's look at those commands in detail.

obr:repos

The `obr:repos` command (`repos` for short, when there are no name conflicts) allows us to manage the repositories of the OBR service.

Its usage is as follows:

```
g! help repos
```

```
repos - manage repositories
    scope: obr
    parameters:
        String    ( add | list | refresh | remove )
        String[]    space-delimited list of repository URLs
```

The `repos add` operation is used to register repositories with the OBR service. For example, let's register our releases repository:

```
g! repos add file:///C:/projects/felixbook/releases/repository.xml
```

Registered repositories are not kept between restarts of the framework. To have repositories automatically registered at startup, set the property `obr.repository.url` in the framework `conf/config.properties` file. Its value is a space-separated list of repository URLs.

For example, the default value for this property is the Felix releases repository:

```
obr.repository.url=http://felix.apache.org/obr/releases.xml
```

The `repos remove` operation unregisters a previously added repository.

The `repos list` operation is used to list the registered repositories, for example:

```
g! repos list
file:/C:/projects/felixbook/releases/repository.xml
http://felix.apache.org/obr/releases.xml
```

Here we have the default repository and the one we've just added.

The `repos refresh` operation will reload the repositories that are passed as a parameter.

obr:list

The `obr:list` command finds bundles in the registered repositories and displays them. The search may be constrained by a filter on bundle names.

Its usage is as follows:

```
g! help list


list - list repository resources
   scope: obr
   flags:
      -v, --verbose    display all versions
   parameters:
      String[]    optional strings used for name matching
```

The `-v` (or `--verbose`) flag is used to display more information on each bundle, including all versions and the bundle-symbolic name.

For example, the following lists the bundles in the repository containing the sub-string book and displays verbose information:

```
g! list -v book
Bookshelf Inventory API
    [com.packtpub.felix.bookshelf-inventory-api] (1.4.0)
Bookshelf Inventory Impl - Mock
    [com.packtpub.felix.bookshelf-inventory-impl-mock] (1.4.0)
```

The output was reformatted for clarity.

obr:info

The obr:info command retrieves and displays the information available in the repository for one or more bundles.

The targeted bundles are passed as a space-separated list, each entry specified by display name, symbolic name, or bundle ID.

The syntax is as follows:

```
g! help info


info - retrieve resource description from repository
    scope: obr
    parameters:
        String[] ( <bundle-name>
                 | <symbolic-name> | <bundle-id> ) [@<version>] ...
```

For example, the following is the repository information of the "Apache Felix Gogo Shell Runtime" (bundle ID 3):

```
g! obr:info 3
-------------------------------
Apache Felix Gogo Shell Runtime
-------------------------------
license: http://www.apache.org/licenses/LICENSE-2.0.txt
symbolicname: org.apache.felix.gogo.runtime
uri: http://repo1.maven.org/maven2/org/apache/felix/gogo/-
    org.apache.felix.gogo.runtime/0.2.0/-
    org.apache.felix.gogo.runtime-0.2.0.jar
```

```
documentation: http://www.apache.org/
category: [org.apache.felix.gogo]
description: Apache Felix Gogo Shell
size: 58198
presentationname: Apache Felix Gogo Shell Runtime
id: org.apache.felix.gogo.runtime/0.2.0
version: 0.2.0
Requires:
    (&(package=org.osgi.framework))
    (&(package=org.osgi.service.command)(version>=0.2.0))
    (&(package=org.osgi.service.packageadmin))
    (&(package=org.osgi.service.threadio)(version>=0.2.0))
    (&(package=org.osgi.util.tracker))
Capabilities:
    {manifestversion=2, symbolicname=org.apache.felix.gogo.runtime,
      presentationname=Apache Felix Gogo Shell Runtime, version=0.2.0}
    {package=org.osgi.service.command, version=0.2.0}
    {package=org.osgi.service.threadio, version=0.2.0}
```

obr:deploy

The `obr:deploy` command is used to download bundles from the repository and install them onto the Felix instance, with the possibility of optionally starting them.

The command usage is as follows:

```
g! help deploy

deploy - deploy resource from repository
    scope: obr
    flags:
        -s, --start    start deployed bundles
    parameters:
        String[]    ( <bundle-name>
                    | <symbolic-name> | <bundle-id> )[@<version>] ...
```

The `-s` (or `--start`) flag is used to request the start of the bundles that were just installed.

We will use this command in a short while to install and start our Book Inventory API and implementation bundles.

obr:source and obr:javadoc

The `obr:source` and `obr:javadoc` commands are used to download a bundle's sources and JavaDocs archives (if present) to a local directory, and to optionally extract them.

The targeted bundles are specified as a space-separated list of references, each reference being the bundle-symbolic name, presentation name, or ID, with an optional version specification.

The `obr:source` and `obr:javadoc` commands have similar usage. The following command is that of the `javadoc`:

```
g! help javadoc
```

```
javadoc - retrieve resource JavaDoc from repository
   scope: obr
   flags:
      -x, --extract    extract documentation
   parameters:
      File    local target directory
      String[]    ( <bundle-name>
                  | <symbolic-name> | <bundle-id> )[@<version>] ...
```

The `-x` (or `--extract`) flag is used to request that the archive be extracted once it is downloaded.

 There is a name conflict between the `obr:source` and `gogo:source` commands. The fully scoped name must be used when calling those commands.

Updating bundles in the repository

As you go through your development cycle, you'll need to refresh the bundles on your framework with their latest versions for testing.

The `obr:refresh` command reloads the repository listing from its source and updates the list of available bundles. However, this does not mean that the bundles have been refreshed. For this, you'll need to `update` the bundle.

The full cycle at each rebuild of a bundle (assuming you're using the same version) would be as follows:

1. Deploy the bundle and update the repository descriptor, using Maven.
2. Refresh the URL; this is done in the Felix console, using the following `obr:refresh` command:

   ```
   -> repos refresh file:/C:/projects/felixbook/releases/repository.
   xml
   ```
3. Update the bundle using the `felix:update <id>` command.

This command finds the latest version of the bundle and installs it. If the bundle was previously started, it will be restarted after the installation.

 Updating a bundle may not work as well as expected if the installation failed because classes were not found. In those cases, it's better to uninstall and then deploy it again.

You will find yourself going through this cycle often. Alternatively, you can use a direct file install using the `felix:install` command and then update the bundle using the `felix:update` command. This is useful for fast deploy-test cycles re-using the same version of the bundle.

Installing the Book Inventory bundles to Felix

In the previous chapter, we deployed the inventory layer bundles to the releases OBR repository. Now that we know more about how to operate the OBR service in Felix, we will pick up where we left off in the last chapter. We're going to install them on our OSGi framework.

If you haven't done so already:

♦ Start up your Felix framework instance (see *Chapter 2, Setting Up the Environment*)
♦ Add the releases repository URL to the OBR service (covered earlier in this chapter)

Time for action – install the book inventory bundles

We start by listing the target bundles, to make sure they're there and to have their names, for easy copy-and-paste.

```
g! list book
Bookshelf Inventory API (1.5.0)
Bookshelf Inventory Impl - Mock (1.5.0)
```

Since we've declared the bookshelf inventory API as a dependency of the mock implementation, we only need to specifically deploy the implementation.

First, we set the initial bundle level to 2 (Tier 3 services), and move the framework level to that level right away:

```
g! bundlelevel -i 2
g! frameworklevel 2
```

Then we use the `obr:deploy` command to deploy the bookshelf implementation:

```
g! deploy -s "Bookshelf Inventory Impl - Mock"
Target resource(s):
-------------------
   Bookshelf Inventory Impl - Mock (1.5.0)


Required resource(s):
--------------------
   Bookshelf Inventory API (1.5.0)


Deploying...
Starting Book Inventory Mock Impl
done.
```

The bundle listing now shows the newly installed bundles:

```
g! lb
START LEVEL 1
   ID|State      |Level|Name
    0|Active     |     0|System Bundle (3.0.1)
    1|Active     |     1|Apache Felix Bundle Repository (1.6.2)
    2|Active     |     1|Apache Felix Gogo Command (0.6.0)
    3|Active     |     1|Apache Felix Gogo Runtime (0.6.0)
    4|Active     |     1|Apache Felix Gogo Shell (0.6.0)
    5|Active     |     1|Bookshelf Inventory API (1.5.0)
    6|Active     |     1|Bookshelf Inventory Impl - Mock (1.5.0)
```

Bundles 5 and 6 are those we've just installed and started.

What just happened?

Alright, this is cool. Let's go back through it step-by-step.

Someone (in this case, it was us) has deployed a bundle onto their OBR. Now this OBR could be local, as it is here, but could also be hosted online (for example, as is the one for the Felix releases at `http://felix.apache.org/obr/releases.xml`).

We have registered our releases OBR with the Bundle Repository service (while we were looking at the `obr:repos add` command earlier), which resulted in it now being aware of the "Bookshelf Inventory API" and the "Bookshelf Implementation - Mock" bundles.

Then we requested the Bundle Repository to start the "Bookshelf Inventory Impl - Mock", calling it by name. The Bundle Repository retrieves the information relating to that bundle, namely, the bundle URI, from its cached listing.

However, the inventory mock implementation bundle declares a dependency on the inventory API. The Bundle Repository matches this dependency with the "Bookshelf Inventory API" bundle and installs it.

Then, as all the dependencies required for the "Bookshelf Inventory Impl - Mock" bundle are satisfied, it installs it.

Having specified the `-s` flag, the installed bundles are started.

When the "Bookshelf Inventory Impl - Mock" bundle is started, its bundle activator's `start()` method is called. This is when our message "Starting Book Inventory Mock Impl" is printed on the standard output.

On dependency management

The example we've just looked at is a simple one, with a shallow level of dependencies; yet it already shows the value gained from the use of a proper dependency management tool. As bundles become richer in features, their dependency on other bundles, whether internal or third party, grows into a complex tree (sometimes a graph with potential cycles).

Keeping a close check on the dependencies of each project reduces the potential issues relating to the deployment of bundle upgrades. It will save you from lengthy searches for the missing dependencies—usually in the late hours of the night.

It is recommended to keep a checklist of those dependencies, the versions of each that have been tested and approved and the version that's currently being used. Also include their assigned OBR repository URL for quick access when using `obr:repos add`.

Pop Quiz

1. What is an OBR?

   a. It's OSGi's way of storing bundles

   b. It's a service for querying repositories hosting OSGi bundles

   c. It's a service that manages installed bundles

2. What's the main difference between the `felix:install` and `obr:deploy` commands?

   a. There's no difference

   b. The main difference is that `obr:deploy` finds and installs dependencies

   c. The main difference is that `obr:deploy` uses the bundle presentation name

3. How do you install and start a bundle using OBR?

   a. I use `obr:deploy`; it will automatically start the bundle when it's installed

   b. I use `obr:deploy` to install the bundle, then `felix:start` to start it

   c. I use `obr:deploy` with the `-s` flag to install and then start the bundle

4. How do you update an OBR repository?

   a. I submit a request to the OSGi alliance; they will update it

   b. I copy the bundle and then manually update the repository XML file

   c. I use the bundle plugin in Maven to update the repository on bundle deploy

Summary

In this chapter, you have learned about OSGi Bundle Repository. You've also looked at:

- The OBR service and the repository XML descriptor
- How to manage the registered OBR repositories using the `obr` scope commands
- How to find and deploy a bundle from an OBR repository to Felix and update it when it is modified

Then you have:

- Installed the bundles from *Chapter 5* to the Felix instance

Next, we're going to implement the first version of the bookshelf service; it is a proof-of-concept, which we will enrich in subsequent chapters.

7

The Bookshelf: First Stab

The bookshelf service is the business logic component of our case study. It will stand as a middle tier between the inventory (or data layer), which we've implemented in Chapter 4, Let's Get Started: The Bookshelf Project, and the presentation layer, which we will implement in later chapters.

In this chapter, we will define the service's API and implement it. We will also create an activator for the service to register it.

Since we do not yet have a presentation layer, we will also make the activator perform a few test actions on the service at startup to ensure that it's working as expected.

You will:

◆ Define the `BookshelfService` interface and implement it

◆ Learn how to get access to a registered service (the inventory service)

◆ Install the bookshelf service bundle onto you Felix framework, running the first test

The Bookshelf Service bundle

In the previous chapters, when we have worked on the Bookshelf Inventory API and mock implementation, we separated the API bundle from that holding the implementation.

In general, it is a good practice to separate them as it enforces the loose coupling between components and prevents the developer from making assumptions about the specifics of the implementation.

As we've seen, this loose coupling makes it easier to replace the specific implementation of the API without impacting the components that depend on it

An added benefit is that it limits the strict dependencies to those required by the API bundle. For example, our `bookshelf-inventory-api` bundle has no dependencies while the `bookshelf-inventory-impl-mock` bundle does. Keeping them separate simplifies the dependency structure.

However, this separation has the downside of increasing the number of bundles we're working with. The lose coupling also adds the overhead of identifying the implementation and installing it separately.

To make the previous points clearer, we will define the API and the implementation in the same bundle for the Bookshelf Service. This way, you'd have seen both cases in action and you can choose which one fits your needs best.

Let's start with the boiler-plate project preparation.

Have a go hero – preparing the bookshelf-service project

We've already gone through those steps before for the `bookshelf-inventory-api` and `bookshelf-inventory-impl-mock` bundles. Let's see if you can go through them on your own. The following is the information that you'll need during your setup.

The bundle identification is:

- **Group Id**: `com.packtpub.felix`
- **Artifact Id**: `com.packtpub.felix.bookshelf-service`
- **Version**: `1.7.0`
- **Packaging**: `bundle`

The project will have dependencies to:

- `com.packtpub.felix.bookshelf-inventory-api` (`1.5.0`)
- `org.osgi.core` (`4.2.0`)

The Java packages will be:

- `com.packtpub.felix.bookshelf.service.api` for the API interfaces and classes
- `com.packtpub.felix.bookshelf.service.impl` for the implementation

The activator will be:

- ◆ `BookshelfServiceImplActivator` in the package `com.packtpub.felix.bookshelf.service.impl.activator`

This information should be all you need to set up the project base structure.

Once you're done with the setup, download the accompanying code and double-check if you've got it all right.

Next, we'll write the API and implementation classes.

Define the main Bookshelf Service interfaces

The `BookshelfService` interface provides the bookshelf business logic and functionality to components that require it. It will perform a few checks before delegating to the inventory tier.

In our example, and for simplicity, the business logic tier also includes the authentication functionality. The authentication functionality is defined by the `Authentication` interface, which the `BookshelfService` interface extends.

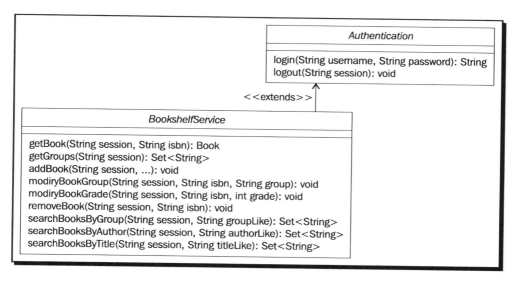

Time for action – writing the APIs

By now, you should have prepared the `bookshelf-service` project structure. Let's write the `BookshelfService` and `Authentication` interfaces. Those will be in the package `com.packtpub.felix.bookshelf.service.api`.

The Authentication interface

The authentication interface here is a very simple one. It is based on a username and password and creates a session when the authentication information is accepted.

```
public interface Authentication
{
    String login(String username, char[] password)
        throws InvalidCredentialsException;

    void logout(String sessionId);

    boolean sessionIsValid(String sessionId);
}
```

Again, here, the exceptions (for example, `InvalidCredentialsException`) are not listed; they are left to you to write on your own.

Typically, this interface would be defined in another bundle to allow for flexibility in the selection of an Authentication and Authorization implementation. We won't worry about this here and will just include it in this bundle.

 The choice of using `char[]` for the password, instead of `String`, is due to the increased security relating to the potentially longer lifespan of a String at garbage collection.

The BookshelfService interface

As said, the `BookshelfService` interface extends `Authentication` to add the authentication functionality to its bookshelf management methods:

```
public interface BookshelfService extends Authentication
{
    Set<String> getGroups(String sessionId);
```

Most of the methods in this interface look a lot like those in the inventory interface. However, they ask for a valid session ID and hide some of the complexity of the third tier.

```
void addBook(
        String session, String isbn, String title,
        String author, String category, int rating)
    throws BookAlreadyExistsException, InvalidBookException;
```

We chose to hide the `MutableBook`, for example, and spread its properties as separate method parameters. Here, this is a choice we have to abstract away from the book factory method.

Depending on the complexity of the bean at hand, you may choose to use the `MutableBook` and `Book` objects instead. It would be interesting, later, if you tried to expose it and implement a locking mechanism when a `MutableBook` is served, thus preventing edits to the entry until it is released.

The modify book operations are restricted to category and rating attribute updates.

```
void modifyBookCategory(
    String session, String isbn, String category)
  throws BookNotFoundException, InvalidBookException;

void modifyBookRating(String session, String isbn, int rating)
    throws BookNotFoundException, InvalidBookException;

void removeBook(String session, String isbn)
    throws BookNotFoundException;

Book getBook(String session, String isbn)
    throws BookNotFoundException;
```

You may have noticed a difference between the way the inventory API and the bookshelf API function. For example, the inventory API would expect you to get a book for modification, then set its category, then save it; while the bookshelf service API makes this operation available as a single method (`modifyBookCategory`).

This introduced difference is not necessary; the same update mechanism could have been replicated at the business layer. It is mainly to show that, even though one may be naturally inclined to replicate an interface when exposing some of its functionality, this replication is not a rule. Thought must always be given to the way the client may use this information. In our case, the methods exposed by the inventory interface are made flexible for a middle tier using them. Those in the middle tier are made simple for easy client integration.

Search functionality is provided by category, author, title, and given rating.

```
    Set<String> searchBooksByCategory(
            String session, String categoryLike);

    Set<String> searchBooksByAuthor(
            String session, String authorLike);

    Set<String> searchBooksByTitle(
            String session, String titleLike);

    Set<String> searchBooksByRating(
            String session, int ratingLower, int ratingUpper);
}
```

This concludes the `BookshelfService` interface definition. Next, we move to its implementation.

Have a go hero – tailor the bundle to your liking

Did you feel that the `BookshelfService` interface is not exactly the way you would have implemented it? Or maybe you want to engage your own creativity while going through this case study?

Before moving onto the implementation of the service, you may want to enrich the interface and extend the scope of work. The following are a few ideas:

- Move the `Authentication` interface to a separate bundle and implement a proper authentication bundle. You can also find an existing authentication implementation for OSGi and redesign that part of the bookshelf service to use it.

- Enrich the `BookshelfService` interface by exposing more search functionality or adding methods such as:
    - `startedBook(String session, String isbn): void`, to tell the service that the user has just started reading this book
    - `finishedBook(String isbn, int rating): void`, to mark this book as finished and give it a rating and then include some additional search functions to retrieve books based on those added book attributes
    - `getNotStartedBooks(): List<String>`, to search for books not marked as started
    - `getUnfinishedBooks(): List<String>`, to search for books not marked as finished, and so on

Implementing the service

Alright, now we'll implement the service and its activator. The following diagram puts it all in perspective.

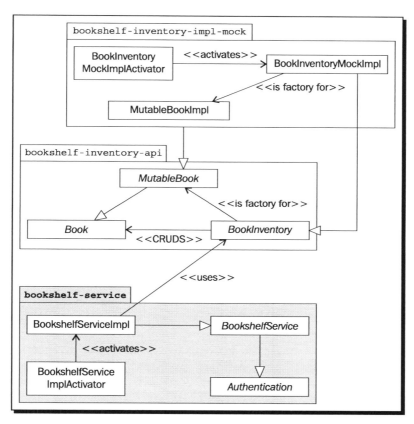

The `bookshelf-service` bundle holds the service classes and it depends on the `bookshelf-inventory-api` bundle. The `bookshelf-inventory-impl-mock` bundle provides the `bookshelf-inventory-api` functionality (implementation).

Time for action – writing BookshelfServiceImpl

We won't go through the whole `BookshelfService` implementation. Let's implement the first part together and then you can go on with the rest of it on your own.

```
public class BookshelfServiceImpl implements BookshelfService
{
    private String sessionId;

    private BundleContext context;
```

The service receives a BundleContext through its constructor, handed to it by the activator (see later). It will keep a reference of it in order to use it for the BookInventory component lookup when it needs the inventory functionality.

```
public BookshelfServiceImpl (BundleContext context)
{
    this.context = context;
}
```

The login, logout, and checkSession methods are plain mocks, only one set of credentials is recognized and only one session is supported at a time. Also, no concurrency checks are made, therefore, we would expect this code to misbehave in a multi-threaded usage.

```
public String login(String username, char[] password)
    throws InvalidCredentialsException
{
    if ("admin".equals(username) &&
            Arrays.equals(password, "admin".toCharArray()))
    {
        this.sessionId =
            Long.toString(System.currentTimeMillis());
        return this.session;
    }
    throw new InvalidCredentialsException(username);
}

public void logout(String sessionId) {
    checkSession(sessionId);
    this.sessionId = null;
}
```

The session check is a simple one: we only allow one active session at a time. If the sessionId is set, it must match the one that's passed, otherwise the check fails.

```
public boolean sessionIsValid(String sessionId) {
    return this.sessionId!=null
        && this.sessionId.equals(sessionId);
}

protected void checkSession(String sessionId) {
    if (!sessionIsValid(sessionId)) {
        throw new SessionNotValidRuntimeException(sessionId);
    }
}
```

We will call this method before every operation of the bookshelf service.

Let's carry onto the implementation of the `BookshelfService` methods.

To retrieve a `Book` from the repository, after session validation, we get an instance of the inventory service to which we delegate the book load request.

```
public Book getBook(String sessionId, String isbn)
        throws BookNotFoundException
{
    checkSession(sessionId);
    BookInventory inventory = lookupBookInventory();
    return inventory.loadBook(isbn);
}
```

The `lookupBookInventory` method will use the stored context reference to retrieve the `BookInventory` service instance from the framework's registered services and then return it.

```
private BookInventory lookupBookInventory() {
    String name = BookInventory.class.getName();
    ServiceReference ref =
        this.context.getServiceReference(name);
    if (ref == null)
    {
        throw new
            BookInventoryNotRegisteredRuntimeException(name);
    }
    return (BookInventory) this.context.getService(ref);
}
```

Since we have loose coupling between the bookshelf service and the inventory component, we need to make sure that there is an implementation registered for the `BookInventory` interface. This is why we check if `ref` is `null` before using it.

Have a go hero – complete service implementation

You have a general idea about this now, right? How about completing the implementation on your own?

I've included the methods missing from the implementation of the `BookshelfService` below for quick reference:

```
public MutableBook getBookForEdit(String sessionId, String isbn)
        throws BookNotFoundException;

public void addBook(
```

```
            String sessionId, String isbn, String title,
            String author, String group, int grade)
        throws BookAlreadyExistsException, InvalidBookException;

    public void modifyBookCategory(
            String sessionId, String isbn, String group)
        throws BookNotFoundException, InvalidBookException;

    public void modifyBookRating(
            String sessionId, String isbn, int grade)
        throws BookNotFoundException, InvalidBookException;

    public Set<String> getCategories(String sessionId);

    public void removeBook(String sessionId, String isbn)
        throws BookNotFoundException;

    public Set<String> searchBooksByAuthor(
            String sessionId, String authorLike);

    public Set<String> searchBooksByCategory(
            String sessionId, String categoryLike);

    public Set<String> searchBooksByTitle(
            String sessionId, String titleLike);

    public Set<String> searchBooksByRating(
            String sessionId, int gradeLower, int gradeUpper);
}
```

We'll get the chance to test some of those in a bit to make sure they're working as expected before adding the client interaction bits.

But before getting there, we still need to write the bundle activator code.

Time for action – implementing the service activator

The bundle activator for this service is straightforward. We basically register the service with the framework on start and keep a reference to it for being able to unregister it on stop.

In *Chapter 9, The Bookshelf: Second Stab with iPOJO*, we'll look at how to declare services using annotations, and, in some cases, remove the need for an activator altogether.

It's also useful, for now, to include a part of the code that tests the service, which would be kicked off at service start. This test code will be removed in the next chapter, in which we'll add shell service integration and start testing it using the text console.

The package containing the activator class, `BookshelfServiceImplActivator`, will be `com.packtpub.felix.bookshelf.service.impl.activator`:

```
public class BookshelfServiceImplActivator
    implements BundleActivator
{

    ServiceRegistration reg = null;

    public void start(BundleContext context) throws Exception
    {
        this.reg = context.registerService(
            BookshelfService.class.getName(),
            new BookshelfServiceImpl(context), null);

        testService(context);
    }

    public void stop(BundleContext context) throws Exception {
        if (this.reg!=null) {
            context.ungetService(reg.getReference());
        }
    }
}
```

Let's write the `testService` method now.

Framework service lookup

Since we have not yet implemented any way of interacting with the service, but we still want to make sure it's working right, we've added a method call that executes on bundle start—`testService()`, which will add a few books. Then perform a search and display the search results on the standard output.

```
    private void testService(BundleContext context)
    {
        // retrieve service
        String name = BookshelfService.class.getName();
        ServiceReference ref = context.getServiceReference(name);
        if (ref==null) {
            throw new RuntimeException(
                "Service not registered: " + name);
        }
        BookshelfService service =
            (BookshelfService) context.getService(ref);
```

This `BookshelfService` lookup seems to be unnecessary, because we've just instantiated the bookshelf service implementation previously. We could have kept a reference to it and used it. However, this allows you to move this test method to a separate unit testing class later without changing it.

Let's continue with our test method. So we first login (the credentials will be hardcoded admin / admin):

```
// authenticate and get session
String sessionId;
try
{
    System.out.println("\nSigning in. . .");
    sessionId =
        service.login("admin", "admin".toCharArray());
}
catch (InvalidCredentialsException e)
{
    e.printStackTrace();
    return;
}
```

Then we can add a few books using the service interface. The goal of the test is to validate the `addBook` and the `searchBooksByAuthor` methods, so we'll add books with attributes that fit the purpose.

```
// add a few books
try
{
    System.out.println("\nAdding books. . .");
    service.addBook(sessionId, "123-4567890100",
        "Book 1 Title", "John Doe", "Group 1", 0);
    service.addBook(sessionId, "123-4567890101",
        "Book 2 Title", "Will Smith", "Group 1", 0);
    service.addBook(sessionId, "123-4567890200",
        "Book 3 Title", "John Doe", "Group 2", 0);
    service.addBook(sessionId, "123-4567890201",
        "Book 4 Title", "Jane Doe", "Group 2", 0);
}
catch (BookAlreadyExistsException e)
{
    e.printStackTrace();
    return;
}
```

```
catch (InvalidBookException e)
{
    e.printStackTrace();
    return;
}
```

The search will look for authors that end with "Doe". The `search` string will therefore be "%Doe".

```
// and test search
String authorLike = "%Doe";
System.out.println(
    "Searching for books with author like: "+authorLike);
Set<String> results = service.searchBooksByAuthor(
    sessionId, authorLike);
for (String isbn : results)
{
    try
    {
        System.out.println(
            " - " + service.getBook(sessionId, isbn));
    }
    catch (BookNotFoundException e)
    {
        System.err.println(e.getMessage());
    }
}
}
}
```

This will do for validation until we get the user interfaces up. The `testService()` method and references to it will be removed in the latter chapters.

 Outside the scope of this book, but nonetheless important to know about, is that you can also include pieces of code dedicated for unit and integration testing as part of the code structure. These pieces can be used in the context of a testing framework (such as `JUnit`) and automatically kicked off by Maven as part of the relevant phase of the build lifecycle.

Trying the BookshelfService

Let's take our service for a short ride. This will be a test for both the `BookshelfService` and `BookInventory` implementations.

Time for action – building the bundle

Build the bundle and deploy it to the releases repository. Here's a reminder of the `build` and `deploy` command:

```
mvn clean deploy
```

```
...
[INFO] Deploying file:/C:/projects/felixbook/releases/com/packtpub/felix/
com.packtpub.felix.bookshelf-service/1.7.0/com.packtpub.felix.bookshelf-
service-1.7.0.jar
[INFO] Writing OBR metadata
[INFO] Uploading repository.xml
[INFO] UNLOCK file:///C:/projects/felixbook/releases/repository.xml
[INFO] ----------------------------------------------------------------
----
[INFO] BUILD SUCCESSFUL
...
```

If the build is successful, the bundle will be deployed to the releases repository and the OBR repository file will be updated. Next, we install the bundle to Felix.

Time for action – installing and testing the service

At this stage, we have the following bundles installed:

```
g! lb
START LEVEL 2
   ID|State      |Level|Name
    0|Active     |    0|System Bundle (3.0.1)
    1|Active     |    1|Apache Felix Bundle Repository (1.6.2)
    2|Active     |    1|Apache Felix Gogo Command (0.6.0)
    3|Active     |    1|Apache Felix Gogo Runtime (0.6.0)
    4|Active     |    1|Apache Felix Gogo Shell (0.6.0)
    5|Active     |    2|Bookshelf Inventory API (1.4.0)
    6|Active     |    2|Bookshelf Inventory Impl - Mock (1.4.0)
```

And the following repositories registered with the OBR service:

```
g! repos list
file:/C:/projects/felixbook/releases/repository.xml
http://felix.apache.org/obr/releases.xml
```

We refresh our releases repository and get the updated list of Bookshelf bundles:

```
g! repos refresh file:///C:/projects/felixbook/releases/repository.xml
g! list book
Bookshelf Inventory API (1.5.0)
Bookshelf Inventory Impl - Mock (1.5.0)
Bookshelf Service (1.7.0)
```

Notice that the bundle we've just deployed now appears on the list. We will download, install, and start the bookshelf service bundle using the `obr deploy` command.

But before doing that—for the fun of seeing things break, let's stop the book inventory implementation.

```
g! stop 6

Stoping Book Inventory Mock Impl

```

This will make the inventory functionality unavailable when the bookshelf service activator tries to run the tests.

Now, let's instruct the OBR service to deploy and start the bookshelf service. We're installing the bookshelf service on start level 3 (Tier 2 services):

```
g! bundlelevel -i 3
g! frameworklevel 3


g! deploy -s "Bookshelf Service"
Target resource(s):
------------------
   Bookshelf Service (1.7.0)

Deploying...
```

Having checked dependencies, it installs the service and attempts to start it. However, when we start with our test, we attempt to get an instance of the BookInventory service—in lookupBookInventory()—and this bit fails (I've reformatted the output and hidden most of the stack trace for clarity):

```
Signing in. . .


Adding books. . .
ERROR: Resolver: Start error -
    com.packtpub.felix.bookshelf-service
    org.osgi.framework.BundleException:
    Activator start error in bundle
        com.packtpub.felix.bookshelf-service [8].
at org.apache.felix.framework.Felix.activateBundle(Felix.java:1909)
at ...


Caused by: com.packtpub.felix.bookshelf.service.impl.
BookInventoryNotRegisteredRuntimeException:
    BookInventory not registered, looking under:
        com.packtpub.felix.bookshelf.inventory.api.BookInventory
at com.packtpub.felix.bookshelf.service.impl.-
    BookshelfServiceImpl.lookupBookInventory(
        BookshelfServiceImpl.java:53)
at ...


done.
```

We'll get to fix this later. Let's take a closer look at the first bit of the start operation.

What just happened?

As the bookshelf-service bundle is started, the activator is invoked. It registers the BookshelfServiceImpl under the class name BookshelfService (fully qualified). It then kicks off the test operations.

Then the activator requests an implementation of the inventory service API from the framework. In regular situations, this would provide it with one. However, none is available on the framework (because we've stopped it).

Time for action – fulfilling the missing dependency

The lookup for the inventory implementation that we tried to make on startup failed and caused the failure of the start operation. This is because we had stopped the "Bookshelf Inventory Impl - Mock" bundle.

Looking at the bundle listing, we find the newly installed bundle in the `Resolved` state:

```
g! lb
START LEVEL 3
   ID|State         |Level|Name
    0|Active        |    0|System Bundle (3.0.1)
    1|Active        |    1|Apache Felix Bundle Repository (1.6.2)
    2|Active        |    1|Apache Felix Gogo Command (0.6.0)
    3|Active        |    1|Apache Felix Gogo Runtime (0.6.0)
    4|Active        |    1|Apache Felix Gogo Shell (0.6.0)
    5|Active        |    2|Bookshelf Inventory API (1.4.0)
    6|Resolved      |    2|Bookshelf Inventory Impl - Mock (1.4.0)
    7|Resolved      |    3|Bookshelf Service (1.7.0)
```

Let's start the mock inventory implementation and make it available again:

```
g! start 6

Starting Book Inventory Mock Impl
```

Now that the dependency is satisfied, starting the Bookshelf Service should work as follows:

```
g! start 8

Signing in. . .

Adding books. . .
Searching for books with author like: %Doe
  - Group 2: Book 4 Title from Jane Doe [0]
  - Group 1: Book 1 Title from John Doe [0]
  - Group 2: Book 3 Title from John Doe [0]
```

Everything looks alright now; a quick check shows all our bundles in `Active` state:

```
g! lb
START LEVEL 3
   ID|State         |Level|Name
    0|Active        |    0|System Bundle (3.0.1)
    1|Active        |    1|Apache Felix Bundle Repository (1.6.2)
    2|Active        |    1|Apache Felix Gogo Command (0.6.0)
    3|Active        |    1|Apache Felix Gogo Runtime (0.6.0)
    4|Active        |    1|Apache Felix Gogo Shell (0.6.0)
    5|Active        |    2|Bookshelf Inventory API (1.4.0)
    6|Active        |    2|Bookshelf Inventory Impl - Mock (1.4.0)
    7|Active        |    3|Bookshelf Service (1.7.0)
```

What Just Happened?

The following image shows the flow of control between the bookshelf service and the inventory implementation bundles.

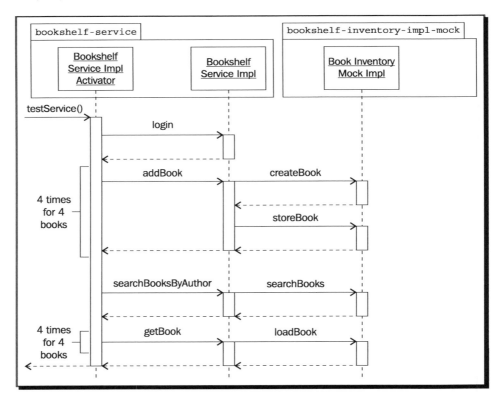

This is a partial flow as the interactions with the `BundleContext` are not shown.

When you decide to replace this inventory implementation with another one, all you'll need to do is uninstall the existing implementation and install the new one. The next lookup will catch the new bundle implementation. The same applies for bundle version upgrades.

On class visibility

Looking up the inventory service from the bookshelf service code gives it access to objects hosted in another bundle (namely, in the `bookshelf-inventory-impl-mock` bundle).

This is not of any great impact in this example, however, it is a good idea to keep in mind that those classes live in different bundles. The wiring made it so that the inventory implementation classes are visible from the bookshelf service context.

When working on more complex bundles that would need to make use of class or resource loaders, the bundle codebases and their class loaders are managed by the Felix framework. It's not always correct to assume that another object's class loader is the same as ours or that we're in the same class space. Remember to use the methods made available by the target bundle `BundleContext` for loading resources from that bundle.

Pop quiz

1. When a bundle is started, it goes through which sequence of states?
   a. RESOLVED, INSTALLED, and then STARTED.
   b. DOWNLOADED, INSTALLED, and then STARTED.
   c. INSTALLED, RESOLVED, STARTING, and then ACTIVE.

2. When are the BundleActivator methods called?
   a. When the bundle is starting.
   b. When the bundle is stopping.
   c. a and b.

Summary

Ok, so by now you know quite a lot about OSGi and bundle development on Felix, and you are well on your way with the bookshelf project.

In this chapter, you have completed the business logic tier of the case study. You have:

- Defined and implemented the `BookshelfService` interface
- Learned how to look up a service on the OSGi framework
- Installed the service bundle onto you Felix framework

In the next chapter, we'll look at the Felix Gogo Shell Service, and more specifically, at how to implement and register our own commands. This will be the first part of the presentation tier (Tier 1).

8

Adding a Command-Line Interface

In the previous chapters, we implemented the core functionality of our Bookshelf service. In a layered architecture, we've implemented the inventory as a memory-based, non-persistent temporary mock, and added the Bookshelf service on top of it. However, we don't yet have any way of interacting with our service.

In Chapter 11, How about a Graphical Interface?, we'll implement a graphical frontend for our service. In the meantime, we'll use a command-line interface (text UI), which we will put in place here.

As you learned earlier in Chapter 3, Felix Gogo, OSGi does not yet specify how users are to interact with the framework and its services through a command-line interface. Such features are left for the different bundle providers to fulfill. We've looked at the RFC 147 draft proposal and the TSL language. You have also covered a few of the commands that are provided by the Felix Gogo Shell service.

In this chapter, you will:

- ◆ Learn about the Apache Felix Gogo Shell Service
- ◆ Discover how to extend it with your own commands

We will also improve our Bookshelf case study by:

- ◆ Implementing the Gogo shell commands, namely, `book:search` and `book:add`
- ◆ Removing the temporary test procedures in the `bookshelf-service` activator

We'll also learn how to:

- ◆ Update a bundle with a newer version
- ◆ Write a script for automating frequently repeated tasks

The Apache Felix Gogo Shell Service

Felix provides a simple but extensible shell service. This service allows bundles to expose commands to the shell user. Commands that are registered by bundles are detected by the shell service and provided to the user on the text console. We will look at how this is done in a bit.

The shell service can be used by any component that wishes to interact with other services by using a simple text command mechanism.

The Apache Felix Gogo Shell waits for user input on the command line and transmits it to the Gogo Runtime Service for execution. The Gogo Runtime Service then matches the command in the transmitted line with one of the registered methods and delegates its execution to the matched method.

In *Chapter 3*, we've looked at the commands that are exposed by the Felix Shell Service. Here, we'll write our own commands that we'll use to manage our books and register them.

Time for action – creating the Bookshelf Service TUI bundle

We will implement the text UI commands in a separate bundle. It is a good practice, in general, to avoid combining functional elements. In this case, it's mainly to separate the TUI bundle delivery cycle from that of the main service.

Take a minute to create a new project for the Bookshelf Service TUI bundle. Here is the information you'll need:

- **Group Id**: `com.packtpub.felix`
- **Artifact Id**: `com.packtpub.felix.bookshelf-service-tui`
- **Version**: `1.8.0`
- **Packaging**: `bundle`

Leave the `dependencies` section empty for now. Later, we'll take a look at it as we go through the commands implementation.

 If you're not sure what needs to be done here, review the part in the beginning of *Chapter 5*, *The Book Inventory Bundle*, where we set up the project for the inventory bundle. There's also more details in *Appendix A*, *Eclipse, Maven, and Felix*, on how to use Eclipse to create Maven projects.

Implementing a Gogo Shell Service command

Creating shell service commands is fairly simple; it consists of the following:

◆ Creating a proxy class that defines the commands—one method per command syntax flavor

◆ Registering the proxy as a service with the OSGi framework, along with properties in the registration dictionary

Those properties declare the commands to be exposed and the scope in which they belong.

Additionally, a set of annotations can be attached to the proxy methods and their parameters to provide further descriptive information. This information would be used when listing the commands or when constructing their `help` output.

There are two service properties used when registering commands:

◆ `osgi.command.scope`: A string that declares the scope of the registered commands

◆ `osgi.command.function`: A string array listing the commands to be exposed from the registered proxy

Here's a diagram that describes the previous setup to our case:

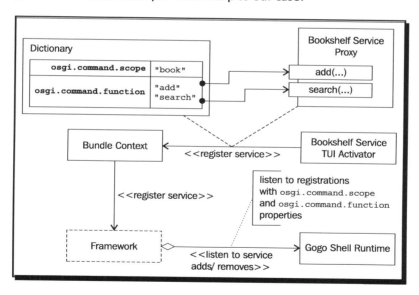

When a service is registered with those dictionary properties, the Gogo Shell Runtime picks them up and constructs command entries for them. Those entries map to the method, or methods, with the same name.

It is possible to have more than one method that matches the function name (with different signatures). The Gogo components will find the best match, based on the command input by the user.

The `BookshelfServiceProxy` is the service that we will register; it will hold the methods that provide the commands. We will first take an end-to-end path with the `search` commands and then take it again when implementing the `add` command.

Implementing the book:search command

The first command we'll implement is the `book:search` command. Since we've left the part of the `bookshelf-service` activator that inserts books to the bookshelf on startup, we can test the `search` command right away.

Time for action – adding the required dependencies

Right now, let's look at the required dependencies. As we go through them, we will add them into the `dependencies` section of the `com.packpub.felix.bookshelf-service-tui` project descriptor: `pom.xml`.

For this functionality, we will need to use the Descriptor annotation, which is provided by the the `org.apache.felix.gogo.runtime` bundle:

```
<dependency>
  <groupId>org.apache.felix</groupId>
  <artifactId>org.apache.felix.gogo.runtime</artifactId>
  <version>0.6.0</version>
</dependency>
```

We will also need to register the implemented command as a service, by implementing a `BundleActivator`, which is provided by the `org.osgi.core` bundle:

```
<dependency>
  <groupId>org.osgi</groupId>
  <artifactId>org.osgi.core</artifactId>
  <version>4.2.0</version>
  <scope>provided</scope>
</dependency>
```

The book search functionality is provided by the `com.packpub.felix.bookshelf-service` bundle:

```
<dependency>
  <groupId>com.packpub.felix</groupId>
  <artifactId>com.packpub.felix.bookshelf-service</artifactId>
```

```
        <version>1.7.0</version>
        <scope>compile</scope>
    </dependency>
```

The two flavors of the search command will return a set of `Books`, which are defined in the `com.packpub.felix.bookshelf-inventory-api` bundle:

```
    <dependency>
        <groupId>com.packpub.felix</groupId>
        <artifactId>
          com.packpub.felix.bookshelf-inventory-api</artifactId>
        <version>1.5.0</version>
    </dependency>
</dependencies>
```

We're now ready to start the `search` command implementation.

Time for action – writing the BookshelfServiceProxy

I've chosen the package `com.packtpub.felix.bookshelf.service.tui` for the proxy and `com.packtpub.felix.bookshelf.service.tui.activator` for the bundle activator.

The `BookshelfServiceProxy` is the main class for the bookshelf command functionality. For easy reference, we will define the `SCOPE` and `FUNCTIONS` constants that define the commands scope ("book") and the functions that are to be exposed. Currently, we will expose one function for the `add` command:

```
public class BookshelfServiceProxy
{
    public static final String SCOPE = "book";
    public static final String[] FUNCTIONS = new String[] {
        "search"
    };
    private BundleContext context;
    public BookshelfServiceProxy(BundleContext context)
    {
        this.context = context;
    }
```

The proxy constructor also takes a `BundleContext`, which will be needed to look up the `BookshelfService` when executing the command operations.

The `search` commands that are exposed have two possible syntax signatures:

◆ `search <username> <password> <attribute> <filter>`: For searches matching books filtering by "author", "title" or "category" `attribute`

◆ `search <username> <password> <attribute> <lower> <upper>`: For searches matching books with a "rating" `attribute` between `lower` and `upper`

Each one of these signatures matches a method in the proxy class:

◆ `Set<Book> search(String username, String password, String attribute, String filter)`

◆ `Set<Book> search(String username, String password, String attribute, int lower, int upper)`

The `@Descriptor` annotation provides additional information on the method and its parameters. Here, for example, we provide some help on the search command and include a hint on each parameter it takes:

```
@Descriptor("Search books by author, title, or category")
public Set<Book> search(
    @Descriptor("username") String username,
    @Descriptor("password") String password,
    @Descriptor(
      "search on attribute: author, title, or category")
      String attribute,
    @Descriptor(
      "match like (use % at the beginning or end of <like>"+
      " for wild-card)")
      String filter)
  throws InvalidCredentialsException
{
    BookshelfService service = lookupService();
    String sessionId = service.login(
        username, password.toCharArray());
    Set<String> results;
    if ("title".equals(attribute))
    {
        results = service.searchBooksByTitle(sessionId, filter);
    }
    else if ("author".equals(attribute))
    {
        results =
            service.searchBooksByAuthor(sessionId, filter);
```

```
        }
        else if ("category".equals(attribute))
        {
            results =
                service.searchBooksByCategory(sessionId, filter);
        }
        else
        {
            throw new RuntimeException(
                "Invalid attribute, expecting one of { 'title', "+
                "'author', 'category' } got '"+attribute+"'");
        }
        return getBooks(sessionId, service, results);
    }
```

The remainder of the method is pretty straightforward, the `attribute` is checked against the valid values and the appropriate search is triggered.

Since the "rating"-based search is supposed to be directed to the method with another signature, we ensure that this method was not selected by mistake (for example, when `upper` is not passed or when it cannot be made into an `int`).

The `lookupService()` method uses the stored `BundleContext` to look up the bookshelf service and return it. It throws a `RuntimeException` if it doesn't find one:

```
    protected BookshelfService lookupService()
    {
        ServiceReference reference = context.getServiceReference(
            BookshelfService.class.getName());
        if (reference == null)
        {
            throw new RuntimeException(
                "BookshelfService not registered, cannot invoke "+
                "operation");
        }
        BookshelfService service =
            (BookshelfService) this.context.getService(reference);
        if (service == null)
        {
            throw new RuntimeException(
                "BookshelfService not registered, cannot invoke "+
                "operation");
        }
        return service;
    }
```

Notice the paired checks of the service reference and the service for null. As we saw earlier, when we stopped the inventory implementation before starting the bookshelf service, the environment can change at any time, such as services are stopped, upgraded, and so on while others are running. This is one of the powers of this service platform, but is also an added responsibility on the developer.

The `getBooks()` method is defined next. It takes a set of ISBNs and returns the corresponding set of `Book` entries:

```java
private Set<Book> getBooks(
    String sessionId, BookshelfService service,
    Set<String> results)
{
    Set<Book> books = new HashSet<Book>();
    for (String isbn : results)
    {
        Book book;
        try
        {
            book = service.getBook(sessionId, isbn);
            books.add(book);
        }
        catch (BookNotFoundException e)
        {
            System.err.println("ISBN " + isbn +
                " referenced but not found");
        }
    }
    return books;
}
```

The second search signature is dedicated to rating-based search. It takes two `int`s, instead of a String filter, for lower and upper bounds of the rating:

```java
@Descriptor("Search books by rating")
public Set<Book> search(
    @Descriptor("username") String username,
    @Descriptor("password") String password,
    @Descriptor("search on attribute: rating") String attribute,
    @Descriptor("lower rating limit (inclusive)") int lower,
    @Descriptor("upper rating limit (inclusive)") int upper)
  throws InvalidCredentialsException
{
    if (!"rating".equals(attribute))
    {
```

```
            throw new RuntimeException(
                "Invalid attribute, expecting 'rating' got '"+
                attribute+"'");
        }
        BookshelfService service = lookupService();
        String sessionId =
            service.login(username, password.toCharArray());
        Set<String> results =
            service.searchBooksByRating(sessionId, lower, upper);

        return getBooks(sessionId, service, results);
    }
```

On Converters

Depending on the number and type of parameters passed to the command on the shell, Gogo will attempt to find (coerce) a best matching method signature for the command request.

The shell can recognize the basic types and convert them for use as parameters when calling the command function. However, for more complex types, it would require the assistance of a helper class.

The Converter (`org.apache.felix.service.command.Converter`) is a service that knows how to convert a String to an object of a specific type and vice-versa.

Without going into too much detail, the converter is registered as a service, along with a property (`osgi.converter.classes`) that lists the classes it supports conversion for. The service exposes the following two methods:

- `convert(...)` that takes the target class (the desired type) and an input object and is expected to return the converted object
- `format(...)` that takes an object to format, a formatting directive, and a Converter for delegation of the formatting of sub-parts

The converters are ordered by `service.ranking` and attempted until one successfully converts or formats the content.

Let's go back to our case study: What's left is the activator to register the service and its commands with the framework and the Gogo Runtime.

Time for action – implementing a bundle activator

The activator for this bundle will only be responsible for registering commands. It's not of greater complexity than the ones we've seen so far.

Create the class `BookshelfTuiActivator` and make it register an instance of the `BookshelfServiceProxy` at start.

The values for the command-related properties were defined in the proxy as constants earlier. Defining them in the service class makes it easier to update them later (for example, when we include the `add` command).

```
public class BookshelfTuiActivator implements BundleActivator
{
    public void start(BundleContext bc)
    {
        Hashtable props = new Hashtable();
        props.put("osgi.command.scope", BookshelfServiceProxy.SCOPE);
        props.put("osgi.command.function",
            BookshelfServiceProxy.FUNCTIONS);
        bc.registerService(
            BookshelfServiceProxy.class.getName(),
            new BookshelfServiceProxy(bc),
            props);
    }

    public void stop(BundleContext bc)
    {
    }
}
```

The service is registered as we did before. The difference is that we also provide the service properties along with the register request.

You still need to configure the bundle plugin in the POM, and you're done. Nothing really special for this configuration, compared to the previous ones. For reference, here's what that section would look like:

```
<plugin>
    <groupId>org.apache.felix</groupId>
    <artifactId>maven-bundle-plugin</artifactId>
    <version>2.1.0</version>
    <extensions>true</extensions>

    <configuration>
```

```
            <instructions>
                <Bundle-Category>sample</Bundle-Category>
                <Bundle-SymbolicName>
                  ${artifactId}
                </Bundle-SymbolicName>
                <Export-Package>
                  com.packtpub.felix.bookshelf.service.tui
                </Export-Package>
                <Bundle-Activator>
  com.packtpub.felix.bookshelf.service.tui.activator.-
  BookshelfTuiActivator
                </Bundle-Activator>
                <Private-Package>
                  com.packtpub.felix.bookshelf.service.tui.activator
                </Private-Package>
            </instructions>
            <remoteOBR>repo-rel</remoteOBR>
            <prefixUrl>
              file:///C:/projects/felixbook/releases</prefixUrl>
            <ignoreLock>true</ignoreLock>
          </configuration>
        </plugin>
```

With this last update, we can build and deploy this bundle for a test run.

Time for action – packaging and installing

Let's bundle it all up, and deploy it, then install and start it on the framework. By now, building and deploying a bundle is second nature for you, so the details for that are not included here.

With the building of the bundle and its deployment to the releases repositories being completed successfully, we prepare the framework for the bundle install.

The shell extension bundles fit on start level 5, as defined in *Chapter 1, Quick Intro to Felix and OSGi*. Here we set the initial start level for all the newly installed bundles to 5 and change the framework level as well.

```
g! bundlelevel -i 5
g! frameworklevel 5
```

Refresh the OBR repository and get the updated list using:

```
g! repos refresh file:///C:/projects/felixbook/releases/repository.xml
```

```
g! list book
Bookshelf Inventory API (1.5.0)
Bookshelf Inventory Impl - Mock (1.5.0)
Bookshelf Service (1.7.0)
Bookshelf Service Gogo commands (1.8.0)
```

Then install (and start) the newly deployed bundle:

```
g! deploy -s "Bookshelf Service Gogo commands"
Target resource(s):
-------------------
   Bookshelf Service Gogo commands (1.8.0)

Deploying...done.
```

The bundle listing should now be something like the following lines:

```
g! lb
START LEVEL 5
   ID|State      |Level|Name
    0|Active     |    0|System Bundle (3.0.1)
    1|Active     |    1|Apache Felix Bundle Repository (1.6.2)
    2|Active     |    1|Apache Felix Gogo Command (0.6.0)
    3|Active     |    1|Apache Felix Gogo Runtime (0.6.0)
    4|Active     |    1|Apache Felix Gogo Shell (0.6.0)
    5|Active     |    2|Bookshelf Inventory API (1.5.0)
    6|Active     |    2|Bookshelf Inventory Impl - Mock (1.5.0)
    7|Active     |    3|Bookshelf Service (1.7.0)
    8|Active     |    5|Bookshelf Service Gogo commands (1.8.0)
```

The newly installed bundle is now active and we can give it a try.

Time for action – trying out the book:search command

If all went well, typing `help` should include our `book:search` command in the listing:

```
g! help
book:search                <-- this is our command!
felix:bundlelevel
felix:cd
felix:frameworklevel
```

```
felix:headers
felix:help
felix:inspect
felix:install
felix:lb
felix:log
felix:ls
...
```

Also check that the help command displays the command syntax as we have intended it to be:

```
-g! help search

search - Search books by rating
    scope: book
    parameters:
        String    username
        String    password
        String    search on attribute: rating
        int    lower rating limit (inclusive)
        int    upper rating limit (inclusive)
search - Search books by author, title, or category
    scope: book
    parameters:
        String    username
        String    password
        String    search on attribute: author, title, or category
        String    match like (use % at the beginning or end of <like> for
wild-card)
```

Notice the two syntax help entries available for the search command, as we had defined them in the service proxy previously—one that takes five parameters (the last two being integers), and the other that takes four Strings.

Let's give it a try with the books we've added during the activation of the `bookshelf-service`. Search for authors ending with "Doe":

```
g! search admin admin author %Doe
Group 2: Book 3 Title from John Doe [0]
Group 2: Book 4 Title from Jane Doe [0]
Group 1: Book 1 Title from John Doe [0]
```

And a more restrictive search for authors starting with "John":

```
g! search admin admin author John%
Group 2: Book 3 Title from John Doe [0]
Group 1: Book 1 Title from John Doe [0]
```

The `search` command works as expected.

Time for action – cleaning up the bookshelf-service activator

Now that we have the `search` command working, we're about to implement the `add` command. Therefore, we will no longer need the part of the `bookshelf-service` activator that inserts books at startup.

Let's remove that call by using:

```java
public class BookshelfServiceImplActivator implements BundleActivator
{
    ServiceRegistration reg = null;
    public void start(BundleContext context) throws Exception
    {
        this.reg = context.registerService(
            BookshelfService.class.getName(),
            new BookshelfServiceImpl(context), null);

        // testService(context);
    }
// ...
```

For now, I've just commented the call to `testService()`, but it can be removed.

 Don't forget to rebuild, package, and deploy the updated `bookshelf-service` bundle! This one will have version `1.8.0`.

Implementing the book:add command

The next thing is to implement the `book:add` command, which is implementing the `add()` method in the `BookshelfServiceProxy` and including the function name in the commands list.

Time for action – implementing the book-add command

In the same manner as we've implemented the `book:search` command, edit the `BookshelfServiceProxy` class and declare the `add()` method:

```
public String add(@Descriptor("username") String username,
                  @Descriptor("password") String password,
                  @Descriptor("ISBN") String isbn,
                  @Descriptor("Title") String title,
                  @Descriptor("Author") String author,
                  @Descriptor("Category") String category,
                  @Descriptor("Rating (0..10)") int rating)
    throws InvalidCredentialsException,
        BookAlreadyExistsException, InvalidBookException
{
    BookshelfService service = lookupService();
    String sessionId = service.login(
        username, password.toCharArray());

    service.addBook(
        sessionId, isbn, title, author, category, rating);
    return isbn;
}
```

This command is named "book:add" and will take the book's ISBN, title, author, category, and rating as arguments, in addition to the authentication user and password. Its implementation is straightforward.

To declare it as part of the exposed functions, we include the method name in the list of functions:

```
public static final String[] FUNCTIONS = new String[] {
    "add", "search"
};
```

This new command implementation is ready. Since we've used the constant from this class during the service registration, we don't need to make any changes to the activator code.

Go ahead hero – building and deploying the changes

To test the changes we've made, we'll need to rebuild the following bundles:

◆ `bookshelf-service`: Was modified to remove the test call at startup. This will be released with version `1.8.0`

◆ `bookshelf-service-tui`: To which we've added the `book:add` command. This will be released with version `1.8.1`

Do you think you can do it on your own? (Hint: this was covered in *Chapter 5*.)

Updating an installed bundle

We have just released new versions of bundles `bookshelf-service` and `bookshelf-service-tui`. Before updating them in the framework, the state of the bundle listing should be something like:

```
g! lb
START LEVEL 5
   ID|State      |Level|Name
    0|Active     |    0|System Bundle (3.0.1)
    1|Active     |    1|Apache Felix Bundle Repository (1.6.2)
    2|Active     |    1|Apache Felix Gogo Command (0.6.0)
    3|Active     |    1|Apache Felix Gogo Runtime (0.6.0)
    4|Active     |    1|Apache Felix Gogo Shell (0.6.0)
    5|Active     |    2|Bookshelf Inventory API (1.5.0)
    6|Active     |    2|Bookshelf Inventory Impl - Mock (1.5.0)
    7|Active     |    3|Bookshelf Service (1.7.0)
    8|Active     |    5|Bookshelf Service Gogo commands (1.8.0)
```

The `repos refresh` command instructs the OBR service to reload the repositories and update its listings:

```
g! repos refresh file:///C:/projects/felixbook/releases/repository.xml
```

Now, by searching for our bundles, we will find:

```
g! list book
Bookshelf Inventory API (1.5.0)
Bookshelf Inventory Impl - Mock (1.5.0)
Bookshelf Service (1.8.0, ...)
```

```
Bookshelf Service Gogo commands (1.8.1, ...)
```

Notice that the bundles "Bookshelf Service" and "Bookshelf Service Gogo commands" now have the newer versions shown in the list of versions available. The list is shortened with ellipses, which means that other (lower) versions have been omitted.

To get a fuller listing, we can use the verbose option:

```
g! list -v book
Bookshelf Inventory API
    [com.packtpub.felix.bookshelf-inventory-api] (1.5.0)
Bookshelf Inventory Impl - Mock
    [com.packtpub.felix.bookshelf-inventory-impl-mock] (1.5.0)
Bookshelf Service
    [com.packtpub.felix.bookshelf-service] (1.8.0, 1.7.0)
Bookshelf Service Gogo commands
    [com.packtpub.felix.bookshelf-service-tui] (1.8.1, 1.8.0)
```

Here the "Bookshelf Service" is available with two versions, namely, 1.7.0 and 1.8.0.

To instruct Felix to update its currently installed bundle with its latest version, we use the update command, which we've seen in *Chapter 3*. It takes the bundle ID as a parameter and updates the bundle with the latest version:

```
g! update 7
DEBUG: Using ResourceSelectionStrategy: newest
DEBUG: Using Version 1.8.0 for bundle com.packtpub.felix.bookshelf-
service
g!
g! update 8
DEBUG: Using ResourceSelectionStrategy: newest
DEBUG: Using Version 1.8.1 for bundle com.packtpub.felix.bookshelf-
service-tui
```

The resulting bundle listing should be as follows:

```
g! lb
START LEVEL 5
   ID|State       |Level|Name
    0|Active      |    0|System Bundle (3.0.1)
    1|Active      |    1|Apache Felix Bundle Repository (1.6.2)
    2|Active      |    1|Apache Felix Gogo Command (0.6.0)
```

```
3|Active        |      1|Apache Felix Gogo Runtime (0.6.0)
4|Active        |      1|Apache Felix Gogo Shell (0.6.0)
5|Active        |      2|Bookshelf Inventory API (1.5.0)
6|Active        |      2|Bookshelf Inventory Impl - Mock (1.5.0)
7|Active        |      3|Bookshelf Service (1.8.0)
8|Active        |      5|Bookshelf Service Gogo commands (1.8.1)
```

And the updated help listing should be:

```
g! help
book:add
book:search
felix:bundlelevel
felix:cd
felix:frameworklevel
felix:headers
felix:help
felix:inspect
...
```

The add command was added to the listing, as expected. Its syntax from the help command is:

```
g! help add
add
    scope: book
    parameters:
        String    username
        String    password
        String    ISBN
        String    Title
        String    Author
        String    Category
        int    Rating (0..10)
```

What just happened?

By deploying newer versions of the `bookshelf-service` and `bookshelf-service-tui` bundles, Maven (with the help of the `maven-bundle-plugin`) has updated our releases repository with new entries.

Then the `repos refresh` command has instructed the OBR service to go and fetch that file again and to update its listing cache with its latest contents. This has added the versions of the newly deployed bundles to the list.

When we've asked Felix to update the bundle (using the `update` command), it has looked at the bundle source location. Bundles installed using the OBR service are given a special URL as the source location (for example, `obr://com.packtpub.felix.bookshelf-service/-1284463217828`).

The OBR service has a stream handler registered for the `obr:` protocol; it will intercept requests for load of this bundle. Then check for newer versions of the bundles and return the latest compatible bundle.

In this case, the bundle is already ACTIVE, so the framework will:

◆ Stop the bundle

◆ Get the newer version, resolve, and install it

◆ Start the bundle again

If you need to, go back to *Chapter 1* to review the states of a bundle in the framework.

Trying the commands

Now that we've updated the code with the `add` command and cleaned up the `bookshelf-service` code, we can give it an end-to-end test.

To empty our memory-based inventory, it's enough to refresh the `bookshelf-inventory-impl-mock` bundle by running the following:

```
g! refresh 6
Stoping Book Inventory Mock Impl

Starting Book Inventory Mock Impl
```

Let's add a couple of books to test the add command using the following:

```
g! add admin admin 9789079350018 "OSGi Service Platform, Core
Specification, Release 4, Version 4.1" "OSGi Alliance" Reference 8
9789079350018
```

```
g!

g! add admin admin 9789079350025 "OSGi Service Platform, Service
Compendium, Release 4, Version 4.1" "OSGi Alliance" Reference 6

9789079350025
```

Of course, the ratings have been assigned for the sake of the example. Both of these books are very good.

Searching for any author would return the following:

```
g! search admin admin author %

Reference: OSGi Service Platform, Service Compendium, Release 4, Version
4.1 from OSGi Alliance [6]

Reference: OSGi Service Platform, Core Specification, Release 4, Version
4.1 from OSGi Alliance [8]
```

Searching for books with a rating between 5 and 7:

```
g! search admin admin rating 5 7

Reference: OSGi Service Platform, Service Compendium, Release 4, Version
4.1 from OSGi Alliance [6]
```

It behaves as expected.

Go ahead hero – implementing the other commands

The two commands, book:search and book:add, are enough for the tasks in this chapter, so we won't go any further in implementing others. However, that does not mean that you should not go ahead and add them on your own!

This is a good place for you to practice what you've learned by implementing some more commands. Here are a few suggestions:

◆ Add a book:get command to retrieve the book information from an exact ISBN match

◆ Add a book:remove command to remove a book from the bookshelf based on its ISBN

◆ Add a book:started command to mark a book as just started, given its ISBN

◆ Add a book:finished command to mark a book as just finished, giving it a rating

◆ Improve the search command to allow multiple simultaneous search criteria

The goal is to allow a full management of your bookshelf through the command-line interface.

Sourcing scripts

Now that we have the add command implemented, we can look at how to write a simple script for adding books into our inventory. Since our inventory implementation does not save the books between inventory service restarts, it is useful to have such scripts.

Time for action – creating a book population script

Writing a script is simple. Create a file (let's call it `populate-books.tsl`) and place it somewhere you can easily access from your Felix installation. I've put it in a directory under the Felix home directory called `scripts/`.

The population script taken as an example here will have the same books as we've used previously. Each command is on a line (below they wrap around because of page width limitations):

```
echo Now adding books to inventory. . .

add admin admin 9789079350018 "OSGi Service Platform, Core
Specification, Release 4, Version 4.1" "OSGi Alliance" Reference 8

add admin admin 9789079350025 "OSGi Service Platform, Service
Compendium, Release 4, Version 4.1" "OSGi Alliance" Reference 6

echo Done.
```

This program can now be executed on framework restart to add those two books to the inventory.

To execute the program, we use the `source` command (introduced in *Chapter 3*). I've refreshed the bundle to clear the books that were added earlier:

```
g! refresh 6
g!
Stoping Book Inventory Mock Impl

Starting Book Inventory Mock Impl
```

Use the `cd` command to change directory and the `ls` command to double-check that the file is there:

```
g! cd scripts
Name              scripts
CanonicalPath     C:\felix\scripts
Parent            C:\felix
Path              C:\felix\scripts
```

AbsoluteFile	C:\felix\scripts
AbsolutePath	C:\felix\scripts
CanonicalFile	C:\felix\scripts
ParentFile	C:\felix

```
g! ls
C:\felix\scripts\populate-books.tsl
```

Now run the following script:

```
g! source populate-books.tsl
Now adding books to inventory. . .
Done.
```

A quick search confirms the books were correctly added.

```
g! search admin admin author %
Reference: OSGi Service Platform, Core Specification, Release 4, Version
4.1 from OSGi Alliance [8]
Reference: OSGi Service Platform, Service Compendium, Release 4, Version
4.1 from OSGi Alliance [6]
```

This scripting capability is very useful. For example, I've constructed a script that helps me restart with a fresh Felix installation in just a few steps as follows:

```
# update obr repos
echo Adding releases obr repository. . .
repos add file:///C:/projects/felixbook/releases/repository.xml

# deploy tier 3
echo Deploying tier 3 \(inventory\) bundles. . .
bundlelevel -i 2
frameworklevel 2
deploy -s "Bookshelf Inventory Impl - Mock"

# deploy tier 2
echo Deploying tier 2 \(business logic\) bundles. . .
bundlelevel -i 3
frameworklevel 3
deploy -s "Bookshelf Service"

# deploy tier 1
echo Deploying tier 1 \(presentation\) bundles. . .
bundlelevel -i 5
frameworklevel 5
deploy -s "Bookshelf Service Gogo commands"
```

```
# populate books
source populate-books.tsl
```

After starting with a clean Felix install (or deleting the `felix-cache` directory), change to the `scripts/` directory:

```
g! cd scripts
Name              scripts
CanonicalPath     C:\felix\scripts
Parent            C:\felix
Path              C:\felix\scripts
AbsoluteFile      C:\felix\scripts
AbsolutePath      C:\felix\scripts
CanonicalFile     C:\felix\scripts
ParentFile        C:\felix
```

And execute the `install.tsl` script. It registers the releases repository with the OBR service and installs the bundles (with the right start levels). It then calls the `populate-books.tsl` script to add the books to the inventory:

```
g! source install.tsl
Adding releases obr repository. . .
Deploying tier 3 (inventory) bundles. . .
Target resource(s):
-------------------
   Bookshelf Inventory Impl - Mock (1.5.0)

Required resource(s):
--------------------
   Bookshelf Inventory API (1.5.0)

Deploying...
Starting Book Inventory Mock Impl
done.
Deploying tier 2 (business logic) bundles. . .
Target resource(s):
-------------------
   Bookshelf Service (1.8.0)

Deploying...done.
Deploying tier 1 (presentation) bundles. . .
```

```
Target resource(s):
-------------------

   Bookshelf Service Gogo commands (1.8.1)

Deploying...done.
Now adding books to inventory. . .
Done.
```

Of course, this script is now as far as we have come in this chapter; it will require a step-by-step update as you go along.

Summary

In this chapter, we've looked at the Apache Felix Gogo Shell Service, the service that provides a way to interact with bundle services through a simple text command line.

You have:

♦ Learned how to extend the Gogo Shell service with your own commands
♦ Implemented the `book:search` and `book:add` commands in a new bundle (`bookshelf-service-tui`)
♦ Learned how to update a bundle with a newer version
♦ Practiced sourcing a script to automate recurrent tasks

In the next chapter, we'll look at Felix iPOJO, which simplifies the registration of services and their retrieval by using declarative registration and injection of dependencies.

9
Improve the Bookshelf Service with iPOJO

So far, you've noticed while implementing our case study that we've used the bundle activator to register services with the framework. We've also looked at them from the framework's perspective when we needed to use them.

However, we've had to look up the service every time it was needed, to ensure that we always have the latest valid instance that is registered with the framework.

A developer may add a listener to framework activity (a service tracker) and update references on changes to dependencies of interest. Not only is this a more complex functionality to implement, but the resulting code is also mostly boiler-plate, that is, it is very similar from bundle to bundle—one usually ends up copying and pasting pieces of code or writing a common library to manage it. This is where iPOJO comes in handy.

In this chapter, we will look at how iPOJO can help keep this process simple, while improving the overall performance. You will:

◆ Look at an overview of the inversion of control component-oriented programming patterns and its application in our context, namely, the service locator, dependency injection, whiteboard, and extender patterns

◆ Introduce iPOJO, the service and Maven plugin, and look at the ways it is used to simplify OSGi integration, using XML configuration as well as annotations

◆ Learn how to use the iPOJO Gogo commands to get a view of registered iPOJO instances and factories

You will also:

◆ Simplify the case study bundles by migrating them to iPOJO, keeping their functionality unchanged.

What is Inversion of Control?

Inversion of control (IoC) is a group of design patterns (part of the Component Oriented Programming paradigm) in which logic, that was otherwise controlled by one component, is provided to it by another one. This logic can be related to the communication with a service, the instantiation of dependencies, their configuration, and so on.

In a classical procedural program, the main code block defines a sequence of steps that constitutes the program's execution flow. The program starts, initializes some variables, sets up connections to external systems, and executes its logic. It needs to:

◆ Know where to get its configuration, how to read it, and initialize the properties of its components

◆ Know which systems it needs to connect to, where they are, the connection adapters, and so on

◆ Know how to perform its business logic

However, from the preceding activities, only the last one is really a necessary responsibility of that piece of code. For example, the configuration could be stored in a file, in a database, or provided by another service—all that this component cares about is it being configured. Similarly, with the connection to external systems, the component should not care which adaptor is providing the connectivity, as long as it follows a defined interface.

The main idea behind IoC is to relinquish the fulfillment of those tasks to other components. The result is that the main component is only responsible for its area of concern, with other components taking care of tasks like providing configuration objects, initializing links to services, updating the service references when they are no longer available, and so on.

The progressive move from monolithically stand-alone applications to framework-based component-oriented designs makes the implementation of this inversion of control more reachable. The framework can provide the functionality needed to facilitate these kinds of patterns and add-on components implement them.

A good example that we've already covered is the bundle activator taking control of the execution flow at the point where a bundle is starting or stopping. In this scenario, the framework performs all the tasks that are common to all bundles—loading, resolving, and so on. The framework then inverts the control by handing it to the bundle activator while the bundle is starting (or stopping). The bundle knows what needs to be done during that part of the process, but doesn't need to know more.

In this section, we'll look at four inversions of control patterns that are of interest in the context of iPOJO. The first two relate to the initialization of references to external services, the other two relate to the tracking and reaction to the registration of other bundles like:

◆ The Service Locator pattern
◆ The Dependency Injection pattern
◆ The Whiteboard pattern
◆ The Extender pattern

The Service Locator pattern

We've already seen one inversion of control pattern earlier in this book without really naming it—the Service Locator pattern, by which a service (for example, the bookshelf service) does not instantiate a bookshelf inventory implementation itself. Instead, it requests one from the framework. The framework is responsible for providing the service implementation for the interface.

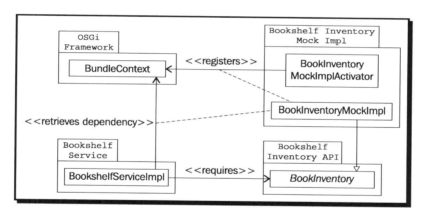

In this case, the bookshelf service does not know where the bookshelf inventory implementation comes from and does not need to worry about instantiating it. That control is inverted and delegated to the framework.

The Dependency Injection pattern

Another inversion of control pattern is dependency injection. In **dependency injection (DI)**, the dependencies of a component are set and managed by an external component.

The external component not only knows how to find the required dependencies, but also injects them into the component that requires them.

The injection mechanism varies, depending on the container and the designer's preferences, but generally it's one of the following:

- ◆ The dependency is passed as a parameter at the construction of the consumer
- ◆ The dependency is passed as a parameter to a setter exposed by the consumer
- ◆ The dependency is assigned to a property declared by the consumer

We will be looking at that last option in this chapter.

In our example, by using iPOJO to provide dependency injection, we delegate keeping track of the available services, registering them when they are started, and also assigning them to declare service instance attributes.

We'll have the following setup:

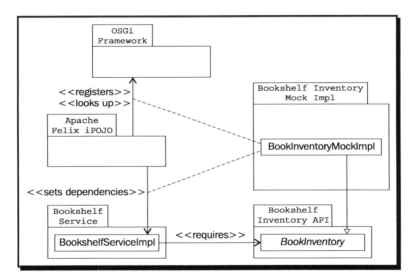

Since we were using the bundle activator of the bookshelf inventory implementation bundle solely for registering the service, we will no longer need it.

The choice of whether to use the Service Locator or Dependency Injection pattern really depends on the context. In here, we clearly see the benefit of using dependency injection, as it greatly simplifies the task of integrating with the framework.

An interesting article to read on inversion of control and dependency injection, by Martin Fowler, can be found at `http://martinfowler.com/articles/injection.html`

The Whiteboard pattern

Also used frequently in the context of OSGi, the whiteboard pattern is basically the matching of service providers to service consumers:

◆ A service consumer, or an agent working on its behalf, registers with the framework to listen for a specific target (the consumed service)

◆ The framework notifies the listener with added and removed instances of the consumed service

The Whiteboard pattern is used as a base for other patterns. For example, a dependency injection mechanism would most probably use the whiteboard pattern to keep track of registered services.

We will also use the whiteboard pattern to register our servlets, instead of registering them directly with the Http Service in *Chapter 11, How about a Graphical Interface?*. In that context, the HTTP whiteboard implementation will listen to registered HttpServlets and will add them to the installed Http Service, thus implementing the Extender Pattern.

The Extender Pattern

Based on the Whiteboard pattern, in the Extender Pattern will react to notifications of bundles starting or stopping and identify those that are of interest to it. This identification is usually through a manifest header or a configuration file in the bundle package. The extender component then registers them with a service provider as extensions.

We will see one example of the extender pattern in *Chapter 13, Improving the Graphics*, when looking at Pax Web. In this scenario, bundles are tagged with a specific manifest header that identifies them as web-applications and provides additional resources (such as a `web.xml` file).

The web extender component listens to bundles starting and stopping, picks those that have the required tag, and registers them with the Http Service.

The following diagram depicts this relationship:

In the preceding example, Bundle A does not carry the required tag and therefore is not included in the extension mechanism.

Bundles B and C are not aware of the steps that are required to register themselves with the Http Service. They will be resolved by the framework. Then, as they are starting, the extender receives a notification, identifies them as extensions, and publishes them with the provider.

Later, when they are stopping, the extender also takes care of un-publishing them and cleaning up the resources that they provided.

The iPOJO Felix sub-project

In short, Apache Felix iPOJO provides dependency injection features for OSGi frameworks. Some of its features simplify the tasks of registering and retrieving services on a framework by taking care of the life-cycle management of declared services. More advanced uses of it involve code manipulation.

iPOJO stands for **injected Plain Old Java Objects** and does not require specific interfaces to be implemented for integration—the components it uses are regular Java objects. It determines the needs of a component instance, based on its characteristics described in the bundle manifest.

The iPOJO components also work following the Extender Pattern, the general mechanism is the same; bundles that require dependency injection and publishing of services are tagged with a specific manifest header. The iPOJO extender components listen to bundles starting and stopping and grab those that have this header declared. The tag contains information on the requirements of the bundles from iPOJO, which fulfills them by interacting with the framework.

The following diagram, which not surprisingly looks a lot like the previous one for the web extender, describes this functional relationship:

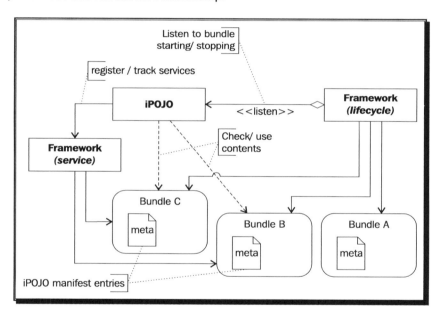

Components and instances

iPOJO recognizes bundles that require its functionality through the `iPOJO-Components` header in the bundle manifest. This header declares the parts of the bundle that require the services of iPOJO. iPOJO will look for the following two kinds of declarations in this header:

◆ **Component**: It describes the characteristics of a component from an abstract point of view—the service it provides, dependencies it requires, and so on.

◆ **Instance**: It declares the need for an instance of a specific component and its configuration.

In a way, components and instances can be compared to class definitions and object instances of those classes.

A component definition describes its requirements and capabilities. A component may:

- ◆ Provide a service, thus request that iPOJO be aware of the interface it provides. In this case, iPOJO will associate the component with that interface and look for components that require it
- ◆ Require a service as a dependency, thus request that iPOJO find implementations for that service and keep references to them up-to-date
- ◆ Require properties to be set on instantiation, and request that iPOJO set the values for those properties before making the service available

Those component declarations are kept by iPOJO and are used when instances are requested.

Instances of a component are managed by iPOJO. It will manage their life-cycle, monitor changes in their dependencies (install, uninstall, update, and so on.), and update their consumers accordingly.

 Components may also ask iPOJO to include their instances in the starting and stopping life-cycle stages, by providing callbacks that iPOJO would invoke at the appropriate time.

All of this information is encoded into the manifest header, which may become a long and complex task to do. Fortunately, the iPOJO Maven plugin allows this header to be generated from a simple metadata XML file.

iPOJO Maven plugin

There is an iPOJO Maven plugin to assist you with the composition of the `iPOJO-Components` manifest header. When it is configured to run as part of the bundle Maven build cycle, it will automatically construct the `iPOJO-Components` manifest header, based on an XML file.

The metadata file

The metadata XML file provided to the iPOJO plugin tells it which components and instances are to be declared for this bundle. If an alternative location is not specified in the configuration, the plugin will look for `meta.xml` in the root of the project or under the resources directory.

The following is a skeleton of this file that contains the placeholders for its parts. We'll look at each of those in greater detail through the following code:

```xml
<?xml version="1.0" encoding="UTF-8"?>
<ipojo
  xmlns:xsi="http://www.w3.org/2001/XMLSchema-instance"
  xsi:schemaLocation="org.apache.felix.ipojo
    http://felix.apache.org/ipojo/schemas/CURRENT/core.xsd"
  xmlns="org.apache.felix.ipojo">

  <component />
  <component />

  <instance />
  <instance />
</ipojo>
```

Components

The component element declares a service that is to be handled by iPOJO. The component's target class is set through the `classname` attribute. An optional `name` can be given to the component and used to reference it.

The component element also declares what it provides to iPOJO, the framework, and what it requires from them.

The `<provides/>` and `<requires/>` elements have a rich set of declarative options, most of which are not covered here. We will focus on the basics needed for the integration.

For example, a component can provide a service, which is registered using the component's interfaces. It can also provide properties to be published with the service.

Examples of things a component can require are lifecycle callbacks (the component provides a method to be called when a lifecycle stage is achieved) or services that it needs set through injection.

Once you're comfortable with the use of iPOJO, it's recommended that you read about some more of those and experiment with them. For now, let's focus on a simple configuration; the one we'll put in place for our bookshelf service:

```xml
<component
    name="BookshelfServiceImpl"
    classname=
      "com.packtpub.felix.bookshelf.service.impl.
BookshelfServiceImpl">
  <provides />
```

The component `classname` is specified along with an optional name. If the name is not set, the class name will be used instead.

The `<provides />` element tags the component as providing a service based on the interfaces it implements. iPOJO will register instances of this component with the framework.

The service also requires its inventory field to be injected with an instance of a `BookInventory`.

```
    <requires field="inventory" />
</component>
```

There's no need to tell iPOJO the type of the required injection. It will find out on its own by inspecting the type this field is declared as in the component class.

Callbacks involve the instances of the component during stages of its life-cycle. Basically, the component optionally provides a method to be called as it is validated and invalidated. In this case, we don't need it, but the syntax would be as follows:

```
    <callback transition="validate" method="start" />
    <callback transition="invalidate" method="stop" />
</component>
```

In the previous syntax, the `start()` method of the component would be called on component validation and the `stop()` method would be called during its invalidation. The callback target method names are arbitrary (that is, they don't have to be called start and stop).

Instances

The instance element requests the creation of an instance of a declared component. It specifies the component that needs to be instantiated, and an optional name for it, as well as the configuration of properties of the instance.

In our case, we're creating an instance of the component `"BookshelfServiceImpl"` that we've previously declared. We will name it `bookshelf.service.impl`; this name will appear later when we inspect the instances that iPOJO has detected.

```
    <instance
      component="BookshelfServiceImpl"
      name="bookshelf.service.impl" />
```

If needed, properties that the component requires can also be set when declaring the instance:

```
    <instance component="name-ref" name="inst-name">
      <property name="propName" value="propValue"/>
    </instance>
```

In our case, the required field is an instance of a component that iPOJO already manages. We, therefore, don't need to worry about setting it here.

Our final iPOJO `meta.xml` would look like this:

```
<ipojo
    xmlns:xsi="http://www.w3.org/2001/XMLSchema-instance"
    xsi:schemaLocation="org.apache.felix.ipojo
        http://felix.apache.org/ipojo/schemas/CURRENT/core.xsd"
    xmlns="org.apache.felix.ipojo">

  <component classname=
    "com.packtpub.felix.bookshelf.service.impl.BookshelfServiceImpl"
    name="BookshelfServiceImpl">

    <provides />

    <requires field="inventory" />
    <requires field="log" />
  </component>

  <instance
    component="BookshelfServiceImpl"
    name="bookshelf.service.impl" />
</ipojo>
```

We will see all this again as we modify our bundles.

> **iPOJO Eclipse plugin**
>
> Writing iPOJO metadata files is fairly simple at this stage, because we're not using all the power it provides. Editing the file as XML is not difficult. As you start exploring more of iPOJO's features, also look at its Eclipse plugin. Among other uses, it speeds up the metadata edition tasks.

Using the plugin

Adding support for iPOJO to a Maven project is fairly simple. It consists of the following two steps:

◆ Including the plugin in the POM's build plugins section and configuring it, optionally overriding the default settings

◆ Declaring components and instances in the iPOJO `meta.xml` file

The iPOJO plugin is used in conjunction with the bundle plugin that we've been using so far. We will place the configuration file in `src/main/ipojo/meta.xml`.

The following is the POM build plugins section used for our bundles:

```
<plugin>
  <groupId>org.apache.felix</groupId>
  <artifactId>maven-ipojo-plugin</artifactId>
  <version>1.6.0</version>
  <executions>
    <execution>
      <goals>
        <goal>ipojo-bundle</goal>
      </goals>
      <configuration>
        <metadata>src/main/ipojo/meta.xml</metadata>
      </configuration>
    </execution>
  </executions>
</plugin>
```

This requests the execution of the `ipojo-bundle` goal and specifies the location of the iPOJO, metadata file. There are other configuration items that can be of interest. I recommend you check the plugin documentation for more information at: (`http://felix.apache.org/site/ipojo-maven-plug-in.html`).

Injecting iPOJOs

Let's modify our use case bundles to use the iPOJO functionality. Here's the plan:

- Modify the `bookshelf-inventory-impl-mock` bundle, adding an iPOJO descriptor for the component and its instance and removing the bundle activator.
- Modify the `bookshelf-service` bundle to have the inventory field injected instead of it performing a lookup in the service and declare it in its descriptor.
- Modify the `bookshelf-service-tui` commands to have as bookshelf service field injected and have them instantiated and registered through iPOJO, here too no longer needing to keep the activator.

As we will soon see, iPOJO allows configuration in XML and using annotations on the component. To practice both technologies, we will modify the `bookshelf-inventory-impl-mock` and `bookshelf-service` bundles to use XML-only and the `bookshelf-service-tui` bundle to use both.

The step-by-step learning of iPOJO will be as follows:

1. The first example (`bookshelf-inventory-impl-mock`) only requires the publishing of a service using XML only.

2. The second example (bookshelf-service) requires both the injection of dependencies and the publishing of a service using XML only.

3. The third example combines two extensions, one for Gogo and the other for iPOJO and requires the injection of dependencies and the publishing of a service. It is also configured for iPOJO using a combination of XML-based and annotation-based declarations.

But first let's install the iPOJO bundle on our Felix framework.

Install the iPOJO service bundle

We'll start the Apache Felix iPOJO bundle directly from the registered Felix OBR, just like we did previously with the other bundles, with the `obr:deploy` command (including the `-s` option):

```
g! deploy -s "Apache Felix iPOJO"
Target resource(s):
-------------------

    Apache Felix iPOJO (1.6.4)

Deploying...done.
```

The service should now be ready for use. The next thing we need to do is to update our bundles to use it.

Let iPOJO register the inventory implementation

When we implemented `BookInventoryMockImpl` in *Chapter 5, The Book Inventory Bundle*, we used a `BundleActivator` and the `BookInventoryMockImplActivator` to register it with the framework on start. It was actually a good idea then, because, while in validation mode, we've also inserted books on start.

As all we need to do is register the service, we'll move it to iPOJO. It's an easy thing to do.

Time for action – creating the iPOJO metadata

So let's start by describing the component in iPOJO terms. The task consists of the addition of the `meta.xml` descriptor under `src/main/ipojo` of the `bookshelf-inventory-impl-mock` project and the modification of the POM to configure the `maven-ipojo-plugin`.

The modification of the POM is usually the step that's forgotten. So let's get that out of the way first.

Update the POM

In our case, as we're moving the component from using a bundle activator to declaring itself using iPOJO, we'll need to do two things:

◆ Remove the bundle activator header from the manifest

◆ Add support for iPOJO in the Maven build cycle

Edit the `pom.xml` file and go to the build plugins section. In the `maven-bundle-plugin` configuration, comment out (or remove) the `Bundle-Activator` instruction. Also, the `Private-Package` instruction is no longer needed, so it will also be commented out:

```
<plugin>
  <groupId>org.apache.felix</groupId>
  <artifactId>maven-bundle-plugin</artifactId>
  <version>2.1.0</version>
  <extensions>true</extensions>
  <configuration>
    <instructions>
      <Bundle-Category>sample</Bundle-Category>
      <Bundle-SymbolicName>${artifactId}</Bundle-SymbolicName>
      <Export-Package>
        com.packtpub.felix.bookshelf.inventory.impl.mock
      </Export-Package>
    <!-- <Bundle-Activator>
com.packtpub.felix.bookshelf.inventory.impl.mock.activator.-
BookInventoryMockImplActivator
      </Bundle-Activator>
      <Private-Package>
      com.packtpub.felix.bookshelf.inventory.impl.mock.activator
      </Private-Package> -->
    </instructions>
  <!-- ... -->
</plugin>
```

You may choose to also delete the `BookInventoryMockImplActivator` class, for completeness.

Next, we hook the `maven-ipojo-plugin`. Do not forget to include the `ipojo-bundle` goal in its execution goals.

```
<plugin>
  <groupId>org.apache.felix</groupId>
  <artifactId>maven-ipojo-plugin</artifactId>
  <version>1.4.2</version>
  <executions>
    <execution>
      <goals>
        <goal>ipojo-bundle</goal>
      </goals>
```

We will also specify an alternate metadata file location:

```
      <configuration>
        <metadata>src/main/ipojo/meta.xml</metadata>
      </configuration>
    </execution>
  </executions>
</plugin>
```

Also, update the project version to `1.9.0` and that's it for the POM. Let's write the metafile now.

Configure bundle for iPOJO

Edit the file `src/main/ipojo/meta.xml`: We will go through the parts of the descriptor while explaining them:

```
<ipojo
    xmlns:xsi="http://www.w3.org/2001/XMLSchema-instance"
    xsi:schemaLocation="org.apache.felix.ipojo
      http://felix.apache.org/ipojo/schemas/CURRENT/core.xsd"
    xmlns="org.apache.felix.ipojo">
```

First, we start by declaring the component. The `classname` designates the name of the component class and points the iPOJO plugin to it for inspection. It retrieves the interface that it will use to register the service.

```
<component
  classname="com.packtpub.felix.bookshelf.inventory.impl.mock.
BookInventoryMockImpl"
  name="BookInventoryMockImpl">
```

The name is arbitrary really; it is used to refer to this component. If it's not set, it defaults to the class name.

This component provides a service; the `<provides />` element tags it as so.

```
        <provides />
    </component>
```

As we saw earlier, declaring a component is not enough to make iPOJO instantiate it. The instance declaration below is also necessary:

```
    <instance component="BookInventoryMockImpl"
       name="bookshelf.inventory.impl.mock" />
    </ipojo>
```

Build and test it

The inventory implementation does not require any service injection, so it's enough to replace its activator with the above iPOJO XML declaration. Let's give it a try.

Rebuild and deploy the bundle to the releases repository and update it in Felix. It should now be at version 1.9.0.

If everything went well, the update should event-less, nothing happens differently in appearance. Test the service to ensure it's working correctly.

Notice that we've modified the inventory implementation bundle, but not the bookshelf service. It still looks up its dependency through the bundle context service locator. Moving one component to iPOJO does not force you to move the others.

Also note that this modification was released with a different version, but we did not need to update the bookshelf-service dependencies. The service depends on the inventory API, not its implementation. This is one of the gains of having decoupled the API bundle from the implementation bundle(s).

What just happened?

Let's take a closer look at what happened in each of the steps. We declared the component and an instance of it in the iPOJO meta.xml file and configured the ipojo plugin to attach its ipojo-bundle goal to the build lifecycle.

During the build cycle, the iPOJO Maven plugin picked up the metadata file and kicked off the manipulation. The plugin manipulates the bundle, based on the metadata file:

```
[INFO] [ipojo:ipojo-bundle {execution: default}]
[INFO] Start bundle manipulation
[INFO] Metadata file : C:\projects\felixbook\sources\-
    com.packtpub.felix.bookshelf-inventory-impl-mock\-
    src\main\ipojo\meta.xml
[INFO] Input Bundle File : C:\projects\felixbook\sources\
    com.packtpub.felix.bookshelf-inventory-impl-mock\
    target\com.packtpub.felix.bookshelf-inventory-impl-mock-1.9.0.jar
[INFO] Bundle manipulation - SUCCESS
```

This is a good part to check when building, looking for any warnings or errors.

Take a look at the changes it made: open the bundle archive (or unzip it somewhere) and inspect the file META-INF/MANIFEST.MF. The header iPOJO-Components was added to it (replacing the Bundle-Activator header, which we have omitted from the plugin configuration).

We don't need to go through it here, but if you inspect it, you'll find that its value is a compilation of the description we've given in the XML file and some additional information that iPOJO extracted from the component class, encoded in a Lisp-like format.

The Felix iPOJO Gogo Command bundle

The Felix iPOJO Gogo Command bundle (previously arch) provides access to the components and instances held by the iPOJO service. It is a useful tool when debugging injection by providing information on the instances and interconnects that iPOJO holds.

It can be started from the following OBR:

```
g! deploy -s "Apache Felix iPOJO Gogo Command"
```

At the time of writing this section, the iPOJO Gogo Command was just released and still had a few install issues (for example, deploying using OBR attempts to install another version of iPOJO). If you face a similar issue, then install it using a direct link to one of the available mirrors:

```
g! start http://www.ibiblio.org/pub/mirrors/apache/felix/org.apache.
felix.ipojo.arch.gogo-1.0.0.jar
```

```
[WARNING] org.apache.felix.ipojo.arch.gogo.Arch : The specification org.
apache.felix.ipojo.arch.gogo.Arch is not implemented by org.apache.felix.
ipojo.arch.gogo.Arch it might be a superclass or the class itself.
```

The warning we just saw can be ignored.

ipojo scope commands usage

The following commands are provided by the iPOJO Gogo Command bundle. They are in the `ipojo` scope:

- `factories`: To list the registered factories
- `factory factoryName`: To display information on the given factory
- `instances`: To list the registered instances
- `instance instanceName`: To display information on the given instance
- `handlers`: To list registered handlers

The factories are our component declarations. Handlers are a more advanced topic, worth exploring if you'd like to extend iPOJO.

For example, the following command is used to list the instances iPOJO currently knows about:

```
g! instances
Instance bookshelf.inventory.impl.mock -> valid
Instance org.apache.felix.ipojo.arch.gogo.Arch-0 -> valid
```

The first item in the list is our bookshelf inventory implementation instance. Its details are retrieved as follows (output reformatted):

```
g! instance bookshelf.inventory.impl.mock
instance
    component.type="BookInventoryMockImpl"
    state="valid"
    bundle="6"
    name="bookshelf.inventory.impl.mock"
        handler
            state="valid"
            name="org.apache.felix.ipojo:provides"
            provides
                service.id="27"
                state="registered"
                specifications=
"[com.packtpub.felix.bookshelf.inventory.api.BookInventory]"
                property value="BookInventoryMockImpl"
                        name="factory.name"
```

```
        property value="bookshelf.inventory.impl.mock"
                  name="instance.name"
    handler
        state="valid"
        name="org.apache.felix.ipojo:architecture"
```

Notice the instance is bound to the `bookshelf-inventory-mock-impl` bundle (ID 6), and it provides the `com.packtpub.felix.bookshelf.inventory.api.BookInventory` service specification.

Migrate the bookshelf service

The bookshelf service is the next item on our list. This component would both provide a service (the `BookshelfService`) and require the injection of the `BookshelfInventory` implementation.

Time for action – removing lookups in the service implementation

We will now update the service implementation, as we want to remove the dependency on the core OSGi framework classes for the lookup of the inventory and declare it as a field for injection.

As a reminder, the `BookshelfServiceImpl` currently starts like this:

```
public class BookshelfServiceImpl implements BookshelfService
{
    private String sessionId;
    BundleContext context;
    public BookshelfServiceImpl(BundleContext context)
    {
        this.context = context;
    }
    private BookInventory lookupBookInventory()
    {
        ServiceReference ref = this.context.getServiceReference(
            BookInventory.class.getName());
        if (ref == null)
        {
            throw new BookInventoryNotRegisteredRuntimeException(
                BookInventory.class.getName());
        }
        return (BookInventory) this.context.getService(ref);
    }
}
```

And continues with its methods that call `lookupBookInventory()` when they need access to the currently registered inventory implementation.

We will declare the inventory field, which will be injected with the registered `BookInventory` implementation:

```
public class BookshelfServiceImpl implements BookshelfService
{
    String session;

    BookInventory inventory;
```

To avoid modifying the whole class and replacing calls to `lookupBookInventory()` with `this.inventory`, we'll update the method to return it.

```
    private BookInventory lookupBookInventory()
    {
        return this.inventory;
    }
```

The `BundleContext` is no longer required. We can remove the `context` property and update the constructor to take no parameters:

```
    public BookshelfServiceImpl()
    {
    }
```

The following OSGi framework imports are also no longer needed and can be removed.

```
import org.osgi.framework.BundleContext;
import org.osgi.framework.ServiceReference;
```

This class is now a POJO that's also container-independent; although it needs a container and service injection to make it functional, it does not specifically need to know how this is going to be achieved. This is one of the most attractive features of dependency injection.

For example, this same bundle can be used in another container, such as Spring, Tapestry, or PicoContainer with the appropriate injection configuration.

 Some dependency injection frameworks require a setter (or a constructor parameter) to be declared for fields that need to be injected.

With these changes, the activator for this bundle fails to compile. This is because it constructs a `BookshelfServiceImpl` passing a `BundleContext`. There's no need to fix it, as it is going to be deleted.

Now, let's write the iPOJO configuration for this bundle.

Time for action – writing the bookshelf service iPOJO configuration

Create the iPOJO configuration file for the `bookshelf-service` bundle
(under `src/main/ipojo/meta.xml`):

```
<ipojo
    xmlns:xsi="http://www.w3.org/2001/XMLSchema-instance"
    xsi:schemaLocation="org.apache.felix.ipojo
            http://felix.apache.org/ipojo/schemas/CURRENT/core.xsd"
    xmlns="org.apache.felix.ipojo">
```

The component we're declaring here is the `BookshelfServiceImpl`:

```
<component
    classname=
    "com.packtpub.felix.bookshelf.service.impl.BookshelfServiceImpl"
    name="BookshelfServiceImpl">
```

And it provides a service, which will be published against the `BookshelfService` interface.

```
<provides />
```

In addition to that, we ask iPOJO to inject the `inventory` field we have just declared:

```
<requires field="inventory" />
</component>
```

And we finish with the instance declaration:

```
<instance
    component="BookshelfServiceImpl"
    name="bookshelf.service.impl" />
</ipojo>
```

Update the POM

The `bookshelf-service` bundle should now have version `1.9.0`. Edit the build plugins
section of the POM, commenting out (or removing) the `Bundle-Activator` instruction:

```
<plugin>
    <groupId>org.apache.felix</groupId>
    <artifactId>maven-bundle-plugin</artifactId>
    <version>2.1.0</version>
    <extensions>true</extensions>
```

```xml
<configuration>
  <instructions>
    <Bundle-Category>sample</Bundle-Category>
    <Bundle-SymbolicName>${artifactId}</Bundle-SymbolicName>
    <Export-Package>
      com.packtpub.felix.bookshelf.service.api,
      com.packtpub.felix.bookshelf.service.impl
    </Export-Package>
<!-- <Bundle-Activator>
com.packtpub.felix.bookshelf.service.impl.activator.
BookshelfServiceImplActivator
    </Bundle-Activator>
    <Private-Package>
      com.packtpub.felix.bookshelf.service.impl.activator
    </Private-Package> -->
  </instructions>
  <!-- ... -->
```

The activator class is also deleted.

Also add the `maven-ipojo-plugin` declaration:

```xml
<plugin>
  <groupId>org.apache.felix</groupId>
  <artifactId>maven-ipojo-plugin</artifactId>
  <version>1.4.2</version>
  <executions>
    <execution>
      <goals>
        <goal>ipojo-bundle</goal>
      </goals>
      <configuration>
        <metadata>src/main/ipojo/meta.xml</metadata>
      </configuration>
    </execution>
  </executions>
</plugin>
```

Notice that the `maven-ipojo-plugin` declaration is the same for all projects. If you're comfortable with Maven multi-projects, this can be moved to a parent POM.

This bundle is now ready to be packaged and deployed.

Deploy and check

Once rebuilt and deployed to the releases repository, and then installed and started in Felix, checking with the `ipojo:instances` command should give:

```
g! instances
Instance bookshelf.inventory.impl.mock -> valid
Instance org.apache.felix.ipojo.arch.gogo.Arch-0 -> valid
Instance bookshelf.service.impl -> valid
```

The newly configured bundle was recognized by iPOJO. Let's check its details as follows:

```
g! instance bookshelf.service.impl
instance
  component.type="BookshelfServiceImpl"
  state="valid"
  bundle="9"
  name="bookshelf.service.impl"
    handler
      state="valid"
      name="org.apache.felix.ipojo:requires"
      requires optional="false" aggregate="false" state="resolved"
      binding-policy="dynamic" proxy="true"
      id="com.packtpub.felix.bookshelf.inventory.api.BookInventory"
      specification=
        "com.packtpub.felix.bookshelf.inventory.api.BookInventory"
...
```

The detailed instance information shows the `bookshelf.service.impl` instance registered as requiring `com.packtpub.felix.bookshelf.inventory.api.BookInventory` and that this requirement is fulfilled (`state="resolved"`).

Testing the `book` commands should show no difference in their behavior. We'll go through a round of tests after updating the text UI bundle. But first, let's learn how to use annotations for component declarations instead of XML.

iPOJO using annotations

An alternative way of tagging components for iPOJO is to annotate them directly in the Java code. iPOJO provides annotations support through the `org.apache.felix.ipojo.annotations` library.

Overview

There are some gains in clarity of the code when using annotations and it also simplifies updates by keeping the configuration closer to its target class or field.

For instance, in the previous declaration of the bookshelf service, we could have replaced the configuration entry in the `meta.xml` file:

```
<component
  classname=
    "com.packtpub.felix.bookshelf.service.impl.BookshelfServiceImpl"
  name="BookshelfServiceImpl">

  <provides />

  <requires field="inventory" />
</component>
```

With annotations to the class `BookshelfServiceImpl`:

```
@Component(name="BookshelfServiceImpl")
@Provides
public class BookshelfServiceImpl implements BookshelfService
{
    @Requires
    BookInventory inventory;
```

Which would have the same effect.

Beginner's annotations

Let's quickly go through the main annotations of interest; the others are left for you to check online through the available iPOJO documentation (`http://felix.apache.org/site/how-to-use-ipojo-annotations.html`).

As a general rule, when declaring components both as annotations and in XML, the XML takes precedence. This is a common pitfall, where one would want to move to annotations but forget to remove the declarations from the XML configuration file, thus getting unexpected results.

@Component

It annotates an implementation class and is used to declare it as a component type (that is, a factory). The `classname` attribute is not available here as it is the class that's annotated. Some of the attributes of interest here are as follows:

◆ **name**: Optional definition of the component name, defaults to the class name if not set

◆ **immediate**: Optionally tag this component as requiring to be created as soon as it has all its requirements met. It is true, by default, when the component does not provide a service. Otherwise it defaults to false. An immediate component is dealt with an eager instantiation mechanism; while a non-immediate component follows a lazy instantiation mechanism (instantiated when first needed).

The other attributes are a bit more advanced, but I recommend you go online and read about them when you get more comfortable using annotations.

@Provides

It annotates an implementation class and is used to declare it as a component that provides a service.

Among the available attributes, one of interest is:

◆ **strategy**: Defines the instantiation strategy (or policy) for the provided service. Its default value is:

 ❑ SINGLETON, meaning that a single instance of the service is shared among the components that require it

 Other values are:

 ❑ INSTANCE, specifying that a separate instance is created per component that requires it

 ❑ SERVICE, refers to the OSGi service factory

 ❑ METHOD, refers to one of the component methods as a factory method

@Requires

It annotates a class field and declares it as a dependency requiring injection.

Some attributes of interest are:

◆ **optional**: Specifies if the field assignment is optional. It's default value is true

◆ **nullable**: Allows the Null object injection when the dependency is not available. Its default value is false.

@ServiceProperty

It annotates a field of a component providing a service and exposes it as a service property.

Its attributes are all optional:

◆ **name**: Provides a name for the property, defaults to the field name

◆ **value**: Provides a value for the property. Otherwise, a value must be provided along with the instance declaration

◆ **mandatory**: Specifies if the property is mandatory (that is, a value is required for it) and is false by default

@Property

It annotates a field or a method and registers an internal property of the component.

Its attributes are as follows:

◆ **name**: Provides a name for the property, defaults to the bean name. For example, if this annotation is attached to a field, then the default name is the field name. If the annotation is attached to a setter of a field, for example, `setMyField()`, then the name of the property would be `MyField`

◆ **value**: Provides a value for the property. Otherwise, a value must be provided along with the instance declaration

◆ **mandatory**: Specifies if the property is mandatory (that is, a value is required for it) and is false by default

 The difference between a `@Property` and a `@serviceProperty` is its visibility to other services: properties are internal to the component, while service properties are made visible to external components.

@Instantiate

It requests the addition of an instance declaration along with the component declaration. This is a slightly limited replacement of the `<instance />` element in the configuration. It annotates the component class and does not take data parameters.

Instantiating annotated components

The separation between the component declaration and the instantiation is an important separation of concerns. The idea is very close to the class/instance relationship; components can be considered as types, or factories, and the instance is an occurrence of this component.

Items that apply to the type definition and behavior are defined at the level of the component, while others, such as the setting of property values, are related to the instance.

This is one of the reasons why the @Instantiate annotation does not allow naming or configuration.

The best practice is to define the instance of the component outside of the component definition; thus allowing the added flexibility of configuring different instances in different ways. Items such as properties and service properties can be configured either in the instance declaration or using the Config Admin service.

When both configuration and annotation based declarations are found by iPOJO, the configuration based declaration takes precedence in the shaping of a component.

Update the text UI bundle

The last bundle to update is the bookshelf-service-tui. This bundle will be updated to use iPOJO annotations.

The defined Gogo commands make use of the BookshelfService, which we'll declare as a field of the service proxy and configure it for injection.

Time for action – updating the BookshelfServiceProxyImpl

Edit the BookshelfServiceProxyImpl class. We will walk through the changes step-by-step.

The @Component annotation at class level declares this class as a component definition, and sets its name. The @Provides annotation flags this component as providing a service (in this can it's the BookshelfServiceProxy service).

```
@Component(name="BookshelfServiceProxy")
@Provides
public class BookshelfServiceProxyImpl
    implements BookshelfServiceProxy
{
```

We have dropped the BundleContext field, since we're going to have iPOJO inject the BookshelfService instance into this newly added bookshelf field. It is tagged as a requirement of the component:

```
@Requires
private BookshelfService bookshelf;
```

Then, when we define the service properties, those properties will be attached to the service at registration time:

```
@ServiceProperty(name = "osgi.command.scope", value=SCOPE)
String gogoScope;

@ServiceProperty(
    name = "osgi.command.function", value=FUNCTIONS_STR)
String[] gogoFunctions;
```

The FUNCTIONS_STR is a new constant added to the BookshelfServiceProxy interface, with the value "[search]". It is needed because the annotation value for a service property is a String.

The constructor is updated removing its BundleContext parameter and the lookupService() method is updated to return the bookshelf field value.

```
public BookshelfServiceProxyImpl() {
}
protected BookshelfService lookupService() {
    return this.bookshelf;
}
// ...
}
```

The remainder of the class remains unchanged.

Time for action – writing the iPOJO meta.xml

With most of the iPOJO configuration annotated into the class, the XML configuration only holds the instance information. Create the meta.xml file under src/main/ipojo/ with the following contents:

```
<ipojo
    xmlns:xsi="http://www.w3.org/2001/XMLSchema-instance"
    xsi:schemaLocation="org.apache.felix.ipojo
            http://felix.apache.org/ipojo/schemas/CURRENT/core.xsd"
    xmlns="org.apache.felix.ipojo">

  <instance
    component="BookshelfServiceProxy"
    name="bookshelf.service.tui" />
</ipojo>
```

Next, we'll update the POM and take the updated bundle for a short ride.

Time for action – updating the POM

The last item to update is the project `pom.xml` file. Its contents are very close to the ones we've already seen relating to iPOJO, with a few differences that we will look at here. The version of the `bookshelf-service-tui` bundle will now be 1.9.0.

The Maven dependency for the iPOJO annotations we've used previously need to be added to the dependencies section:

```
<dependency>
   <groupId>org.apache.felix</groupId>
   <artifactId>org.apache.felix.ipojo.annotations</artifactId>
   <version>1.6.4</version>
</dependency>
```

The build plugins sections for `maven-bundle-plugin` and `maven-ipojo-plugin` will look like:

```
<plugin>
   <groupId>org.apache.felix</groupId>
   <artifactId>maven-bundle-plugin</artifactId>
   <version>2.1.0</version>
   <extensions>true</extensions>
   <configuration>
     <instructions>
       <Bundle-Category>sample</Bundle-Category>
       <Bundle-SymbolicName>${artifactId}</Bundle-SymbolicName>
       <Export-Package>
         com.packtpub.felix.bookshelf.service.tui
       </Export-Package>
     </instructions>
     <remoteOBR>repo-rel</remoteOBR>
     <prefixUrl>file:///C:/projects/felixbook/releases</prefixUrl>
     <ignoreLock>true</ignoreLock>
   </configuration>
</plugin>

<plugin>
   <groupId>org.apache.felix</groupId>
   <artifactId>maven-ipojo-plugin</artifactId>
   <version>1.4.2</version>
   <executions>
     <execution>
       <goals>
```

```
            <goal>ipojo-bundle</goal>
          </goals>
          <configuration>
            <metadata>src/main/ipojo/meta.xml</metadata>
          </configuration>
        </execution>
      </executions>
    </plugin>
```

You'll notice that it is only slightly different than the others we've seen so far.

Have a go hero – updating the bundles to use annotations

We've practiced iPOJO using both XML-based and annotation-based configuration of components. How about you try to move the other two bundles (`bookshelf-inventory-impl` and `bookshelf-service`) to use annotations?

Items to keep in mind while doing this:

◆ Remember that the XML configuration takes precedence over annotations. You'll need to remove component declarations from the XML configuration to switch to newly added annotations.

◆ Unless for very simple cases, it's not recommended to use the Instantiate annotation to request an instance of the component (see previous topics for a short discussion on that).

The result would functionally be the same as what we currently have.

Have a go hero – implementing a file-based bookshelf-inventory

One of the nice features of iPOJO is that it manages a component's dependencies out of the box. This means that it will ensure the dependency is injected with its implementation, when one is available.

Also, we now know how to define a component's required properties.

This is an opportune time to write another implementation of the `BookInventory` service, as a new bundle (say, `bookshelf-inventory-impl-file`), which would store the book data to a file.

Here are some hints for this:

◆ Make the component require a property, which is the path to store the books in, relative to the framework's persistent storage area. Access to the framework's persistent storage area is provided by the `BundleContext`'s `getDataFile()` method

◆ Make the service load the contents of the stored books on start-up and index them for search. This is done by specifying a callback on `validate` that will load all stored books.

When the implementation is complete, it's enough to uninstall the older one (`bookshelf-inventory-impl-mock`) and install and start the new implementation (`bookshelf-inventory-impl-file`). The new implementation will be injected into the bookshelf service inventory field automatically.

Summary

In this chapter, we've introduced iPOJO and the way it simplifies integrating with a framework by providing inversion of control functionality.

By now, you should be able to:

◆ Declare a component to be registered by iPOJO without the need for a `BundleActivator` using both iPOJO configuration means (XML and annotations)

◆ Declare fields that a component requires and ask iPOJO to inject them, when they become available, and update them as they move through their life-cycle

We have also migrated our case study to use iPOJO. We have:

◆ Updated the `bookshelf-inventory-impl-mock` bundle to use iPOJO to register its inventory implementation

◆ Updated the `bookshelf-service` and `bookshelf-service-tui` to also use iPOJO to register them and to inject their dependencies (`BookInventory` and `BookshelfService` respectively.)

10
Improving the Logging

Logging is one of the functionalities frequently given lower priority during the development of an application; the price is usually paid later, when the application does not behave as expected and there's the need to investigate where things aren't right.

It's crucial that the components of an application log activity and unexpected situations properly. This allows us to trace the root cause of issues, in which scenarios they occur, and improves the chances of finding a fix for them.

In our case study so far, we've made poor use of logging and written a few messages to the standard error stream when things went wrong. Now that we've had a good look at the principles of integrating with an OSGi framework, it's time to take a closer look at the logging side of things.

In this chapter, we will:

◆ Learn a little bit about logging in general and in the context of OSGi

◆ Look at the Apache Felix Log Service implementation and its `log` command

◆ Update our bundles to use the framework logging system

On logging

Logging is an important facet of any application. When things don't go as expected, proper logs provide a great deal of information that can be used in the troubleshooting and root cause analysis activities.

Proper logging is a fine balance between giving useful contextual information and error traces and keeping it at low volume to avoid visibility clutter and performance impact. Being able to fine-tune the level of detail of the information that is received while the service platform is available (at runtime) is a valuable functionality. It allows the operational support team to drop down to a low level of details when additional information is needed, while keeping the system at the highest performance when it is running as expected.

Logging levels

To better classify logged activity and error situations, a log entry is typically tagged with a level of severity. The log levels defined for the OSGi Log Service are:

Level Name	Level Severity	Level Description
DEBUG	4	Use the 'debug' level to log relatively "verbose" information, usually targeted at the developer/tester of the component.
		Debug level log entries containing contextual information on the details of the execution progress, they may contain information such as entry into a method, the parameter values, algorithm steps, return of calls, and so on.
INFO	3	Use the 'info' level to log light notifications on component activity or changes in state.
		Info level log entries do not contain information that relates to error situations.
WARNING	2	Use the 'warning' level to notify the encounter of a situation that's currently not a problem, but may be the hint of upcoming errors. It may also be used to send a notification of an unexpected error situation that was recovered.
		Warning level logs must contain enough contextual information to be used by a monitoring system for attempts to determine a root cause or correlate multiple messages.
ERROR	1	Use the 'error' level to notify of encountered error situations that require immediate attention.
		Error level log entries are usually also accompanied with an exception that was thrown. They must also contain enough contextual information for use by monitoring systems.

The log severity represents that level numerically—severity 1 is the highest. This numeric value is used to set a threshold on the level of logs to filter when showing log entries. For example, a threshold at WARNING level (=2) would show only WARNING and ERROR (=1) log entries, but not INFO and DEBUG.

Some of the logging APIs also include the 'trace' and 'critical' or 'fatal' log levels. The 'trace' level is finer than 'debug' and would be used for very verbose logs. The 'critical' or 'fatal' levels would be used to notify of an unrecoverable error state, typically requiring immediate system maintenance.

Who's listening?

Depending on the logging system that's in place, the logs that the application sends may be treated in many ways: they can be written to file, kept in memory, transmitted to an external logging component, and so on.

It is also possible (and recommended) to set up an external platform monitoring system that would react to warnings and error messages by sending an alert to an administrator or taking some corrective action. This stresses the importance of picking the right logging level when sending log messages. Typical monitoring systems only listen to warning and errors. Using an incorrect logging level may result in the monitoring system ignoring the message.

The contents of the log message are of equal importance. On large systems, with many components running (and logging) at the same time, logs from those components will most likely be interlaced. It is therefore important to include contextual information in the logged messages, as well as include a unique key (message code) that can be easily extracted by a monitoring tool.

Say, for example, that you're trying to connect to a URL and are including logging for when this connection fails:

```
try
{
    log.debug("Connecting to: " + url);
    connection = connect(url);
}
catch (IOException e)
{
    log.error("Error connecting", e);
}
```

The error message follows the info message, so one would say the URL information was already provided—wrong. This piece of code could be called by different parties at the same time. The error message for one call may not follow its info message directly. Furthermore, if a monitoring component only logs errors, it won't have access to the URL.

Consider the following as a better alternative:

```
try
{
    log.info("Connecting to: [{0}]", url);
    connection = connect(url);
}
catch (IOException e)
{
    log.error("Error connecting to [{0}]", e, url);
}
```

Making sure each message holds enough contextual information to know what's going on is crucial; it allows an easier analysis of error situations.

Notice also the other difference with the initial code block, which is the use of a message pattern and passing of the URL as a parameter. This has quite a few benefits such as allowing the externalization of the message patterns and potentially localizing them (including alternative language translations). It also avoids concatenation in the main code and delaying it to a later time.

Another piece of information that's usually included with log messages is the identity of the sender; this is also important. In addition to it providing information on the context of the log, it also allows filtering based on the source of the message.

The OSGi Log Service

Developers who are used to a logging tool, such as log4j, are compelled to use the same logging setup in an OSGi framework. After overcoming the initial first obstacles relating to codebase separation and resource visibility, the developers succeed in making it work. The result would typically look like the following diagram:

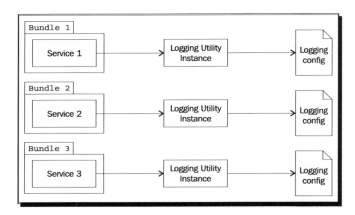

Such structures would work. However, they usually require a complex configuration to be set up and maintained. A better option is the use of a common logging service.

The OSGi Compendium specifications define a set of Log Service interfaces that are intended to provide a common logging service for an OSGi framework.

The Log Service applies separation of concerns by splitting functionality into the following two services:

◆ The Log Service interface is used by bundles that need to send logs—this is the service end

◆ The Log Reader Service interface set is used by bundles that need to read logs—this is the service provider end

Let's take a closer look at those.

The Service end

The Log Service interface exposes a simple, but expandable, logging API for use by the bundles that need to send log events. Those bundles would all depend on a single logging interface.

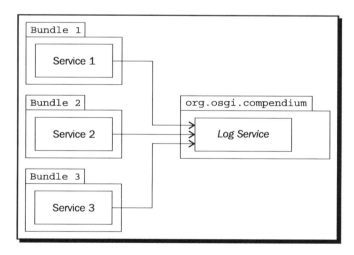

The Log Service interface method declarations are variations of `log()`:

```
log(int level, String message)
```

For logging a message at a log level.

The log levels are declared as constants in the same interface:

- **LOG_DEBUG**: An integer with the value 4 for debug level logs
- **LOG_INFO**: With value 3 for info logs
- **LOG_WARNING**: With value 2 for warning logs
- **LOG_ERROR**: With value 1 for error logs

To also pass an exception with the log entry, the signature with the `Throwable` parameter is used:

```
log(int level, String message, Throwable exception)
```

The same methods are also provided with a `ServiceReference` as the first parameter:

```
log(ServiceReference sr, int level, String message)

log(ServiceReference sr, int level, String message,
        Throwable exception)
```

In this case, the log message is registered as relating to the bundle with the provided service reference (instead of relating to the bundle invoking the `log()` method).

Usage of the Log Service

The Log Service is used just like any other service on an OSGi framework.

To get access to a Log Service instance using the service locator, the look-up is done with the class name:

```
LogService log = null;

ServiceReference ref = context.getServiceReference(
    LogService.class.getName());
    if (ref != null)
    {
        log = (LogService) context.getService(ref);
    }
```

Using iPOJO, the `LogService` is declared as a field of the service:

```
LogService log;
```

Then the field is declared for injection in the service component declaration in the iPOJO configuration:

```
<requires field="log" />
```

We will go through this again in a bit, when adding logging to our services.

The service provider end

What was just mentioned is all that's required when developing the bundle. At runtime, a Log Service implementation is needed.

In this section, we'll look at the service provider side of the Log Service in OSGi. It is not strictly necessary to know how it works. However, it's interesting to go through it for completeness.

According to the OSGi compendium specifications, the Log Service provider is to abide to the following setup:

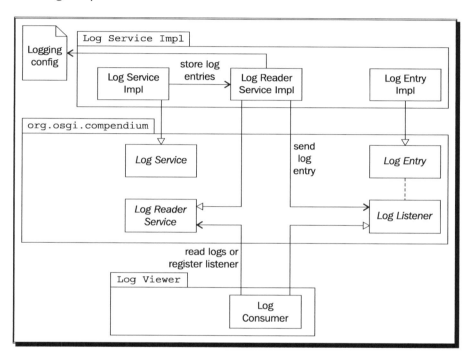

The Log Service implementation packs received logs as Log Events and posts them with the Log Server Reader implementation.

The Log Service Reader exposes a means to access held log events, as well as the ability to register Log Listeners.

Registered Log Listener implementations receive log events and process them as they see fit. Some listeners may write the log entries to a file, others may forward them to an external logging component.

Apache Felix Log Service

In this chapter, we will use the Apache Felix Log Service implementation as a logging service provider. The Felix Log Service provides a simple implementation of the required functionality. It holds the log entries in memory and notifies listeners.

Install it just like we did with previous bundles:

```
g! bundlelevel -i 1
g! deploy -s "Apache Felix Log Service"
Target resource(s):
-------------------
   Apache Felix Log Service (1.0.0)


Deploying...done.
```

For memory usage considerations, the Log Service's default configuration instructs it not to keep debug messages in its history and to limit the history size to 100 entries.

This configuration can be changed by setting values to the following system properties:

- `org.apache.felix.log.maxSize`: The maximum number of entries in the log reader history. Set to `-1` for infinite
- `org.apache.felix.log.storeDebug`: Whether or not to store the debug messages in history.

> It is not recommended to set `maxSize` to `-1` for long-lived framework runs. The used memory will increase as components send log events until there's no memory left. Also, a large load of debug messages is to be expected.

To change this default configuration, edit the configuration file under `conf/config.properties` of your Felix instance.

At the end of the file, I've added the following:

```
#
# Apache Felix Log Service properties
#

org.apache.felix.log.maxSize=500
org.apache.felix.log.storeDebug=true
```

I've set the `storeDebug` to `true` because we're in development mode. Remember to change it back to `false` later!

The log command

The Felix Log Service also adds a shell command to inspect the log entries. The `log` command takes an optional integer parameter to limit the number of log entries displayed and another optional parameter for log-level filtering:

```
g! help log

log - display some matching log entries
   scope: felix
   parameters:
      int      maximum number of entries
      String   minimum log level [ debug | info | warn | error ]

log - display all matching log entries
   scope: felix
   parameters:
      String   minimum log level [ debug | info | warn | error ]
```

The log-level filter shows log entries with a level smaller or equal to that passed. For example, `log info` will show entries with levels info (=3), warn (=2), and error (=1).

For example, having just installed the Log Service, by listing the logs, we find the service startup logs:

```
g! log 5 info
2010.09.22 15:27:57 INFO - Bundle: org.apache.felix.log -
   BundleEvent STARTED
2010.09.22 15:27:57 INFO - Bundle: org.apache.felix.log -
   [org.osgi.service.log.LogReaderService] - ServiceEvent REGISTERED
2010.09.22 15:27:57 INFO - Bundle: org.apache.felix.log -
   [org.osgi.service.log.LogService] - ServiceEvent REGISTERED
```

Here we have set a limit to the number of entries to show (5) and we filtered for info severity logs previously.

Creating the log helper bundles

To simplify the integration with the Log Service, we will define a log helper service. This log helper service will be responsible for processing message formatting and then forwarding them to the Log Service.

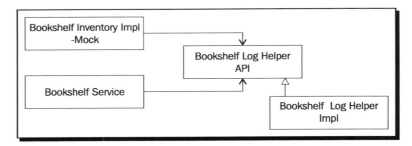

Let's create the `bookshelf-log-api` bundle for the API definition and the `bookshelf-log-impl` for the helper implementation.

Time for action – creating the bookshelf-log-api bundle

The `bookshelf-log-api` bundle is straightforward and only contains the service interface definition.

Start a new project and configure it as we've done for the `bookshelf-inventory-api` bundle. The project identification information is as follows:

- Group ID: `com.packtpub.felix`
- Artifact ID: `com.packtpub.felix.bookshelf-log-api`
- Version: `1.10.0`
- Packaging: `bundle`

And configure the `maven-bundle-plugin` POM build instructions to export its API package, `com.packtpub.felix.bookshelf.log.api`.

The `BookshelfLogHelper` interface abstracts away from the `LogService` priority constants by creating a method per log severity. It also takes a message pattern along with arguments, instead of the actual message.

The interface is defined as follows:

```
public interface BookshelfLogHelper
{
    void debug(String pattern, Object... args);
    void debug(String pattern, Throwable throwable, Object... args);
```

```
    void info(String pattern, Object... args);
    void warn(String pattern, Object... args);
    void warn(String pattern, Throwable throwable, Object... args);
    void error(String pattern, Object... args);
    void error(String pattern, Throwable throwable, Object... args);
}
```

That's it for this bundle. Package it up and deploy it to the releases repository.

Let's implement the service next.

Time for action – creating the log helper implementation

The `bookshelf-log-impl` will provide a `BookshelfLogHelper` implementation that keeps a reference to a Log Service and forwards log requests to it after processing their message formatting.

Start another project, the `bookshelf-log-impl` bundle:

The following are the project identification information:

- Group Id: `com.packtpub.felix`
- Artifact Id: `com.packtpub.felix.bookshelf-log-impl`
- Version: `1.10.0`
- Packaging: `bundle`

This bundle will have the `bookshelf-log-api` as a dependency because it implements the service interface defined in it. It also has a dependency on the `org.osgi.compendium` bundle, which defines the `LogService` interface.

Therefore, dependencies of this bundle are as follows:

```
<dependencies>
  <dependency>
    <groupId>com.packtpub.felix</groupId>
    <artifactId>com.packtpub.felix.bookshelf-log-api</artifactId>
    <version>1.10.0</version>
  </dependency>
  <dependency>
    <groupId>org.osgi</groupId>
    <artifactId>org.osgi.compendium</artifactId>
    <version>4.2.0</version>
  </dependency>
</dependencies>
```

This bundle also uses iPOJO for the injection of the `LogService` instance, as well as the publishing of the service. We will look at the iPOJO configuration after implementing the service.

Notice that neither of the previous dependencies is Felix-specific. Even though we have selected the "Apache Felix Log Service" as a Log Service implementation, the bundle that uses it does not depend on it. This bundle can be used on any framework with any Log Service implementation.

Implementing the BookshelfLogHelper service

The implementation of the `BookshelfLogHelper` interface will be named `BookshelfLogHelperImpl` and defined in the package `com.packtpub.felix.bookshelf.log.impl` as follows:

```
public class BookshelfLogHelperImpl implements BookshelfLogHelper
{
    LogService log;

    public void debug(String pattern, Object[] args) {
        String message = MessageFormat.format(pattern, args);
        this.log.log(LogService.LOG_DEBUG, message);
    }
}
```

The caller passes a message pattern as a string and an array of arguments. Those are used to construct a log message, which is mapped to the right `LogService` method signature.

Here we've used the `java.text.MessageFormat` Java class, which allows flexible formatting for message text.

The pattern is encoded with placeholders that are used to insert the formatted arguments. For example, the placeholder $\{n\}$ is used for the insertion of the nth argument:

```
String pattern = "Expecting integer, got ''{0}''.";
Object[] args = new Object[] { "value" };
System.out.println(MessageFormat.format(pattern, args);
```

This would produce:

`Expecting integer, got 'value'.`

It also provides some additional cool formatting features—refer to the API Javadocs for a detailed description. (`http://download.oracle.com/javase/1.4.2/docs/api/java/text/MessageFormat.html`)

The remaining methods are similar, each calling a method from the `LogService` interface using the appropriate log level.

The iPOJO configuration for this service is as expected:

```
<ipojo>
  <component
    classname=
      "com.packtpub.felix.bookshelf.log.impl.BookshelfLogHelperImpl"
    name="BookshelfLogHelperImpl">

    <provides />
    <requires field="log" />
  </component>

  <instance
    component="BookshelfLogHelperImpl"
    name="bookshelf.log-helper.impl" />
</ipojo>
```

Complete the project configuration and then package and deploy it to the releases repository.

We are now ready to make changes to the `bookshelf-service` and `bookshelf-inventory-impl-mock` bundles to use this newly created service.

Add logging to the bookshelf-service

In this section, we will add logging to the `BookshelfServiceImpl` class in the bookshelf-service bundle by making it use the `bookshelf-log-api` calls instead of `System.out`. We will also define our log messages a little more rigorously.

Time for action – updating the bundle POM

The `BookshelfLogHelper` interface is a new dependency to our project—it needs to be added to the `bookshelf-service` POM:

```
<dependency>
  <groupId>com.packtpub.felix</groupId>
  <artifactId>com.packtpub.felix.bookshelf-log-api</artifactId>
  <version>1.10.0</version>
</dependency>
```

Now that the dependency is added, we can start making the changes to the bookshelf service implementation class.

Time for action – updating the bookshelf service logging calls

Next, we'll edit the `BookshelfServiceImpl` class. Add the logger field (an instance of `BookshelfLogHelper`). This will be set up for injection in a bit:

```
public class BookshelfServiceImpl implements BookshelfService
{
    private String sessionId;

    BookInventory inventory;

    BookshelfLogHelper logger;
```

For flexibility, we'll also add a getter for this field. This will allow us to change the means for looking up the service easily, if it is needed in the future:

```
private BookshelfLogHelper getLogger()
{
    return this.logger;
}
```

If you don't want to use iPOJO, then this is the place where you'd perform the service look-up using a `BundleContext` instance, initialized during service construction.

In our case, we'll configure this property for injection in the iPOJO XML configuration file (`src/main/ipojo/meta.xml`):

```
<component
    classname=
    "com.packtpub.felix.bookshelf.service.impl.BookshelfServiceImpl"
    name="BookshelfServiceImpl">
    <provides />

    <requires field="inventory" />
    <requires field="logger" />
</component>
```

The integration setup is now complete. We can carry on with the update of the bookshelf service methods.

Time for action – logging to BookshelfLogHelper

We've gone through a few methods where we had printed to the System.out stream. It's now time to replace them with calls to the BookshelfLogHelper service.

Next, I'll take two examples and comment on them. The others will be left for you to do on your own:

```
public MutableBook getBookForEdit(String session, String isbn)
    throws BookNotFoundException
{
    getLogger().debug(LoggerConstants.LOG_EDIT_BY_ISBN, isbn);
    checkSession(session);
    MutableBook book = this.inventory.loadBookForEdit(isbn);
    debug("Got book for edit: " + book);
    return book;
}
```

The call is logged as a debug message, including the ISBN parameter received by the method. In this implementation, the checkSession() method also logs session check attempts and failures.

Here a new interface was defined, the LoggerConstants interface, which holds the pattern strings for the log messages. For example, the declaration for the above constant would be as follows:

```
public interface LoggerConstants
{
    String LOG_EDIT_BY_ISBN =
        "LOG_EDIT_BY_ISBN: Get book for edit: [isbn={0}]";
}
```

Once the full bundle is migrated to use the BookshelfLogHelper service, this interface would contain the listing of all log messages, along with the expected arguments for each.

Let's go back to the BookshelfServiceImpl and migrate another method, namely, the addBook() method:

```
public void addBook(
    String sessionId, String isbn, String title, String author,
    String category, int rating)
throws BookAlreadyExistsException, InvalidBookException
{
    getLogger().debug(LoggerConstants.LOG_ADD_BOOK,
```

```
            isbn, title, author, category, rating);
        checkSession(sessionId);

        BookInventory inv = lookupBookInventory();

        getLogger().debug(LoggerConstants.LOG_CREATE_BOOK, isbn);
        MutableBook book = inv.createBook(isbn);
        book.setTitle(title);
        book.setAuthor(author);
        book.setCategory(category);
        book.setRating(rating);

        getLogger().debug(LoggerConstants.LOG_STORE_BOOK, isbn);
        inv.storeBook(book);
    }
```

It's typical to log something before an operation that may fail to keep a record of its context in the log files. In our case, the operations that may fail are the check for the session, the creation of the book, and its update in the store.

The above log calls have resulted in the following additional constants in the `LogConstants` interface:

```
String LOG_ADD_BOOK =
    "LOG_ADD_BOOK: Add book: [isbn={0}] [title={1}] "+
    "[author={2}] [category={3}] [rating={4}]";

String LOG_CREATE_BOOK =
    "LOG_CREATE_BOOK: Create new book [isbn={0}]";

String LOG_STORE_BOOK =
    "LOG_STORE_BOOK: Store book [isbn={0}]";
```

The above messages can easily be recognized by an external monitoring system and parsed for useful information.

Update bookshelf-service-tui dependency

The one last thing to do before we're ready to test our changes is to update the `bookshelf-service-tui` dependency on the `bookshelf-service`.

Having released the `bookshelf-service` bundle with a new version (`1.10.0`), edit the `bookshelf-service-tui` project descriptor and update the dependency version:

```
<dependency>
  <groupId>com.packtpub.felix</groupId>
  <artifactId>com.packtpub.felix.bookshelf-service</artifactId>
```

```
<version>1.10.0</version>
<type>bundle</type>
<scope>compile</scope>
</dependency>
```

 This shows the downside of having joined service API and implementation in the same bundle for `bookshelf-service`. The change we have just made was to the implementation only: releasing a new version of the implementation without changing the interface. However, since both API and implementation are in the same bundle, they are released together.

Have a go hero – adding the remaining logs

Continue what we've started here and update the remaining logging calls in the other bundles. Then update those in the `BookInventoryMockImpl` class in the `bookshelf-inventory-impl-mock` bundle and those in the `BookshelfServiceProxyImpl` class in the `bookshelf-service-tui` bundle.

Trying it out

If you haven't done so already, build and deploy your three updated bundles to the releases repository:

- `bookshelf-inventory-impl-mock`
- `bookshelf-service`
- `bookshelf-service-tui`

All with version `1.10.0`.

Then start the newly created `bookshelf-log-api` and `bookshelf-log-impl` bundles:

```
g! repos refresh file:///C:/projects/felixbook/releases/repository.xml
g! list book
Bookshelf Inventory API (1.5.0)
Bookshelf Inventory Impl - Mock (1.9.0, ...)
Bookshelf Log Helper API (1.10.0)
Bookshelf Log Helper Impl (1.10.0)
Bookshelf Service (1.10.0, ...)
Bookshelf Service Gogo commands (1.10.0, ...)
```

The log helpers belong to the "Common Services" layer on start level 1.

```
g! bundlelevel -i 1


g! deploy -s "Bookshelf Log Helper API"
Target resource(s):
------------------
   Bookshelf Log Helper API (1.10.0)


Deploying...done.
g! deploy -s "Bookshelf Log Helper Impl"
Target resource(s):
------------------
   Bookshelf Log Helper Impl (1.10.0)


Deploying...done.
```

The bundle listing should be as follows:

```
g! lb
START LEVEL 5
   ID|State      |Level|Name
    0|Active     |    0|System Bundle (3.0.1)
    1|Active     |    1|Apache Felix Bundle Repository (1.6.2)
    2|Active     |    1|Apache Felix Gogo Command (0.6.0)
    3|Active     |    1|Apache Felix Gogo Runtime (0.6.0)
    4|Active     |    1|Apache Felix Gogo Shell (0.6.0)
    5|Active     |    2|Apache Felix iPOJO (1.6.4)
    6|Active     |    2|Bookshelf Inventory Impl - Mock (1.9.0)
    7|Active     |    2|Bookshelf Inventory API (1.5.0)
    8|Active     |    3|Bookshelf Service (1.10.0)
    9|Active     |    3|Bookshelf Log Helper API (1.10.0)
   10|Active     |    5|Apache Felix iPOJO Gogo Command (1.0.0)
   11|Active     |    5|Bookshelf Service Gogo commands (1.10.0)
   12|Active     |    1|Apache Felix Log Service (1.0.0)
   13|Active     |    1|Bookshelf Log Helper Impl (1.10.0)
```

If you have not restarted the "Bookshelf Inventory Impl - Mock" since our last change in the previous chapter, a quick search on all authors should give:

```
g! search admin admin author %
Reference: OSGi Service Platform, Service Compendium, Release 4,
    Version 4.1 from OSGi Alliance [6]
Reference: OSGi Service Platform, Core Specification, Release 4,
    Version 4.1 from OSGi Alliance [8]
```

Looking at the last three logs on the Log Reader (output reformatted):

```
g! log 3 debug
2010.09.22 17:48:10 DEBUG - Bundle:
    com.packtpub.felix.bookshelf-log-impl -
    LOG_SEARCH_BY_AUTHOR: Searching by author like %
2010.09.22 17:46:03 DEBUG - Bundle:
    org.apache.felix.ipojo -
    [DEBUG] IPOJO-Extender : Creator thread is waiting - Nothing to do
2010.09.22 17:46:03 INFO - Bundle:
    com.packtpub.felix.bookshelf-log-impl -
    [INFO] BookshelfLogHelperImpl : Instance bookshelf.log-helper.impl
    from factory BookshelfLogHelperImpl created
```

 Programmer's reflex will look at the last line for the latest update. Notice that the newest logs here are on top!

The log entry is typically composed of a time-stamp, the log level, the name of the logging bundle, and the message. For example, the last log entry we have seen previously should be understood as:

- Time-stamp: `2010.09.22 17:48:10`
- Log level: `DEBUG`
- Logging bundle: `com.packtpub.felix.bookshelf-log-impl`
- Message: `LOG_SEARCH_BY_AUTHOR: Searching by author like %`

Using other Log Service implementations

In most situations, you'll need a more complete logging implementation—to log to a file or send log messages to a remote logging system.

Fortunately, replacing the logging implementation does not impact the bundles that use the Log Service. Here are a few to look at (among others):

◆ Pax Logging

◆ Apache Sling

◆ Eclipse Equinox Log Service

Some others may also have emerged by the time you read this.

Summary

In this chapter, we've covered logging in the context of an OSGi framework. We have:

◆ Learned about some logging principles

◆ Looked at the Log Service architecture

◆ Gotten an introduction to the Apache Felix Log Service and the `log` command

We also covered the following:

◆ Implemented logging using the `LogService` in our bundles

◆ Inspected the resulting logs

11

How About a Graphical Interface?

Most applications would require more than a command-line interface for human interaction. The majority of operations, except for a few administrative tasks, would be best exposed to the user in the form of a nice graphical frontend.

In this chapter, we work towards implementing a simple servlet-based graphical interface for the bookshelf case study, in which we will expose some of the operations that we've implemented earlier.

In this chapter, you will:

◆ Learn a bit about the OSGi Http Service

◆ Look at the Felix Http Service and Felix Http Whiteboard implementations

◆ Create our bookshelf-servlet bundle, a simple first stab at a web application-based graphical interface

Se let's start with some context around HTTP services on an OSGi framework.

The OSGi HTTP Service

In *Chapter 10, Improving the Logging*, we saw the Log Service, one of the service interfaces defined in the OSGi compendium specification. In this chapter, we'll see another one, namely, the Http Service.

The Http Service provides a means for bundles to expose servlets or resources to be accessed through Http and to provide content in HTML, XML, and so on. The bundles register their content and servlets in a dynamic manner, providing context information as part of the registration.

The `HttpService` implementation will take care of initializing the registered servlets, interfacing with the outside world, delegating requests to the corresponding servlet, and providing the resulting content back to the requesting party.

This separation of concern offers a great flexibility in the implementation of web-based applications. The bundle providing the servlet only worries about its requirements in terms of dependencies and content it provides and delegates the rest of the initialization work to the Http Service, while having access to the other services on the framework like any other bundle does.

For example, if a servlet is registered with the `HttpService` implementation with the alias `/myServlet`, then, by default, it will receive requests from users accessing the URL `http://localhost:8080/myServlet`. The customization of the base URL is part of the configuration of Http Service implementation.

Component structure

The following is a simplified view of the component structure related with the Http Service. Many details have been omitted for clarity.

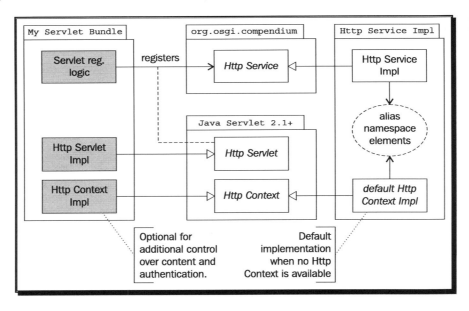

On the left, we have the functionality and objects provided by a bundle that uses the `HttpService`; this is the servlet code. On the right is an `HttpService` implementation; it's the service provider side of things. The middle is the interface specifications, which consist of the OSGi compendium `HttpService` interface (and others, not shown here) and the Java Servlet API specification (2.1+).

The right side is the bundle providing the Http Service implementation. It keeps track of registered servlets mapped to their contextual information.

Registration of servlets

The registration of a servlet with the HttpService is pretty straightforward. It consists of providing the Http Service implementation with:

◆ An instance of the servlet (that implements `HttpServlet`)

◆ The alias (base context name) of the servlet

◆ An optional `HttpContext` implementation

The Http context implementation is optional and will be set to the default implementation provided by the Http Service implementation:

```
Hashtable initParams = new Hashtable();
initParams.put("paramName", "paramValue");

getHttpService().registerServlet(
    "/alias", new MyServlet(), initParams, null);
```

This will make the Http Service aware of the instance of `MyServlet` and will delegate the processing of requests that it receives for `http://localhost:8080/alias` to `MyServlet`.

 The servlet alias must be unique in the context of the Http Service!

The initialization parameters are accessible to the servlet through the `ServletConfig` instance given to it at init (by calling `getInitParameter()`), as would be in a regular web container.

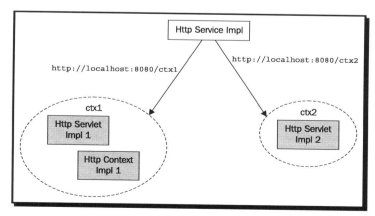

Typically, the bundle would have an activator that registers the servlet(s) at bundle start, as shown in the previous code. However, in this chapter, we will look at how to use iPOJO to achieve the same result.

In a similar fashion, servlets are unregistered by calling the unregister method of the Http Service as follows:

```
getHttpService().unregister("/alias");
```

iPOJO and the Whiteboard Extender

As mentioned in *Chapter 9, Improving the Bookshelf Service with iPOJO*, we will use the whiteboard pattern to register our servlets, instead of registering them directly with the Http Service.

In this context, the HTTP whiteboard implementation will listen to registered HttpServlets and will add them to the installed Http Service.

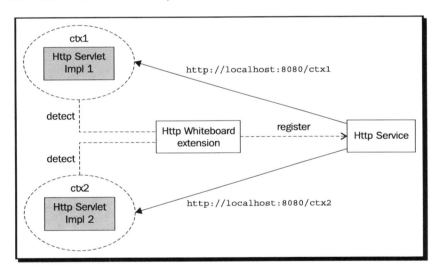

In *Chapter 9*, we also saw how to simplify service registration using iPOJO. Combining iPOJO service declaration along with an http whiteboard extender reduces the publishing of an Http Servlet to the following steps:

◆ Write an HttpServlet implementation
◆ Declare its component and instance using iPOJO
◆ Deploy and start on the framework

The iPOJO service detects the bundle and registers its service with the framework. Next, the whiteboard extension recognizes it as a servlet and publishes it with the Http Service.

One of the main gains from using this approach is to avoid having a direct dependency on the `HttpService` interface, which, in this case, is only used to publish the servlet. All the bundle knows is that it implements the `HttpServlet` interface, iPOJO publishes the service, and the Http Whiteboard extender recognizes it as a servlet and publishes it with the Http Service.

Http Service implementations

There are quite a few implementations of the OSGi Http Service specification out there. In this chapter, we'll use the one provided by the Felix project. Later, in *Chapter 13, Improving the Graphics*, we'll also look at the Pax Web implementation as another example.

The Apache Felix Http Service

The Felix project provides a simple, but effective, Http Service implementation. It allows registration of servlets, as well as provides other non-standard features.

The bundles provided are as follows:

◆ **Apache Felix Http Jetty**: Implements the Http Service on Jetty, an embedded Http server

◆ **Apache Felix Http Whiteboard**: Provides an implementation of the whiteboard pattern

Also, for using the host application server in bridged mode (instead of an embedded Jetty), the bundles are:

◆ **Apache Felix Http Bridge**

◆ **Apache Felix Http Proxy**: Is needed inside a WAR that is deployed in bridged mode

The "Apache Felix Http Bundle" bundle provides all of the above in a single bundle.

> A servlet bridge allows a standard web application container, such as Apache Tomcat, to delegate HTTP requests to another application (in this case, the OSGi framework). Using a container in bridged mode adds the flexibility of using a stable and well-supported container, instead of an Http Service implementation bundle, while still gaining from the flexibility of the OSGi service platform.

For our project, we will use the implementation with embedded Jetty. This will save us the need to install and configure an external web server. We will also use the whiteboard-based registration right away. Let's install those two bundles now, before going on to implementing the servlet bundle.

Time for action – installing the Apache Felix Http Service

You will install Felix Http Service (which includes an embedded Jetty server) and the Felix Http Whiteboard implementation. It's straightforward:

```
g! bundlelevel -i 4
g! deploy -s "Apache Felix Http Jetty"
Target resource(s):
-------------------
   Apache Felix Http Jetty (2.0.4)

Deploying...done.
g!
g! deploy -s "Apache Felix Http Whiteboard"
Target resource(s):
-------------------
   Apache Felix Http Whiteboard (2.0.4)

Deploying...done.
```

The environment is now ready to receive bundles that register `HttpServlet` services.

We've kept the default configuration in place. It can be modified either by setting configuration properties or by the means of the Configuration Admin service.

For more details on the service and its configuration, refer to the documentation page: `http://felix.apache.org/site/apache-felix-http-service.html`.

A simple bookshelf web application

Alright, we're now ready to implement our first servlet. We'll call the bundle `bookshelf-servlet` and start with version `1.11.0`.

Create this new project and configure its POM. This bundle will use iPOJO for the servlet registration.

The following are the required dependencies:

```
<dependencies>
  <dependency>
    <groupId>javax.servlet</groupId>
    <artifactId>servlet-api</artifactId>
    <version>2.5</version>
  </dependency>
  <dependency>
    <groupId>com.packtpub.felix</groupId>
    <artifactId>com.packtpub.felix.bookshelf-service</artifactId>
    <version>1.10.0</version>
  </dependency>
  <dependency>
    <groupId>com.packtpub.felix</groupId>
    <artifactId>
      com.packtpub.felix.bookshelf-inventory-api</artifactId>
    <version>1.5.0</version>
  </dependency>
  <dependency>
    <groupId>com.packtpub.felix</groupId>
    <artifactId>com.packtpub.felix.bookshelf-log-api</artifactId>
    <version>1.10.0</version>
  </dependency>
</dependencies>
```

Notice the re-use of our log wrapper service.

Time for action – implementing the servlet

The bundle will contain one class, the servlet implementation; we'll configure the rest as iPOJO declarations.

In the accompanying code, the servlet class is defined in the package `com.packtpub.felix.bookshelf.servlet`. We'll start with a skeleton to define the iPOJO injection points and complete the configuration.

```
public class BookshelfServletImpl extends HttpServlet
{
    private String alias;
    private BookshelfService service;
    private BookshelfLogHelper logger;
    private String sessionId;
    public void init(ServletConfig config) {
    }
```

```
        protected void doGet(
            HttpServletRequest req, HttpServletResponse resp)
        {
        }
    }
```

We'll give the method `doGet()` a fuller body in a bit. Let's configure the iPOJO declarations.

The iPOJO configuration

The iPOJO configuration declares the component as providing a service. From the point of view of iPOJO, this component is a regular service that has requirements and capabilities. The fact that it extends `HttpServlet` will be of interest to the Http Whiteboard at activation time.

```
<ipojo>
  <component
    name="BookshelfServletImpl"
    classname=
      "com.packtpub.felix.bookshelf.servlet.BookshelfServletImpl"
    immediate="true">

    <provides>
      <property name="alias" field="alias" />
    </provides>
```

The `alias` property will be used by the whiteboard pattern implementation to publish the servlet.

The component also requires injection of the `service` field (a `BookshelfService`) and the `logger` field (a `BookshelfLogHelper`):

```
    <requires field="service" />
    <requires field="logger" />
  </component>
```

The instance declaration sets the `alias` value to `/bookshelf`.

```
<instance
    name="bookshelf.servlet"
    component="BookshelfServletImpl">
  <property name="alias" value="/bookshelf" />
</instance>
</ipojo>
```

This will delegate processing of requests to `http://localhost:8080/bookshelf` to our servlet implementation `BookshelfServletImpl`.

Implementing the operations

Okay, let's implement the servlet's `doGet()` method to process the following requests:

◆ Listing of categories: Requested with the operation `categories`.

◆ Listing of books by category: Requested using the `byCategory` operation, with the parameter `category` as the search filter.

◆ Listing of books by author: Requested using the `byAuthor` operation, with the parameter `author` as the search filter.

◆ Adding a book: Requested using the `addBook` operation, with the parameters `isbn`, `author`, `title`, `category`, and `rating`. An additional operation, `addBookForm`, provides the html form for submitting the `addBook` operation.

Let's start by preparing the constants for those operations.

Time for action – declaring the parameter constants

The servlet is a simple implementation that behaves based on the value of an 'operation' parameter (`op`) that is passed as part of the request.

```
private static final String PARAM_OP = "op";
```

The `op` operation can take one of the values: `categories`, `byCategory`, `byAuthor`, `addBookForm`, and `addBook`.

The `categories` operation requests a listing of the currently registered categories.

```
private static final String OP_CATEGORIES = "categories";
```

The `byCategory` and `byAuthor` operations request a listing of the books in a given category and by a given author, respectively.

```
private static final String OP_BYCATEGORY = "byCategory";
private static final String OP_BYAUTHOR = "byAuthor";
```

Their `category` and `author` parameters are passed using:

```
private static final String PARAM_CATEGORY = "category";
private static final String PARAM_AUTHOR = "author";
```

The `addBookForm` operation requests the display of the form for adding a book:

```
private static final String OP_ADDBOOKFORM = "addBookForm";
```

It will pass the parameters of the book using the `category` and `author` keys, as defined previously along with the `isbn`, `title`, and `rating`:

```
private static final String PARAM_ISBN = "isbn";
private static final String PARAM_TITLE = "title";
private static final String PARAM_RATING = "rating";
```

The parameters for adding a book are passed to the `addBook` operation as follows:

```
private static final String OP_ADDBOOK = "addBook";
```

And last, but not least, the authentication form is displayed with the `loginForm` operation and the authentication request using the `login` operation, along with the `user` and `pass` parameters.

```
private static final String OP_LOGINFORM = "loginForm";
private static final String OP_LOGIN = "login";
private static final String PARAM_USER = "user";
private static final String PARAM_PASS = "pass";
```

Those constants will be used in the code and embedded in the generated HTML.

Time for action – implementing the operations

We won't go through the whole servlet implementation code. For that, I suggest you download the accompanying code for this chapter.

The servlet will provide `HTTP GET` operations by overriding `doGet()`:

```
protected void doGet(
        HttpServletRequest req, HttpServletResponse resp)
    throws ServletException, java.io.IOException {
```

Retrieve the operation parameter and prepare the response content type:

```
String op = req.getParameter(PARAM_OP);
resp.setContentType("text/html");

this.logger.debug(
    "op = " + op + ", session = " + this.sessionId);
```

Then check authentication-related operations. If the operation is a login request, then it is executed:

```
if (OP_LOGIN.equals(op))
{
    String user = req.getParameter(PARAM_USER);
    String pass = req.getParameter(PARAM_PASS);
```

```
        try
        {
            doLogin(user, pass);
            htmlMainPage(resp.getWriter());
        }
        catch (InvalidCredentialsException e)
        {
            htmlLoginForm(resp.getWriter(), e.getMessage());
        }
        return;
    }
```

Otherwise, if it's a request for displaying the login form, or if the session is not valid, then the login form is displayed:

```
    else if (OP_LOGINFORM.equals(op) || !sessionIsValid())
    {
        htmlLoginForm(resp.getWriter(), null);
        return;
    }
```

With the authentication checks out of the way, we then check the operations and process them. The default page is the welcome page:

```
    try {
        if (op == null)
        {
            htmlMainPage(resp.getWriter());
        }
```

Then, in the case of each known operation, call the appropriate response method as follows:

```
        else if (OP_CATEGORIES.equals(op))
        {
            htmlCategories(resp.getWriter());
        }
        else if (OP_BYCATEGORY.equals(op))
        {
            String category = req.getParameter(PARAM_CATEGORY);
            htmlByCategory(resp.getWriter(), category);
        }
        else if (OP_BYAUTHOR.equals(op))
        {
            String author = req.getParameter(PARAM_AUTHOR);
            htmlByAuthor(resp.getWriter(), author);
        }
```

```
        else if (OP_ADDBOOKFORM.equals(op))
        {
            htmlAddBookForm(resp.getWriter());
        }
        else if (OP_ADDBOOK.equals(op))
        {
            htmlTop(resp.getWriter());
            doAddBook(req, resp);
            htmlBottom(resp.getWriter());
        }
```

If the operation is not recognized, then just display the welcome page:

```
        else
        {
            htmlMainPage(resp.getWriter());
        }
    }
    catch (InvalidCredentialsException e)
    {
        resp.getWriter().write(e.getMessage());
    }
}
```

We'll look at the details of the `categories` operations now (and `addBook` a little later).

The `htmlCategories()` method is called, when processing the `categories` operation, to display the list of currently registered categories:

```
private void htmlCateories(PrintWriter printWriter)
    throws InvalidCredentialsException
{
    htmlTop(printWriter);
    printWriter.println("<h3>Categories:</h3>");
    printWriter.println("<ul>");
    for (String category : this.service.getCategories(session))
    {
        printWriter.println(
            "<li><a href=\"" + browseByCategoryUrl(category)
            + "\">" + category + "</li>");
    }
    printWriter.println("</ul>");
    htmlBottom(printWriter);
}
```

The methods `htmlTop()` and `htmlBottom()` are not listed here. They write boiler-plate html for the top part of the page with menu options and the bottom part respectively.

Notice that the call to `this.service.getCategories()` (highlighted in the previous code) is almost too casual. In fact, no additional fuss is needed! A point that will be more obvious when we give this implementation another pass using JSP in *Chapter 13*.

The categories are listed as links to the `byCategory` operation, which shows the books in a selected category.

The outcome of `htmlCategories()` is something like the next screenshot. Not really the fanciest web page, but it's enough to show the idea.

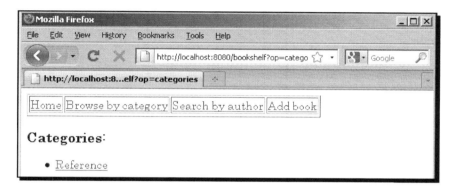

For convenience, the action URLs are encoded in separate methods. For example, the `browseByCategoryUrl()` method retrieves the action to call when requesting the `byCategory` operation:

```
private String browseByCategoryUrl(String category)
{
    return "?" + PARAM_OP + "=" + OP_BYCATEGORY
        + "&" + PARAM_CATEGORY + "=" + category;
}
```

Clicking on the **References** link would kick this request off and retrieve the books in that category:

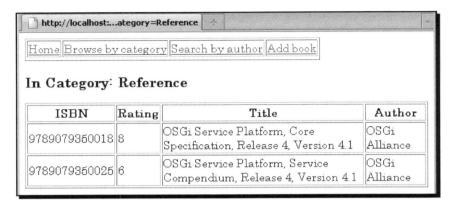

Not shown here, the `htmlAddBookForm()` method displays a form with the input fields for creating a new book entry:

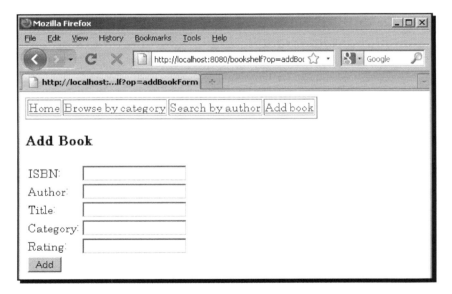

The request for the `addBook` operation is directed to the `addBookUrl()` method:

```
private String addBookUrl()
{
    return "?" + PARAM_OP + "=" + OP_ADDBOOK;
}
```

Executing the `addBook` operation is a matter of extracting the parameters and calling the appropriate method from `BookshelfService`.

```
private void doAddBook(
        HttpServletRequest req, HttpServletResponse resp)
    throws IOException
{
    String isbn = req.getParameter(PARAM_ISBN);
    String category = req.getParameter(PARAM_CATEGORY);
    String author = req.getParameter(PARAM_AUTHOR);
    String title = req.getParameter(PARAM_TITLE);
    String ratingStr = req.getParameter(PARAM_RATING);
    int rating = 0;
    try
    {
        rating = Integer.parseInt(ratingStr);
    }
    catch (NumberFormatException e)
    {
        resp.getWriter().println(e.getMessage());
        return;
    }
    try
    {
        this.service.addBook(
            session, isbn, title, author, category, rating);
    }
    catch (Exception e)
    {
        resp.getWriter().println(e.getMessage());
        return;
    }
    resp.getWriter().println("Added!");
}
```

Have a go hero – implementing the remaining operations

Pretty straightforward, so do you think you can implement the remaining methods?

The `htmlByAuthor()` can be both the search and result display page. It would omit the results section when the author property is not set.

It's not worth spending any time on the aesthetics of the graphical interface. We will soon re-implement this using JSP.

Trying it out

Give it a try. Package and deploy the bookshelf-servlet bundle to the releases repository, and then install and start it (`deploy -s`) in Felix. Remember that the `bookshelf-servlet` belongs to the Tier 1 Services start level (5).

Checking the logs, you will find entries for the successful creation of the iPOJO instance and the registration of the service:

```
2010.09.23 17:03:21 INFO -
    Bundle: com.packtpub.felix.bookshelf-servlet -
    [INFO] BookshelfServletImpl : Instance bookshelf.servlet from
        factory BookshelfServletImpl created
2010.09.23 17:03:21 INFO -
    Bundle: com.packtpub.felix.bookshelf-servlet -
    [javax.servlet.Servlet, java.io.Serializable,
        javax.servlet.ServletConfig] - ServiceEvent REGISTERED
```

If all went well, you should be able to access your new servlet at `http://localhost:8080/bookshelf`.

 The embedded Jetty may take a little time to start and to be ready. Look for a message that looks like `Started jetty 6.1.x at port 8080` to know that Jetty is ready to accept requests.

What just happened?

This is a nice example of the collaboration of extenders, each having a separate concern towards a common purpose. From the bundle's point of view, all we've done is define an iPOJO component that is also an Http Servlet and configure it for injection of service instances and properties.

When the bundle is started on the framework, the iPOJO service will instantiate the component and register it as a service. At this point, the whiteboard extension will recognize it as a servlet and publish it with the Http Service.

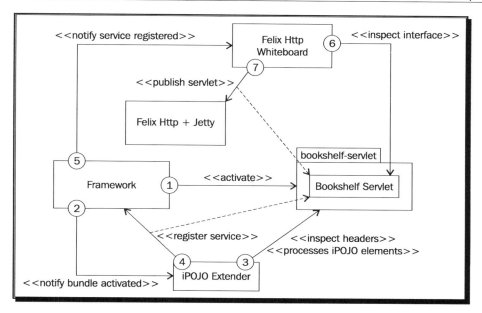

The preceding flow diagram shows the steps of this activation sequence. They are as follows:

1. The bundle is installed and started, it is active.
2. The framework dispatches a bundle STARTED event, one of the listeners is the iPOJO Extender.
3. The iPOJO Extender inspects the bundle, processes its iPOJO components, and prepares the instances.
4. The iPOJO Extender registers the Bookshelf Servlet service.
5. The Framework dispatches a service REGISTERED event, one of the listeners is the Http Whiteboard.
6. The Http Whiteboard inspects the service and finds it extends HttpServlet.
7. It registers the servlet with the installed Http Service, using the alias for defining the context.

At this point, the servlet is initialized by the Http Service and made available on the embedded Jetty container.

Pop Quiz

1. Which design pattern is one where a component requests a service from service registrar?

    a. The whiteboard pattern

    b. The service locator pattern

    c. The dependency injection

2. How can you register a servlet with an Http Service?

    a. Invoke the `registerServlet` method

    b. Through the Http Service whiteboard extension and register the servlet with the bundle context

    c. Through the Http Service whiteboard extension and using iPOJO to register the servlet

    d. All of the above

Summary

In this chapter, we've started the exploration of the "web" side of OSGi and its available services and we've implemented our first (very simple) graphical interface to the bookshelf.

You have:

◆ Learned about the OSGi Http Service, its architecture, and the way to register servlets with it

◆ Learned about the whiteboard pattern and its application in OSGi

◆ Covered the Felix Http Service and Felix Http Whiteboard implementations and installed them

Then you have:

◆ Implemented the `bookshelf-servlet` bundle with a simple servlet-based graphical interface implementation

Now that we've started playing with web applications, in the next chapter, we will look at a useful one that helps manage the framework—the Felix Web Console.

12

The Web Management Console

So far, we've used the command-line Text UI to administer our Felix instance. It's a good interface when the administrator has direct access to the host where Felix is running.

However, in many situations, especially on production platforms, the backend servers and their OS processes are managed by monitoring systems that ensure they are running and restart them when they fail. In those cases, it's hard to have and keep a command-line interface such as the one provided by default.

There are services that provide the same kind of command-line shell access remotely, through Telnet, if a command-line operation is necessary or a graphical interface is not possible.

However, when possible, it's easier to manage a set of services graphically. Using a graphical interface improves the readability of the provided content by structuring it and displaying it with a nice style. The Web Management Console is an extension that registers itself with the Http Service and provides a **Graphical User Interface (GUI)** *for the management of the instance.*

In this chapter, you will:

- ◆ Install the Felix Web Management Console
- ◆ Learn how to transform a regular JAR for use in an OSGi framework
- ◆ Take a brief walk around it, going through some of its menu tabs
- ◆ Extend it with the iPOJO WebConsole Plugins, which extend the Web Console with the iPOJO inspection functionality

Getting started

The Web Management console provides a visual representation of operations we've already seen when using the Shell TUI commands.

Let's start by installing it. Later, we'll go over its pages and describe a few of them.

Installing the Web Console

The Web Management Console has a few mandatory and optional dependencies. The mandatory dependencies are:

◆ **OSGi Http Service**: Provides the web container functionality

◆ **Apache Commons IO**: Library that provides common I/O functionality

◆ **Apache Commons FileUpload**: For file upload functionality

◆ **JSON**: For JavaScript Object Notation, a library that implements this simple data interchange format

We've already installed the Felix Http Service implementation of the OSGi Http Service in *Chapter 11, How about a Graphical Interface?*, so this one's covered.

The last three dependencies are to be installed manually. To simplify this process, the Web Console comes in two flavors—the full bundle, which also contains those last three dependencies, and the bare bundle, which doesn't.

 Personally, I find it useful to keep a very close check on dependency versions. This allows updating one of those dependencies if a bug fix comes out. Therefore, I'll take you through the steps to install the bare bundle. If you're not interested, then you'll want to get the link to the full bundle and install it.

The optional dependencies are used if they are found. They are as follows:

◆ **OSGi Log Service**: If installed, the console provides access to the log entries

◆ **OSGi Configuration Admin Service** and **OSGi Metatype Service**: If installed, the console provides configuration administration functionality

◆ **Apache Felix Declarative Services**: If installed, the console provides functionality to inspect declared components

In our case, we have the log service installed, so this functionality will be enabled.

Time for action – installing commons-fileupload and commons-io

A quick search online gives us a few places where our dependencies can be found. I found a copy of the artifacts on one of the Maven repositories (here `Ibiblio`, a widely used online repository, under `http://mirrors.ibiblio.org/pub/mirrors/maven2/`).

The manifests for `commons-fileupload` and `commons-io` already contain OSGi information, so we can install them right away. Those bundles belong to the Common Services start level (1).

```
g! bundlelevel -i 1
```

To save us some typing, we'll declare a common variable for the Maven repository base URL:

```
g! mvnrepo = http://repo2.maven.org/maven2
http://repo2.maven.org/maven2
```

Install and start the `commons-io` bundle:

```
g! start $mvnrepo/commons-io/commons-io/1.4/commons-io-1.4.jar
```

And the `commons-fileupload` bundle:

```
g! start $mvnrepo/commons-fileupload/commons-fileupload/1.2.1/commons-
fileupload-1.2.1.jar
```

Notice that we've used the `start` command to install and then start the bundles in one request.

Time for action – installing json

I could not find a version with OSGi headers for the remaining dependency, `json`. Maybe they'll be added by the time you cast your eyes on this (a little research before the selection of the dependency to install is always recommended).

However, depending on functionality in a JAR that doesn't hold OSGi headers is not an unlikely predicament to find yourself in.

The steps to work around such situation are not complicated. Here, you'll see one way of doing it—the manual way, which works well for very simple JARs like this one. In Chapter 14, *Pitfalls and Troubleshooting*, you'll be introduced to another way of achieving a similar result, using the BND tool. This tool goes deeper into the analysis of the JAR to be augmented with OSGi headers.

The following are the steps to follow:

1. Download the dependency and save it somewhere on your disk. It can be found in the Maven repository used previously: `http://repo2.maven.org/maven2/org/json/json/20090211/json-20090211.jar`. I've saved the JAR in the following directory: `P:/projects/felixbook/repackaged/`.

2. Unzip it and edit the `META-INF/MANIFEST.MF`. Not a lot of headers are needed for a simple library dependency—the exported packages and a few additional headers for a clean display and proper version registration (for potential updates later).

   The Manifest should look like the following:

```
Manifest-Version: 1.0
Created-By: 1.6.0_07 (Sun Microsystems Inc.)
Export-Package: org.json
Bundle-Name: JSON
Bundle-Version: 20090211
Bundle-SymbolicName: org.json
```

3. Re-bundle the JAR with the updated manifest, using a ZIP archiver. Ensure that the files in the archive are under the correct root. This is a common JAR manipulation human error. In this case, the classes must be under `org/json`. To keep the original JAR separate from the repackaged JAR, I've repackaged the updated one as `json-20090211-osgi.jar`.

4. Install and start it on the framework:

```
g! repack = file:///P:/projects/felixbook/repackaged/
g! start $repack/json-20090211-osgi.jar
```

   The dependencies should now be satisfied and the result should be:

```
g! lb
START LEVEL 5
```

ID	State	Level	Name
0	Active	0	System Bundle (3.0.1)
1	Active	1	Apache Felix Bundle Repository (1.6.2)
2	Active	1	Apache Felix Gogo Command (0.6.0)
3	Active	1	Apache Felix Gogo Runtime (0.6.0)
4	Active	1	Apache Felix Gogo Shell (0.6.0)
5	Active	2	Bookshelf Inventory API (1.5.0)
6	Active	1	Apache Felix iPOJO (1.6.4)
7	Active	2	Bookshelf Inventory Impl - Mock (1.9.0)

```
 8|Active        |    1|Bookshelf Log Helper API (1.10.0)
 9|Active        |    1|Apache Felix Log Service (1.0.0)
10|Active        |    1|Bookshelf Log Helper Impl (1.10.0)
11|Active        |    3|Bookshelf Service (1.10.0)
12|Active        |    5|Apache Felix iPOJO Gogo Command (1.0.0)
13|Active        |    5|Bookshelf Service Gogo commands (1.10.0)
14|Active        |    4|Apache Felix Http Jetty (2.0.4)
15|Active        |    4|Apache Felix Http Whiteboard (2.0.4)
16|Active        |    5|Bookshelf Servlet (1.11.0)
17|Active        |    1|Apache Commons IO Bundle (1.4.0)
18|Active        |    1|Apache Commons FileUpload Bundle (1.2.1)
19|Active        |    1|JSON (20090211.0.0)
```

Let's install and start the web management console.

Time for action – installing and starting the Web Console

Now that the dependencies are satisfied, we can install and start the Web Console. Remember to install the Web Console bundle on the Tier 1 Services start level:

```
g! bundlelevel -i 5
g! start $mvnrepo/org/apache/felix/org.apache.felix.webconsole/3.1.2/
org.apache.felix.webconsole-3.1.2-bare.jar
```

The Web Console is now started. We'll go through an overview of its functionality next.

 The web management console uses the OSGi Config Admin Service for its configuration. Refer to the Web Console online documentation for more information on how to customize it at http://felix.apache.org/site/apache-felix-web-console.html.

A quick overview

Let's go through a quick overview of the management console.

If everything went well in the previous steps, then pointing a browser to http://localhost:8080/system/console should pop up an authentication request.

The authentication mechanism used is a simple one (the default administrator username and password for the Web Console are `admin` / `admin`) and it allows for a single user to be set up. Those defaults can be modified by reconfiguring the Web Console (refer to the previous note).

After authentication, the Web Console opens its default page, the bundles listing.

We'll go over a few of those tabs here, just to show you around.

Bundles

The **Bundles** tab, which is the default view, shows a listing that groups the functions of the system service. It combines many of the command-line bundle-related operations seen earlier, such as `lb`, `start`, `stop`, and `update`.

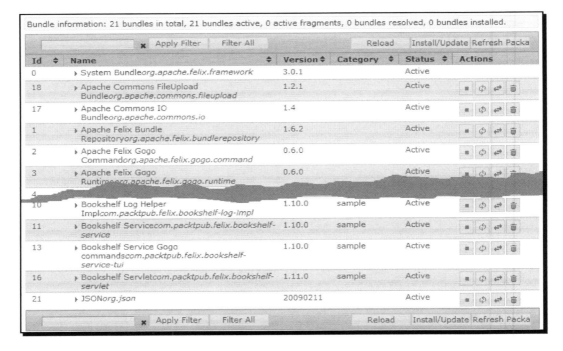

Clicking on the bundle name shows the bundle information details page, a combination of information from the bundle manifest and framework bundle instance-related information such as the bundle ID or the bundle location.

Additional operations on the top (and bottom) strip allow filtering for the listing, as well as installing or updating a bundle from a file:

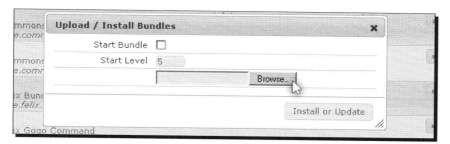

This is the same as using the `install` command; it can be used to install bundles that are located on the system such as the JSON bundle (`json-20090211-osgi.jar`) that we've repackaged earlier in the chapter.

Log Service

The **Log Service** tab integrates with the log reader, if one is installed, and displays the available log entries based on the severity filter criterion on the top-right. It is a graphical version of the `log` command.

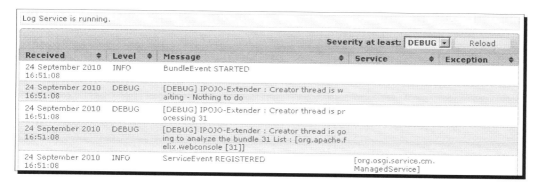

The page must be reloaded to see new log entries.

OSGi Repository

The **OSGi Repository** tab provides a graphical view to the OBR service. The top view lists the currently registered repositories along with operations to refresh and remove each one of them or add new ones.

This part combines the `obr:repos` command operations.

The lower portion of the page lists the bundles available in the repositories along with an indication if a version of the bundle is installed.

Those can be filtered using the browse links and the search bar. Here, for example, I've searched for **book**:

Resource entries can be expanded to show a list of the available versions for a bundle. Each links to a page that displays the details of the version along with the deploy operations. We will use this later in this chapter to install the iPOJO WebConsole Plugins bundle.

Services

The **Services** tab shows the bundle listing from the perspective of the services they have registered. It also includes (when expanding an entry) the service properties and the bundles that use it.

Here, for example, we find the `bookshelf-inventory-impl-mock` bundle providing a service that implements the `BookshelfInventory` type that we've installed in *Chapter 5*, *The Book Inventory Bundle*, along with the name of the factory (the component) and instance, and get a confirmation that the `bookshelf-service` is using it.

Clicking on the bundle name in the right column displays the bundle information details page.

Shell

When the right shell service is installed, the **Shell** tab acts as a user interface for the shell service. This version of the Web Console has not yet been updated to use the Gogo Shell service and therefore shows a **Shell Service not available** message.

The Gogo Shell replaces the older Shell Service. You can install it if you want to see this tab in action (`deploy -s "Apache Felix Shell Service"`). If you do, the result is a web-based command console.

 There is a great difference in the command-line syntax between the Shell Service and the Gogo Shell. Not all commands learned in Chapter 3, *Felix Gogo*, apply if you use the older shell.

System Information

The **System Information** tab gives access to additional system bundle operations as well as Virtual Machine statistics.

The **System Start Level** was introduced in *Chapter 1, Quick Intro to Felix and OSGi*, and used in later chapters. The **Default Bundle Start Level** is the start level at which a bundle is placed, by default. In this case, it's set at 5, as we've just changed it before installing the Web Console bundle.

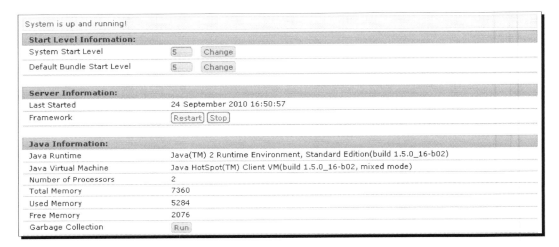

The **Server Information** section allows the stop and restart of the server. And the **Java Information** provides some statistics on the Java environment and its memory consumption.

Apache Felix iPOJO WebConsole Plugin

The Web Management Console has a plugin mechanism that allows third parties to add functional tabs. It's a simple mechanism, but beyond the scope of this book. Visit http:// felix.apache.org/site/extending-the-apache-felix-web-console.html for more on extending the Web Console.

The iPOJO project extends the Web Management Console with its own plugin that provides functionality, which corresponds to the ipojo scope commands. The graphical view of this information makes inspecting the output a little easier.

Let's use the Web Console to install the **iPOJO WebConsole Plugin bundle**. To do that, go to the OSGi Repository tab and search the resources (for example, by "ipojo").

By expanding the **Apache Felix iPOJO WebConsole Plugin** resource entry, you can select the version you want to inspect (and potentially deploy).

> Apache Felix iPOJO URL Handler (org.apache.felix.ipojo.online.manipulator)
>
> ▼ Apache Felix iPOJO WebConsole Plugin (org.apache.felix.ipojo.webconsole)
>   1.4.0
>   1.4.4
>
> ▶ Apache Felix iPOJO White Board Pattern Handler (ipojo.event.admin.handler.wbp)

Here I picked version **1.4.4**. To deploy and start it, just click on the **Deploy and Start** button.

Resource	Deploy	Deploy and Start	☐ deploy optional dependencies
Name	Apache Felix iPOJO WebConsole Plugins		
Description	iPOJO plugin for the Apache Felix Web Console. This plugin allows introspecting an iPOJO system with the Apache Felix Web Console.		
Symbolic name	org.apache.felix.ipojo.webconsole		
Version	1.4.4		
URI	http://repo1.maven.org/maven2/org/apache/felix/org.apache.felix.ipojo.webconsole/1.4.4 /org.apache.felix.ipojo.webconsole-1.4.4.jar		
Documentation	http://felix.apache.org/site/ipojo-webconsole-plugin.html		
License	http://www.apache.org/licenses/LICENSE-2.0.txt		
Size	21082		
▶ Exported services	1		
▶ Imported packages	11		

The click seems uneventful, but the bundle is installed and started.

If you refresh your browser, you should get a new tab in the menu bar: **iPOJO**.

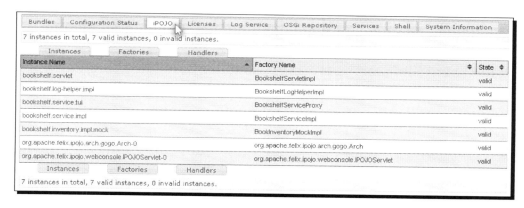

The default view for this tab is the instances listing, along with their factories and state. This corresponds to the `ipojo:instances` Gogo command.

Most of the previously shown entries are familiar to us. We find the ipojo scope commands service instance, which was installed by the Apache Felix iPOJO Gogo Command bundle in Chapter 9, *Improving the Bookshelf Service with iPOJO*, along with our iPOJO-ized services and commands.

We also find the bookshelf and the iPOJO WebConsole Plugin servlets.

Summary

In this chapter, we've installed and gone through a brief overview of the Felix Web Management Console bundle, which provides a graphical management interface alternative to the command-line TUI.

We've covered the following:

◆ The Web Console install procedure

◆ How to use a JAR library that's not OSGi-enabled

We've also:

◆ Had a quick overview of the Web Console

◆ Extended it with the iPOJO plugins

13
Improving the Graphics

In Chapter 11, How about a Graphical Interface?, we've implemented a servlet-based graphical user interface, giving web access to our bookshelf service. However, as you must have noticed, writing servlets for generating HTML is tedious. One quickly finds it useful to move to JSP.

In this chapter, we will look at OSGi Web Containers, opening the door to the world of web applications. We'll look at how to use a Web Container to register JSP resources by implementing the bookshelf-webapp *bundle.*

You will learn about the following:

- ◆ Web Containers and their use in the context of an OSGi framework
- ◆ Pax Web, an Http Service extension that provides Web Containers
- ◆ How to install Pax Web to our local Felix instance

You will also:

- ◆ Create the bookshelf-webapp bundle and implement it with JSP
- ◆ Learn how to register the JSPs with the Web Container
- ◆ Learn how to get a service reference from the JSP code

So let's get started with Web Containers.

OSGi Web Containers

The OSGi specifications are in continuous evolution to meet the market needs. As a result of recent interaction that has gone on between members from OSGi and SpringSource teams, concepts around the support for web applications, and their integration in a simple manner in an OSGi framework have been compiled, and OSGi Web Containers were introduced in the OSGi Service Platform Enterprise Specification.

The idea behind a Web Container is to extend on the Http Service functionality to allow for the registration of additional content such as JSPs, registration of filters to the Http Service namespace, as well as the ability to react to lifecycle changes in the context. In our case, for example, we'll register resources (stylesheets) and JSPs.

Another goal would be to simplify the deployment of **Web Application Bundles** (**WAB**s) by specifying a `Web-ContextPath` header in the manifest.

There are a few bundles out there that provide Web Container services. A good implementation is SpringSource's Spring dm Server (SpringSource is a division of VMware), which is the reference implementation of the specification. For the relative ease of installation and configuration, we'll use Pax Web for this example.

Pax Web

The Pax Web bundle set, by the **Open Participation Software for Java (OPS4J)** community, is an OSGi Http Service extension that attempts an implementation of the Web Container functionality along with a set of extensions for JSP and WAR support. Although it may not be up-to-date with the final specifications that were released (see later), it will do the job we need.

In this chapter, we will replace the HTTP service implementation we installed in *Chapter 11* with the following bundles from Pax Web:

- **OPS4J Pax Web - Jetty Bundle**: The Pax Web implementation with the Jetty Web Container embedded
- **OPS4J Pax Web - Extender - WAR**: Extender for WAR support
- **OPS4J Pax Web - Jsp Support**: JSP support for the container

Read more on Pax Web at the following address: `http://wiki.ops4j.org/display/paxweb/Pax+Web`.

Time for action – installing the Pax Web bundles

Let's prepare the framework by uninstalling the previous Http Service implementation and installing those bundles listed previously.

Uninstall previous http support

We will install the Pax Web bundles on start level 4, which contains frontend support functionality.

Let's start by dropping to start level 3 (for Tier 1 Service Providers maintenance) and uninstalling the previously used http implementation bundles:

```
g! frameworklevel 3
g! lb
START LEVEL 3
 ID|State       |Level|Name
  0|Active      |    0|System Bundle (3.0.1)
  1|Active      |    1|Apache Felix Bundle Repository (1.6.2)
  2|Active      |    1|Apache Felix Gogo Command (0.6.0)
  3|Active      |    1|Apache Felix Gogo Runtime (0.6.0)
  4|Active      |    1|Apache Felix Gogo Shell (0.6.0)
  5|Active      |    2|Bookshelf Inventory API (1.5.0)
  6|Active      |    1|Apache Felix iPOJO (1.6.4)
  7|Active      |    2|Bookshelf Inventory Impl - Mock (1.9.0)
  8|Active      |    1|Bookshelf Log Helper API (1.10.0)
  9|Active      |    1|Apache Felix Log Service (1.0.0)
 10|Active      |    1|Bookshelf Log Helper Impl (1.10.0)
 11|Active      |    3|Bookshelf Service (1.10.0)
 12|Resolved    |    5|Apache Felix iPOJO Gogo Command (1.0.0)
 13|Resolved    |    5|Bookshelf Service Gogo commands (1.10.0)
 14|Resolved    |    4|Apache Felix Http Jetty (2.0.4)
 15|Resolved    |    4|Apache Felix Http Whiteboard (2.0.4)
 16|Resolved    |    5|Bookshelf Servlet (1.11.0)
 17|Active      |    1|Apache Commons IO Bundle (1.4.0)
 18|Active      |    1|Apache Commons FileUpload Bundle (1.2.1)
 19|Active      |    1|JSON (20090211.0.0)
 20|Resolved    |    5|Apache Felix Web Management Console (3.1.2)
 21|Resolved    |    5|Apache Felix iPOJO WebConsole Plugins (1.4.4)
```

The bundles we want to uninstall are `Apache Felix Http Jetty` and `Apache Felix Http Whiteboard`. We'll also uninstall the `BookshelfServlet` bundle, as it will no longer be needed.

```
g! uninstall 14 15 16
```

Install PAX Web bundles

We will install the Pax Web bundles directly from the links provided on the project download page (`http://wiki.ops4j.org/display/paxweb/Download`).

The Pax Web main bundle, with Jetty embedded:

```
g! bundlelevel -i 4
g!
g! ops4j = http://repo2.maven.org/maven2/org/ops4j/pax/web/
g!
g! start $ops4j/pax-web-jetty-bundle/0.7.3/pax-web-jetty-bundle-0.7.3.jar
```

The web extender bundle:

```
g! start $ops4j/pax-web-extender-war/0.7.3/pax-web-extender-war-0.7.3.jar
```

And the JSP support Pax Web extension:

```
g! start $ops4j/pax-web-jsp/0.7.3/pax-web-jsp-0.7.3.jar
```

Double-check the http service implementation

To make sure the http service implementation replacement was successful, go back to start level 5 (Tier 1 services):

```
g! frameworklevel 5
g! lb
START LEVEL 5
   ID|State      |Level|Name
    0|Active     |    0|System Bundle (3.0.1)
    1|Active     |    1|Apache Felix Bundle Repository (1.6.2)
    2|Active     |    1|Apache Felix Gogo Command (0.6.0)
    3|Active     |    1|Apache Felix Gogo Runtime (0.6.0)
    4|Active     |    1|Apache Felix Gogo Shell (0.6.0)
    5|Active     |    2|Bookshelf Inventory API (1.5.0)
    6|Active     |    1|Apache Felix iPOJO (1.6.4)
    7|Active     |    2|Bookshelf Inventory Impl - Mock (1.9.0)
```

```
 8|Active    |    1|Bookshelf Log Helper API (1.10.0)
 9|Active    |    1|Apache Felix Log Service (1.0.0)
10|Active    |    1|Bookshelf Log Helper Impl (1.10.0)
11|Active    |    3|Bookshelf Service (1.10.0)
12|Active    |    5|Apache Felix iPOJO Gogo Command (1.0.0)
13|Active    |    5|Bookshelf Service Gogo commands (1.10.0)
17|Active    |    1|Apache Commons IO Bundle (1.4.0)
18|Active    |    1|Apache Commons FileUpload Bundle (1.2.1)
19|Active    |    1|JSON (20090211.0.0)
20|Active    |    5|Apache Felix Web Management Console (3.1.2)
21|Active    |    5|Apache Felix iPOJO WebConsole Plugins (1.4.4)
22|Active    |    4|OPS4J Pax Web - Jetty Bundle (0.7.3)
23|Active    |    4|OPS4J Pax Web - Extender - WAR (0.7.3)
24|Active    |    4|OPS4J Pax Web - Jsp Support (0.7.3)
```

You can use the Felix Web Management Console to test that the replacement was successful. It should both work exactly as it did before.

What just happened?

In the steps we've just followed, we have replaced the OSGi Http Service implementation we're using: we've switched from the Apache Felix Http Service to the Pax Web implementation.

From a strict point of view, it is not necessary to change start levels before applying this replacement. However, it's usually a good idea to drop the level and put the frontend support in maintenance mode while changing the http service implementation.

The framework is now ready to receive web application bundle deployments, so let's start writing ours.

Our bookshelf-webapp

We'll implement a simple JSP application to investigate the way the web application integrates with the the framework services. The examples will cover some of the bookshelf service operations. Let's say:

◆ Listing the categories, which will also be the main page (the index), it displays a list of the categories in the bookshelf, each entry linking to the 'list books in a category' page.

◆ Listing the books in a category, given a `category` name as parameter.

- Searching for books by filtering on author takes an `author` as search criterion and displays a list of results. This page will link to itself displaying the search bar on top of the results.

- Adding a book to the bookshelf, which is made of a submit form page which takes in the user input and a confirmation page.

We'll also need a few pages dealing with authentication and session management.

Those pages will embed commonly used JSP chunks. For example, the initialization code or the code that checks if the session is valid, as well as the common menu at the top of most pages. The result display code is also broken down to chunks that can be included into pages.

The JSP application we'll implement is simple. It doesn't make use of many of JSP's cool extensions; it focuses on the OSGi bits. It's up to you to turn it into the JSP app of your dreams.

Time for action – creating the bookshelf-webapp bundle

Let's start by creating a new project for the bookshelf web application. I've chosen the name `bookshelf-webapp`. Its project descriptor is very close to the others. For now, just take a copy of one of the others; we'll come back to it in a bit to add the dependencies and slightly modify the bundle plugin configuration.

The artifact identification section will look like:

```
<groupId>com.packtpub.felix</groupId>
<artifactId>com.packtpub.felix.bookshelf-webapp</artifactId>
<version>1.13.0</version>
<packaging>bundle</packaging>
<name>Bookshelf Web-App</name>
```

The structure of the code base will contain both Java code and resources. The resources of this WAB will be located under `./src/main/resources/` and are structured as follows:

- `./`: The root of the directory for JSP files

- `./WEB-INF`: For the web application configuration, namely, the `web.xml` file

- `./css`: For the cascading stylesheets

Let's look at the OSGi configuration and the contents of the simple `web.xml` file in the next section.

Web application registration

The Web Container allows for a few ways to register web content; one of them is to use its `WebContainer` service API, another is by relying on automatic detection of the web application bundle by the extender.

The API-based registration will require you to write a bundle activator and get an instance of the Web Container service and then call its `registerJsps()` method. This method is available in addition to the other Http Service operations (`WebContainer` extends `HttpService`).

For this example, we won't use a bundle activator. Instead, we will add an entry to the bundle manifest and create a very simple `WEB-INF/web.xml` file.

Time for action – setting up the web application bundle

This setup is composed of two steps:

1. Specifying the `Web-ContextPath` OSGi manifest entry.

2. Optionally including a `WEB-INF/web.xml` configuration.

 The preceding are the steps based on the (recently) released OSGi Service Platform Enterprise Specification 4.2 and may be updated in the Pax Web implementation by the time you read this. In the meantime, we need to use the `Webapp-Context` manifest entry.

```
<plugin>
  <groupId>org.apache.felix</groupId>
  <artifactId>maven-bundle-plugin</artifactId>
  <version>2.1.0</version>
  <extensions>true</extensions>

  <configuration>
    <instructions>
      <Bundle-Category>sample</Bundle-Category>
      <Webapp-Context>bookshelf</Webapp-Context>
      <!--
        <Web-ContextPath>/bookshelf</Web-ContextPath>
      -->
```

I've included the `Web-ContextPath` element (commented out) in the plugin configuration for the sake of compatibility with the specifications.

Next is the `web.xml` file. It is located under `src/main/resources/WEB-INF/`. Its contents are kept to a minimum:

```
<?xml version="1.0" encoding="UTF-8"?>
<web-app>
  <display-name>Bookshelf Web-app</display-name>
</web-app>
```

We don't need more.

What just happened?

Based on the bundle manifest entry (and the `web.xml` file), the Web Container will identify this bundle as a web application bundle and deploy its contents under the given context path. Once deployed, JSP content will be served under `http://localhost:8080/bookshelf/`.

So let's finish our preparation work and get to the JSP side of things.

Time for action – specifying dependencies

Edit the `pom.xml` file for this project. We will ensure that the dependencies are defined.

This web application depends on the OSGi core and compendium bundles:

```
<dependencies>
  <dependency>
    <groupId>org.osgi</groupId>
    <artifactId>org.osgi.core</artifactId>
    <version>4.2.0</version>
    <scope>provided</scope>
  </dependency>
  <dependency>
    <groupId>org.osgi</groupId>
    <artifactId>org.osgi.compendium</artifactId>
    <version>4.2.0</version>
  </dependency>
```

Also, the JSP code will need the classes from the Servlet API, as well as those from the `bookshelf-service` (for operation requests) and from the `bookshelf-inventory-api` (for the `Book` bean interface):

```xml
<dependency>
  <groupId>javax.servlet</groupId>
  <artifactId>servlet-api</artifactId>
  <version>2.5</version>
</dependency>
<dependency>
  <groupId>com.packtpub.felix</groupId>
  <artifactId>com.packtpub.felix.bookshelf-service</artifactId>
  <version>1.10.0</version>
</dependency>
<dependency>
  <groupId>com.packtpub.felix</groupId>
  <artifactId>
    com.packtpub.felix.bookshelf-inventory-api</artifactId>
  <version>1.5.0</version>
  <optional>false</optional>
</dependency>
```

There will be one more change to this file before it is ready; we'll come back to it. Let's move onto how the JSP integrates with the OSGi framework.

Getting a service reference in JSP

Access to OSGi framework functionality from a JSP is very simple. The Web Container will prepare the servlet context with the bundle's OSGi bundle context bound to the `osgi-bundlecontext` attribute.

The Java code can be embedded in the JSP as follows:

```jsp
<%  BundleContext ctx = (BundleContext)
       getServletContext().getAttribute("osgi-bundlecontext");
```

This bundle context is the same that would have been passed to a `BundleActivator`, if one were defined.

```java
ServiceReference ref =
  ctx.getServiceReference(BookshelfService.class.getName());
```

Getting an instance of the `BookshelfService` is then straightforward:

```
BookshelfService bookshelf =
    (BookshelfService) ctx.getService(ref);
%>
```

Alternatively, the code can be moved outside of the JSP, into a JavaBean. We will create a `SessionBean`, in which will be kept references to session information such as the bookshelf service reference and the session ID.

Time for action – writing the session bean

The `SessionBean` class definition is straightforward. It will be placed in the package `com.packtpub.felix.bookshelf.webapp.beans`.

```
public class SessionBean
{
    static final String OSGI_BUNDLECONTEXT = "osgi-bundlecontext";

    private BundleContext ctx;

    private String sessionId;

    public void initialize(ServletContext context) {
        this.ctx = (BundleContext)
            context.getAttribute(OSGI_BUNDLECONTEXT);
    }
```

The bean's `initialize()` and `getBookshelf()` methods together hold similar code to the code that would have been embedded in the JSP, as described previously.

Here, `initialize()` takes the `ServletContext` as the parameter and keeps it for later use in `getBookshelf()` to retrieve the service reference:

```
public BookshelfService getBookshelf() {
    ServiceReference ref = ctx.getServiceReference(
        BookshelfService.class.getName());
    BookshelfService bookshelf =
        (BookshelfService) ctx.getService(ref);
    return bookshelf;
}
```

It also holds a shortcut for checking if the session is valid:

```
public boolean sessionIsValid() {
    return getBookshelf().sessionIsValid(getSessionId());
}
```

The rest of its methods are the setters and getters for the `bookshelf` and `sessionId` properties.

This bean will be defined in a common JSP, `init-no-check.inc.jsp`, which declares the variable `sessionBean` and initializes it with the servlet context when the bean is created:

```
<jsp:useBean id="sessionBean"
    class="com.packtpub.felix.bookshelf.webapp.beans.SessionBean"
    scope="session">
  <%  sessionBean.initialize(getServletContext()); %>
</jsp:useBean>
```

From this point on, any JSP that includes this block has reference to the bookshelf service by calling `sessionBean.getBookshelf()`.

What just happened?

At the point when the Web Container picks up a JSP and makes a servlet out of it, it will create a servlet context assigned to it. This servlet context is populated with a reference to the bundle context of the bundle holding the JSP.

Here we had passed this servlet context to our bean when it was created. It will use it to initialize its `BookshelfService` reference, which will be available through its getter.

Complete the authentication pages

The main initialization JSP is `init.inc.jsp`, which in addition to initializing also checks if the `sessionId` is valid.

```
<%@ include file="init-no-check.inc.jsp" %>
<%  // check session
    if (!sessionBean.sessionIsValid()) {
        response.sendRedirect("login.jsp");
    }
%>
```

If the session is not valid, it redirects the user to the `login.jsp` page. Otherwise, the rest of the page is loaded.

The `login.jsp` page is a simple username/password submit form that sends the request to the `login.action.jsp` page. It will look like the following:

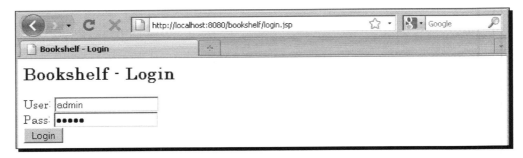

The `login.action.jsp` page takes `user` and `pass` as parameters, attempts a login with the bookshelf service, and then updates the `sessionId` if it is successful:

```
<%  // get authentication paramters
    String user = request.getParameter("user");
    String pass = request.getParameter("pass");

    if (user==null || user.equals("")) {
        response.sendRedirect("login.jsp");
    }
%>
```

As this page is setting the authentication information, we include the `init-no-check. inc.jsp` which does not check for the validity of the session:

```
<%@ include file="init-no-check.inc.jsp" %>
```

Then just set the session to the one newly assigned by the bookshelf service:

```
<%  try {
        sessionBean.setSessionId(sessionBean.getBookshelf().
            login(user, pass.toCharArray()));
    }
    catch (Throwable t) {
        response.sendRedirect("login.jsp");
    }
    // if success then forward to index.jsp
    response.sendRedirect("index.jsp");
%>
```

The JSP `init.inc.jsp` will be included at the beginning of all remaining JSPs.

Time for action – using the service

For example, let's implement the list categories functionality in `index.jsp`. Our index page will list the available categories. For that, it accesses the bookshelf service instance that was stored in the session.

```
<%@ page import="java.util.Set"%>

<%@ include file="init.inc.jsp" %>

<html>
  <head>
    <title>Bookshelf - Browse Categories</title>
    <link rel="stylesheet" type="text/css" href="css/style.css" />
  </head>
<body>
  <%@ include file="menu.inc.jsp" %>

  <h2>Bookshelf - Browse Categories</h2>
  <% Set<String> categories =
        sessionBean.getBookshelf().getCategories(
            sessionBean.getSessionId());
  %><ul>
  <% for (String category : categories) { %>
      <li>
        <a href="byCategory.jsp?category=<%= category %>">
          <%=category%></a>
      </li>
  <% }
  %></ul>
</body>
</html>
```

Each entry in the list links to the `byCategory.jsp` page, which takes a `category` as a parameter and lists the books in that category.

The `menu.inc.jsp` file is a menu table with links to the available operations. It is not listed here.

A first smoke test

The bundle contents are now ready for a first run! Some of the links won't work, but at least we'll confirm if the registration and connection to the bookshelf service work.

Go through the build cycle and deploy it to the OBR repository. Then refresh the repository in Felix.

```
g! repos refresh file:/C:/projects/felixbook/releases/repository.xml
g!
g! list book
Bookshelf Inventory API (1.5.0)
Bookshelf Inventory Impl - Mock (1.9.0, ...)
Bookshelf Log Helper API (1.10.0)
Bookshelf Log Helper Impl (1.10.0)
Bookshelf Service (1.10.0, ...)
Bookshelf Service Gogo commands (1.10.0, ...)
Bookshelf Servlet (1.11.0)
Bookshelf Web-App (1.13.0)
```

Now install and start it:

```
g! deploy -s "Bookshelf Web-App"
Target resource(s):
-------------------
   Bookshelf Web-App (1.13.0)


Deploying...done.
```

If all went well, when you browse to the URL `http://localhost:8080/bookshelf/index.jsp`, you'll get redirected to the login page.

A successful login takes you to the main page, which is the categories list page:

The link to list the books in a category is not yet ready, so how about we implement that now?

Implement the remaining pages

The remaining pages aren't too complex. I'll go through the list of the next one. I'll leave the remaining ones out to avoid repetition.

Time for action – implementing the list books by category page

The list books by category page (byCategory.jsp) will have a similar beginning as the list categories page. The page starts with the imports and the included initialization JSP.

```
<%@ page import="java.util.*"%>

<%@ include file="init.inc.jsp" %>
```

This page takes a category as parameter:

```
<%  // get category to browse, if none go to categories view
    String category = request.getParameter("category");
    if (category==null || category.equals("")) {
        response.sendRedirect("index.jsp");
    }
%>

<html>
  <head>
    <title>Bookshelf - Browse Category: <%= category %></title>
    <link rel="stylesheet" type="text/css" href="css/style.css" />
  </head>
  <body>
```

Include the menu bar:

```
<%@ include file="menu.inc.jsp" %>
<h2>Bookshelf - Browse Category: <%= group %></h2>
```

Then perform the search operation, based on the passed group parameter:

```
<%@ include file="menu.inc.jsp" %>
<h2>Bookshelf - Browse Category: <%= category %></h2>

<%
Set<String> isbns =
    sessionBean.getBookshelf().searchBooksByCategory(
        sessionBean.getSessionId(), category); %>
```

```
        <table class="BookList">
        <%@ include file="bookListHeader.inc.jsp" %>
        <%  for (String isbn : isbns) { %>
            <jsp:include page="bookListEntry.inc.jsp">
              <jsp:param name="sessionBean" value="<%=sessionBean%>"/>
              <jsp:param name="isbn" value="<%=isbn %>" />
            </jsp:include>
        <%  } %>
        </table>
    </body>
</html>
```

For each result in the table, we've included a table row JSP chunk, which retrieves the book information from the bookshelf service and displays it as a separate row.

The result looks like this:

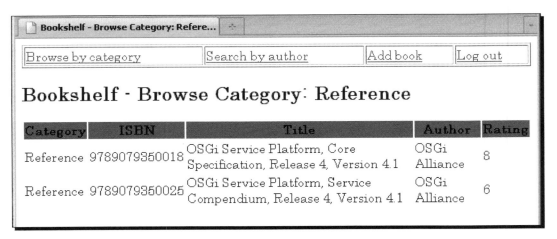

Of course, the style is mediocre. A lot more can be done with just a few cascading `stylesheet` classes, tag libraries, and so on, but learning JSP is outside the scope of this book.

A note on JSP imports

The JSP code that we've written so far uses the `SessionBean` to access the bookshelf service reference. When the bundle plugin analyzes the Java code, it will detect the need for the import of the package `com.packtpub.felix.bookshelf.service.api`, for example, and add it to the bundle Manifest.

However, the bundle plugin does not analyze the JSP's `<%@ page import` directives, for example, the JSP included when listing book entries, `bookListEntry.inc.jsp`, shown here. It imports the package `com.packtpub.felix.bookshelf.inventory.api`, which is not imported by the class `SessionBean`.

```
<%@page import="com.packtpub.felix.bookshelf.inventory.api.*" %>

<%@include file="init.inc.jsp" %>

<%  String isbn = request.getParameter("isbn");

    Book book = null;
    try {
      book = sessionBean.getBookshelf().getBook(
          sessionBean.getSessionId(), isbn); %>
      <tr class="BookListEntry">
        <td><%= book.getCategory() %></td>
        <td><%= book.getIsbn() %></td>
        <td><%= book.getTitle() %></td>
        <td><%= book.getAuthor() %></td>
        <td><%= book.getRating() %></td>
      </tr>
<%  }
    catch (BookNotFoundException e) { %>
      <tr class="BookListEntry">
        <td>-</td>
        <td><%= isbn %></td>
        <td>"<%= e.getMessage() %>"</td>
        <td>-</td>
        <td>-</td>
      </tr>
<%  }
%>
```

Imports of packages in JSPs must be manually declared in the POM (using `Import-Package`) when they are not imported by a Java class in the same bundle. If they are not, the generated servlet will fail at runtime because it cannot see the classes of that package.

Time for action – explicit package imports

Edit the project POM build plugins section; the `maven-bundle-plugin` will be configured to include additional imports that may not be used in the class-set:

```
<plugin>
  <groupId>org.apache.felix</groupId>
  <artifactId>maven-bundle-plugin</artifactId>
  <version>2.1.0</version>
  <extensions>true</extensions>

  <configuration>
    <instructions>
      <Bundle-Category>sample</Bundle-Category>
      <Webapp-Context>bookshelf</Webapp-Context>
      <!--
        <Web-ContextPath>/bookshelf</Web-ContextPath>
        -->
      <Bundle-SymbolicName>${project.artifactId}
          </Bundle-SymbolicName>
      <Import-Package>
        com.packtpub.felix.bookshelf.inventory.api,*
      </Import-Package>
    </instructions>
```

Notice the last imported package (*); it will be replaced by the other packages detected by the bundle plugin during the manifest file generation.

Have a go hero – implementing the remaining pages

You get the gist of it, right? How about you implement the remaining pages? Here are the ones remaining from the initial scope:

Search with authors

A `searchAuthors.action.jsp` page takes an optional author parameter as search criterion. If none is passed, then it displays the search form:

When the form is submitted, the page performs the search against the bookshelf service and displays the results:

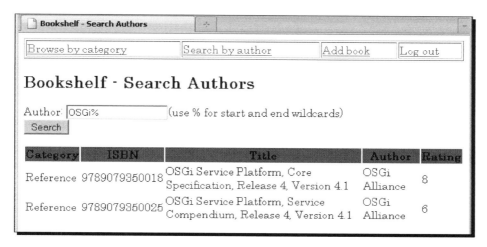

Add book

Also design an `addBook.jsp` form for submitting a request to add a new book to the bookshelf along with the `addBook.action.jsp` page to perform the add action and display a page confirming its success.

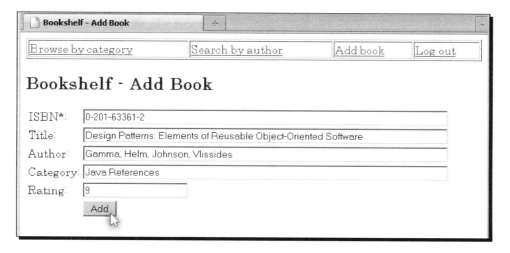

The confirmation results page re-uses the book details embedded JSP bit:

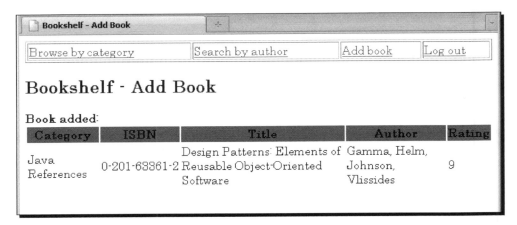

Have a go hero – extending the application

This obviously doesn't cover all the features the bookshelf service provides, especially if you had extended its interface earlier!

There are quite a few more additions that can be made to this:

- Improve the search pages, say, instead of a search by author only, make it search on all criteria, including only those that were set when invoking the service method
- Add edit and delete icons to the book row entries

This concludes this case study. If you've followed it carefully, then you've mostly not encountered any problems and have learned a lot on the way. You'd have learned more if you did encounter some issues!

The next chapter looks at some of the common issues and proposes some means to investigate their root cause and resolve them.

How about a quick quiz to jog your memory?

Pop Quiz

1. Which service interface would you use to register a set of JSP pages from a web application bundle?

    a. Web Container

    b. Web Context

    c. Service Reference

2. How do you get access to a service from within a JSP?

    a. Use the `BundleContext` provided at construction

    b. Use the servlet context, retrieving the `osgi-bundlecontext` attribute

    c. Use injection

Summary

Using a Web Container in an OSGi framework improves the servlet development experience by extending the Http Service with JSP and WAR support.

In this chapter, we've looked a little closer at Web Containers and implemented the bookshelf-webapp. We've also improved the graphical interface to the bookshelf-service.

By now, you should know the following:

*   What Web Containers are and the benefits they give
*   About Pax Web and its extensions
*   How to install Pax Web and its extensions
*   How to register JSPs with the Web Container
*   How to interact with a service from the JSP code

14

Pitfalls and Troubleshooting

The sequence of steps described in this book's chapters guided you in constructing the case study. If you have followed these steps faithfully, you should not have encountered any major issues in building the components of this project.

As I have worked on this application, starting from scratch, going through the same steps, I've written the issues that I've encountered down here. I have also added a few that I had seen earlier.

This is by far not a complete list of the things that can possibly go wrong; the online forums and FAQ pages hold a wealth of information and answers to problems that other beginners and more advanced users have encountered. Be sure to consult those useful resources when you're stuck!

We'll also look at a few ways to troubleshoot your application to find hints on what's causing it to misbehave, as part of a root cause analysis activity.

The following are the common pitfalls that we'll look at in this chapter:

- ◆ I start my bundle, but nothing happens
- ◆ I update my bundle, but I can't see any change
- ◆ I refresh my OBR, but the bundles don't get updated
- ◆ The artifact JAR I need doesn't have OSGi entries in its manifest
- ◆ I get a "No impl service available." error with any TUI command
- ◆ I get a "No LogReaderService available" error with the log command

- ◆ I can't add/connect to an OBR
- ◆ I'm getting a "Jsp support is not enabled" error message
- ◆ My JSP can't find a class that it needs

We'll also look at the following troubleshooting tips:

- ◆ How to get debug logs from the Felix Log Service
- ◆ How can remote debugging help?
- ◆ Where to get answers online

Common pitfalls

This section describes some of the issues that may be encountered when developing an application on an OSGi framework in general and on the Felix framework in specific. Be sure to also read the next section, which shows a few ways to investigate your issue in an attempt to discover the root cause.

I start my bundle but nothing happens

I've created a bundle which includes a `BundleActivator` implementation and installed it onto the OSGi framework. When I start the bundle, I'm expecting a debug message to be printed, but I get none.

Have you declared your bundle activator in the manifest?

The framework knows which class to use as the bundle activator through the `Bundle-Activator` entry in the manifest.

If you're using Maven to build your project, as described in this book, to assist you in constructing the bundle OSGi headers, then the first thing to check is whether your bundle activator class is declared in the `maven-bundle-plugin` configuration of the POM build plugins section. Here's an example of the `test.MyActivator` activator:

```
<build>
  <plugins>
    <plugin>
      <groupId>org.apache.felix</groupId>
      <artifactId>maven-bundle-plugin</artifactId>
      <extensions>true</extensions>
      <configuration>
        <instructions>
          <!-- ... -->
          <Bundle-Activator>test.MyActivator</Bundle-Activator>
```

```
        </instructions>
      </configuration>
    </plugin>
  </plugins>
</build>
```

 Refer to *Chapter 5, The Book Inventory Bundle*, for a review on how to write a bundle activator and how to declare it for inclusion as part of the bundle OSGi manifest headers.

If you're not using a tool to help you generate your OSGi headers, which is not recommended because manual header construction can be very tedious and error prone, then you should double-check the `Bundle-Activator` entry in the manifest. The `Bundle-Activator` manifest entry for the previous example would look like the following:

```
Bundle-Activator: test.MyActivator
```

Do you have the correct logging level set?

It may be that the bundle activator is correctly set up and your messages are not showing because they're hidden.

The framework is configured to not store debug messages because of their volume and their impact on memory usage and performance.

 Refer to the Troubleshooting tips, in the following section, for more information on how to get debug level logs from the Felix Log Service.

I update my bundle, but I can't see any change

After having installed a bundle onto Felix, I've modified the source code, re-built and deployed it, and then updated it in Felix using the `update` command. But it looks like the old classes are still being used.

Are you updating the right bundle?

Okay, it's silly, but just in case, it's worth clearing this doubt first: if you have a large number of bundles installed on your framework, it's easy to type the wrong bundle ID in your update command without paying attention.

Double-check if the bundle ID is the right one by listing the installed bundles using the `lb` command on the shell console.

Are you updating the right bundle location?

In case you're not using the OBR service and instead have installed your bundle with a direct URL using the `install <URL>` command, make sure that you're still deploying to that same URL.

When a bundle is installed using a URL, the framework downloads it and keeps that location for future updates. This location can be overridden by specifying a new location URL when updating the bundle (refer to the section on the `update` command in *Chapter 3, Felix Gogo*).

In the case where the OBR service is used, the URL that is given to the bundle has an `obr://` scheme. When this URL is opened for updates, the open stream request is intercepted and the newest compatible version of that bundle is loaded. However, when the bundle is installed using, for instance, a `file://` or `http://` scheme URL, the same target location is used every time.

If you've changed the bundle version after making those modifications, the deployed bundle is now located at a different URL because the bundle version is typically part of the bundle JAR name.

On Felix, you can find out the source location of a bundle by using the `lb -l` command and flag.

If you are using the OBR to update your bundles, make sure you've refreshed the OBR before you update the bundle! Use the `repos refresh <url>` command to instruct the OBR service to get a fresh listing of the bundles deployed to that repository.

Have you refreshed the bundle dependencies?

This does not apply to private classes, that is, those that are visible and used only within the bundle.

Classes that are accessible from other bundles, public classes that are in an exported package, can be used by other bundles in the framework. If another bundle depends on a package exported by your bundle and references one of those classes, there are cases where this reference does not get updated.

To request the framework to update those references to exported packages, you use the `refresh` command—either by refreshing all the bundles (without any parameters) or by refreshing a selected set of bundles (`refresh <id> . . .`).

I refresh my OBR but the bundles don't get updated

I'm trying to use the OSGi Bundle Repository to update my bundle. I install and deploy my bundle using the `maven-bundle-plugin`, but when I list the bundles in the OBR using the `obr:list` command, my bundle doesn't show up.

Is the remote OBR being updated?

By default, the `maven-bundle-plugin` doesn't update the remote repository when the bundle is deployed. If you look closely at the build logs, you'll find the following message towards the end, a bit before the build successful message:

```
[INFO] Remote OBR update disabled (enable with -DremoteOBR)
```

To enable the remote OBR update during the deploy cycle, include the `-DremoteOBR` directive on the command line or the `<remoteOBR />` instruction in the plugin configuration.

We've set the `<remoteOBR/>` instruction in the POM in this book. Here's an example of how to enable it using the command-line directive:

```
mvn -DremoteOBR clean deploy
```

Now this works well in the case when the project packaging is set to `bundle`:

```
<project>
  <!-- ... -->
  <packaging>bundle</packaging>
```

If it's not the case, refer to the bundle online documentation for the configuration required to enable projects with other packaging types for bundle deploy.

 Also refer to *Chapter 5* for a review on how to set up your `distributionManagement` configuration for bundle deploy.

The artifact JAR I need doesn't have OSGi entries in its manifest

I have a dependency on a library that doesn't have any OSGi entries in its manifest. When I install it on the framework, the packages it holds are not registered and my dependency is not satisfied.

Creating the bundle manually

In Chapter 13, *Improving the Graphics*, we've looked at one way of adding the missing OSGi manifest entries, the manual way. Basically, it consists of inspecting the package contents of the Java Archive and creating the bundle manifest based on those.

This is only suitable for the simplest cases, namely, the ones where the JAR being modified doesn't have external dependencies (or where you deem those dependencies can be ignored), and where the resulting manifest entries are simple enough to be safely filled manually.

Using the BND tool

For more complex cases, it's recommended to use a tool to generate the manifest entries. Luckily, such a tool exists.

The `maven-bundle-plugin` that we've used in this book as part of the build process is based on the BND tool created by Peter Kriens (OSGi Technical Officer). BND is a powerful tool that helps in creating and diagnosing OSGi bundles.

A more detailed set of documentation (as well as the download links) is available on the tool's web page (`http://www.aqute.biz/Code/Bnd`).

The following instructions only target to solve the specific problem described here, but the tool provides a larger set of useful features. The version of the BND tool available at the writing of this is `0.0.384`.

Let's take the example of the `json` JAR we worked with in *Chapter 13*. If you run the following command:

```
java -jar bnd-0.0.384.jar wrap json-20090211.jar
```

The tool will analyze the contents of the JAR and generate `json-20090211.bar`—a new archive that contains the modified manifest file.

Unzip the archive and take a look at the generated manifest:

```
Manifest-Version: 1.0
Export-Package: org.json
Bundle-Version: 0
Tool: Bnd-0.0.384
Bnd-LastModified: 1279997110578
Bundle-Name: json-20090211
Bundle-ManifestVersion: 2
Created-By: 1.6.0_10-rc (Sun Microsystems Inc.)
Import-Package: org.json;resolution:=optional
Bundle-SymbolicName: json-20090211
Originally-Created-By: 1.6.0_07 (Sun Microsystems Inc.)
```

Most of the legwork is already done for you; there's just a few additional steps to make it complete. The previously highlighted lines show the entries to be modified:

◆ Modify the `Bundle-Version` to be that of the artifact (in this case, 20090211).

◆ Modify the `Bundle-SymbolicName`, removing the version from it. This will allow a straightforward upgrade in the framework when a newer version of the artifact is available. Optionally, you can also modify it to be fully qualified (`org.json`).

The following listing shows the updated manifest:

```
Manifest-Version: 1.0
Export-Package: org.json
Bundle-Version: 20090211
Tool: Bnd-0.0.384
Bnd-LastModified: 1279997110578
Bundle-Name: json-20090211
Bundle-ManifestVersion: 2
Created-By: 1.6.0_10-rc (Sun Microsystems Inc.)
Import-Package: org.json;resolution:=optional
Bundle-SymbolicName: org.json
Originally-Created-By: 1.6.0_07 (Sun Microsystems Inc.)
```

All that's left is to repackage the artifact, optionally changing its extension to `.jar`.

I get a "No impl service available" error with any shell command

I've installed a bundle using the `obr:deploy` command, which has failed for some reason, but now I get an error message "No impl service available" for every command I run on the shell.

Re-initialize the environment

This problem will occur if the install has caused the shell service to stop and it was unable to start again. The easiest way to fix this is to reset the environment.

To reset the environment to the way it was initially, delete the `bundle-cache` directory. You'll need to reinstall the bundles that you had added. For that, you can use a script such as the one I have used in *Chapter 8, Adding a Command-Line Interface*.

I get a "No LogReaderService available" error with the log command

I want to check the logs so I've tried the log command, but I'm getting a "No LogReaderService available" error message:

`g! log info`

`No LogReaderService available`

Do you have a Log Service installed?

The availability of the `log` command does not necessarily mean that a Log Service or that a Log Reader Service is installed. It merely provides a means to access the installed Log Reader Service's stored log entries.

This message means that an active Log Reader Service was not found on the framework. You need to install and start one.

 Refer to *Chapter 10, Improving the Logging*, for more details on the Log Service and how to install the simple Felix Log Service and Log Reader service implementations.

I can't add/connect to an OBR

I've tried adding a remote OBR to my list of repositories using the `repos add` command, but I get an error message and the URL doesn't show in the `repos list` command output.

Is that URL valid?

First of all, double-check that the URL that you're using is valid, that is, it's well formed and actually points to a repository file.

A quick check is to point your web browser to that URL; you should be able to see the repository XML contents. If your browser cannot load that file, it means that the URL is no good.

Does the OBR have the right format?

Another possibility for this problem could be the format of the XML file located by the URL. The OBR service expects the repository descriptor to have a specific format. There are some repositories that do not follow this format and cannot be used with the Felix Bundle Repository service.

As a next step to the previous check, make sure that the contents of the repository file follow the required structure.

 For more details on the OSGi Bundle Repository, have a look at *Chapter 6, Using the OSGi Bundle Repository*.

Do you need a proxy to access the Internet?

If your browser requires a proxy to access the internet, then so will the Bundle Repository Service. You need to provide the proxy configuration to the framework. This can either be done as a command-line directive using `-D<prop>=<value>` entries in the startup script, or in the `system.properties` file under the `conf` directory.

The following are the property names that are used for proxy configuration:

- `http.proxyHost`: The host name or IP address of the proxy server
- `http.proxyPort`: The port of the proxy server
- `http.proxyAuth`: The username and password to use when connecting to the proxy server, separated by a colon (for example, `myuser:mypass`)

Check the Felix online configuration documentation for more details on this.

I'm getting a "Jsp support is not enabled" error message

I'm trying to start my web application bundle, but I get error messages about JSP support not being enabled, like:

```
2010.06.22 19:10:12 ERROR - Bundle:com.packtpub.felix.bookshelf-webapp -
[ERROR] com.packtpub.felix.bookshelf.webapp.Activator :
[com.packtpub.felix.bookshelf.webapp.Activator-0]
The callback method validate has thrown an exception : Jsp support is not
enabled. Is org.ops4j.pax.web.jsp bundle installed? -
java.lang.UnsupportedOperationException: Jsp support is not enabled. Is
org.ops4j.pax.web.jsp bundle installed?
```

Did you install JSP support?

Check if the JSP extension for your selected Web Container implementation is installed. If you're using Pax Web, then refer to *Chapter 13* for the installation procedure.

My JSP can't find a class that it needs

I've written a JSP which imports a class that's in another bundle. The bundle with that class is correctly installed on the framework, but my JSP is failing to compile; there's an error saying that this class cannot be resolved to a type.

For example, here I have a JSP (`index.jsp`) that imports the class `test.example.ExternalClass`:

```
<%@ page import="test.example.ExternalClass"%>
```

When attempting to access that JSP in a browser, after starting the web application bundle, I get the error message:

```
Problem accessing /test/index.jsp. Reason:

    Unable to compile class for JSP:

An error occurred at line: 11 in the jsp file: /test/index.jsp

ExternalClass cannot be resolved to a type
```

Mainly, there are two potential reasons for this situation.

Is that class on an exported package?

Make sure that the bundle that's supposed to provide the class (here `ExternalClass`) properly exports its package. The framework will only make classes in exported packages available for other bundles.

To rule this potential root cause out, double-check the `Export-Package` manifest entry in the bundle, that provides this class. It must include the package that contains the class `ExternalClass`.

Does the web application bundle import the required class package?

If you're using the `maven-bundle-plugin` to generate the OSGi manifest entries, it will look for the packages to include in the `Import-Package` manifest entry by inspecting the Java sources. However, it will not look into JSPs to include the packages they import.

The packages required by JSP files need to be specified to be included as part of the `Import-Package` manifest entry.

This is done in the `plugin` configuration section of the project POM:

```
<build>
  <plugins>
    <plugin>
      <groupId>org.apache.felix</groupId>
      <artifactId>maven-bundle-plugin</artifactId>
      <configuration>
        <instructions>
          <!-- ... -->
          <Import-Package>test.example,*
          </Import-Package>
```

```
          </instructions>
        </configuration>
      </plugin>
    </plugins>
  </build>
```

Notice that the package entry is followed by "*". This requests the plugin to also include the other detected packages along with this manually included one.

 Review *Chapter 13* for the steps needed for the implementation of a web application bundle.

If you're not using an automated way to construct the `Import-Package` entry, then just make sure to include the required packages when setting it.

Troubleshooting tips

When encountering an error, or when the application is not behaving the way you're expecting it to, you engage in the exercise of hunting the problem down and trying to find its root cause in order to fix it.

The following gives a few tips to help you troubleshoot issues you may encounter during the development and testing of a bundle on an OSGi framework, in general, or on Felix, in specific.

How to get debug logs from the Felix Log Service

Although the OSGi specifications provide a clear definition of how to log messages with a Log Service, it does not set any constraint on how to configure the Log Service filter levels. This is normal, as it is specific to the implementation.

The configuration of the level of logs that's included in a Log Reader Service implementation differs among providers. The Apache Felix Log Service properties are configured in the `config.properties` file under the `config` directory of the Felix framework instance. The properties are as follows:

- `org.apache.felix.log.maxSize`: Holds the maximum number of log entries to keep in memory at a given time, set to `-1` for 'no maximum size'

- `org.apache.felix.log.storeDebug`: Is a boolean (`true` or `false`) that instructs the service to hold or ignore debug log messages

If you would also like to see debug messages, set the `storeDebug` property to `true`.

Note that setting the `maxSize` to `-1` or `storeDebug` to `true` may have a counter impact on performance and memory consumption. It should only be done in a restricted time frame, for example, while troubleshooting an issue.

 Have a look at *Chapter 10* for more on logging.

How can remote debugging help

Remote debugging allows you to connect to a running remote framework and control its execution flow. By setting breakpoints in the debugger's source code viewer, the execution pauses at specific expressions in the code. It then allows you to step through the execution flow, statement by statement, inspecting the variable values and potentially changing them in some situations.

To set up the JVM running the framework with the previous configuration, the following command-line parameters are included:

```
java
-Xrunjdwp:transport=dt_socket,address=8787,server=y,suspend=n
-Xdebug -jar bin/felix.jar
```

The `suspend=n` requests that the JVM not wait for the remote debugger to connect before starting the application.

 Refer to Appendix A, *Eclipse, Maven, and Felix*, for a more detailed, step-by-step set of instructions for using Eclipse as a remote debugging tool, as well as for running Felix, embedded in Eclipse.

Where to get answers online

There's no doubt that the web has the biggest wealth of information. When you encounter a problem, chances are someone else has encountered it already and has posted a question on one of the many available forums. When stuck with an issue, Google it!

You'll find useful material on provider online documentation pages, FAQs, blogs, discussion forums, and so on. If you've searched thoroughly and have not found the answer to your queries, then consider posting questions to relevant forums yourself.

Discussion forums are a very good source of information. However, be sure to really do your research before posting a message on a forum. As much as forum lurkers want to be helpful and will do their best to assist, it is frustrating to answer questions that can be found through a few online searches.

The following are a few sites, among many others, that are a good source of information:

- OSGi Alliance site, `www.osgi.org`, where you can find specifications, white papers, interesting articles, and links to forums and local user groups
- Apache Felix project site, `felix.apache.org`, with online documentation and information on its mailing lists
- Open OSGi Forum and Discussion Central, `www.osgiforum.com`
- OSGi Users' Forums, `www.orgiusers.org`

Summary

In this chapter, we have looked at some of the common issues that may be encountered while developing a bundle on the Felix framework. It's a compilation of some of the problems that I have found while preparing the case study for this book as well as a selection of a few others that users have encountered and raised questions about online.

We have also covered a few general tips that will help you in the process of troubleshooting your issues.

A
Eclipse, Maven, and Felix

Writing Java code can be fun with just a simple text editor like vi *and* javac
*to compile, at times. However, when the project grows bigger than just a
few classes and starts having many dependencies, the need for an IDE, a
dependency management, and a build process system become a must.*

*A good selection of tools that integrate well with one another improves
the overall productivity while reducing the impact of human intervention
in repetitive, day-to-day processes, which can be automated.*

*In this appendix, we will go over a short introduction to those tools. Then we'll
look at a few ways to use Eclipse in the process of developing and testing Felix
bundles and the Maven project setup for building and packaging them.*

*It is not supposed to be a complete overview of how to use Eclipse or Maven; so
additional research and online reading will be required. However, it will give us
some basics to help us to get going. Some of the more experienced developers
will most probably just whiz through it looking for the main pointers.*

In this appendix, you will learn how to:

- ◆ Extend Eclipse with plugins that integrate it with Felix and Maven
- ◆ Set up a new project using Eclipse and Maven
- ◆ Configure the JVM launch options to set up a Felix framework for remote debugging
- ◆ Configure Eclipse to connect to the standalone Felix as a remote debugger
- ◆ Embed Felix into Eclipse
- ◆ Debug bundles with an embedded Felix

Productivity tools

Using development tools speeds up the development cycle and reduces issues due to manual intervention in the build process. They ensure that the correct dependencies are available, the bundling contains the right descriptors, and that the bundles are deployed to the expected target with the expected name. The build process becomes a simple exercise that's automated by the selected tools.

The first two tools that a serious developer should invest time in selecting are a good IDE and a build management system.

An Integrated Development Environment

An IDE is a software application that provides developers with a set of integrated components that assist in the development activity. An IDE will provide source code and resource editors frequently with contextual assistance on parts of the content and integration with a build management system. Many also provide integration with source code management and issue tracking systems.

There are many good IDEs for free! Take a look at the following:

- Netbeans (`http://www.netbeans.org/`)
- Eclipse (`http://www.eclipse.org/`)

Or you can just Google 'Java IDE' for a wide selection of choices for IDEs and build management systems.

For this project, I've picked Eclipse as my IDE. Eclipse is an extensible application framework (OSGi-based) with a rich feature-set and plugins. If you're interested, visit the Eclipse website for more information (`http://www.eclipse.org/`).

A build management system

Build management systems assist in the build side of things, they help in automating many of the repetitive tasks involved such as from the compilation of source code to the deployment of the end result to a common location.

The main outcome of this automation is the ability to develop components following a continuous integration strategy, whereby the different components of a system are unit tested and integration tested as they are developed. In those setups, a close eye must be kept on the automated integration and testing units.

One well-known build system is Apache Ant (`http://ant.apache.org/`), which allows the description of the sequence of tasks to be performed to build a system in one or more xml files; they act as build scripts.

I've picked Maven as the dependency management and build system (`http://maven.apache.org`). In addition to allowing automation of the build, packaging, and deployment of bundles with little configuration, it structures the build process in lifecycles and can be extended with a rich selection of plugins (Maven is described in greater detail in *Chapter 2, Setting up the Environment*).

Setting up Eclipse and plugins

Installing Eclipse typically consists of downloading the latest distribution and unzipping it to a chosen location. Maybe then you can add a shortcut to its executable from a convenient place.

There are a few Eclipse packages based on the core Eclipse functionality and bundled with a selection of plugins that are mostly useful for a target application. For example, you'll find distributions for C/C++, PHP, or Java EE developers.

I'm working with Helios for Java EE. It comes with a combination of plugins that is suitable for a good range of Java development, and as all packages, it can be extended with a variety of plugins for additional features.

The two additional plugins that we're using in this appendix are:

- The `m2clipse` plugin (`http://m2eclipse.sonatype.org/`): It automates a lot of the Maven project creation processes and also integrates with the "Run As..." for Maven operations
- The `OSP4J Pax Runner` plugin (`http://paxrunner.ops4j.org/space/Pax+Runner`): It provides Eclipse launch configurations for major OSGi frameworks

Maven integration plugin

The integration of Maven with Eclipse is a great tool. It assists in the creation of new Maven projects by doing the leg work involved in the construction of the directory structure. It also configures the project to reflect its POM settings, adding JARs to the classpath, and so on.

Although I usually still prefer to use the `mvn` shell commands for the build, package, and deploy cycles of the main releases. The `m2clipse` plugin integration points with Maven provide hooks into the build cycle phases for quick test cycles between releases.

The most commonly used Maven phases can be launched through the run configurations provided (under the **Run As** and **Debug As** shortcuts). More customized build sequences can be configured using the "Maven build..." run configuration.

We'll install m2clipse in the following section.

 Another Maven plugin for Eclipse that's worth investigating is **IAM** (**Integration for Apache Maven**). To know more, you can go to http://www.eclipse.org/iam/.

OSGi framework container plugin

Another tool that's useful to have when developing for a framework is an embedded framework container. Embedding a framework in an IDE provides a test environment that's easy to obtain. This is especially useful in early testing phases, where there's a good chance that bundles are frequently updated to avoid disturbing the common continuous integration environment.

OSP4J Pax provides an Eclipse plugin, Pax Runner, which serves as a container to the most common OSGi frameworks, including Equinox, Knopflefish, and Felix.

Pax Runner will be installed in a bit and will be configured and used in the final sections of this appendix.

Choosing the workspace

A developer typically works on multiple project streams at a time, each with a set of deliverable projects. In Eclipse, workspaces are used to group projects that are related. A workspace keeps the related projects in a directory structure and uses that structure to add Eclipse and plugin-specific configuration. Then this configuration is applied to the Eclipse environment when switching workspaces.

Unless instructed otherwise, on startup, Eclipse will pop up the Workspace Launcher to prompt which workspace it should use. Otherwise, the workspace can also be switched through the **File -> Switch Workspace** menu option.

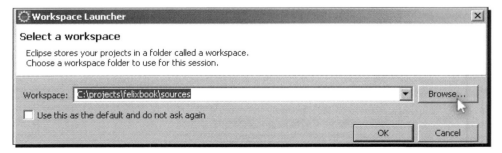

In the example that we're using here, the code is structured under the directory
`C:/projects/felixbook/sources/`. We will use this same location as our workspace.

Installing the Eclipse plugins

Installing plugins for Eclipse is pretty straightforward. Eclipse connects to a remote update
site and downloads a descriptor that contains the plugins made available.

In this section, you'll cover the step-by-step approach for installing a plugin, using Pax Runner
as an example. The information for the `m2clipse` plugin is provided later. Just follow the
same process to install them both.

Installing Pax Runner

Eclipse has the concept of an update site, which is conceptually very closely related to the
OBR repositories described in *Chapter 6, Using the OSGi Bundle Repository*. Each provider
publishes a set of descriptors that list the software that it provides, made available at a URL.
The user adds the update sites that are of interest to them and uses them to install new
software components or to update existing software components.

To install Pax Runner, first launch the **Install new software...** wizard (through the **Help**
menu item).

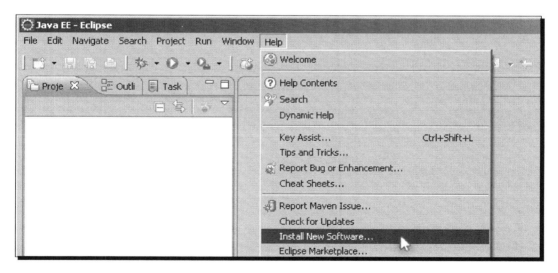

Then add a new update site for OPS4J Pax by clicking on **Add...**. The update site details for OSP4J Pax are as follows:

◆ Update site name to OPS4J Pax Update Site

◆ Update site URL to `http://www.ops4j.org/pax/eclipse/update/`

 The name of the update site is an arbitrary display name that you give to an update site. You can change it to a name of your choice.

With the update site added and selected, Eclipse will connect to the remote update site and retrieve a list of the available plugins.

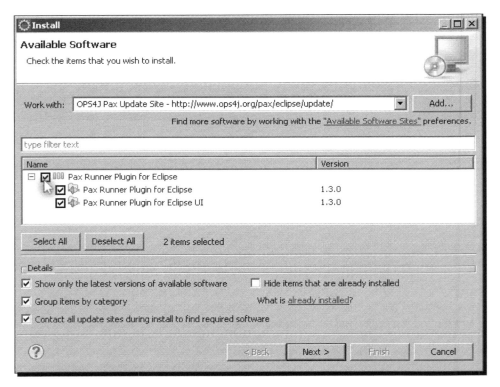

Select the two **Pax Runner** plugins and continue by clicking **Next**. Eclipse will check for dependencies and determine the plugins to be installed. It then provides you with the plugin license terms.

Accept the terms of the licenses and finish the install. Once the installation is complete, restart Eclipse (if requested). If all went well, this set of plugins is now installed and you should be ready to use it to set up embedded OSGi platforms such as Felix.

To double check that your plugins are indeed installed, you can inspect the current installation through the **Help -> About Eclipse** menu sequence.

Installing m2clipse

Follow the previous procedure to install the m2clipse plugin, using the following update site details:

+ Update site name to m2clipse Update Site
+ Update site URL to `http://m2eclipse.sonatype.org/sites/m2e/`

For the m2clipse install, you select the one provided plugin. For reference, the installation procedure can be found at the m2clipse site (`http://m2eclipse.sonatype.org/installing-m2eclipse.html`).

Setting up a new Maven project in Eclipse

In this example, we will use the **Bookshelf Inventory Impl - Mock** bundle from *Chapter 5, The Book Inventory Bundle*, showing the parts that are specific to Eclipse and the m2clipse plugin.

A lot of what you'll see here relating to Maven is exactly the same as what you've seen in *Chapter 5*. The only difference is that the project contents are edited in Eclipse. We will mainly focus on the specifics around the setup and operation in the Eclipse environment.

If you already have the project setup, as described in *Chapter 5*, to add it to Eclipse, follow the steps in the upcoming *Importing a Maven project into Eclipse* section.

Creating the Maven project

At this point, Eclipse is open in Java perspective, with the m2clipse plugin installed and configured. We will now create a new Maven project in Eclipse. Let's quickly go through the project creation steps.

Go to the File menu and select **New > Project...**

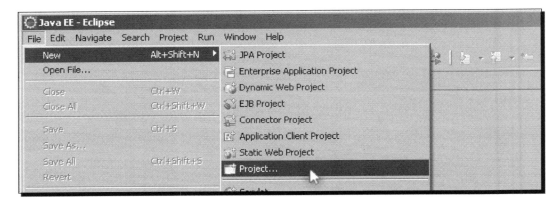

This will open the **New Project** dialog, which requests the selection of the type of project to be created. This shows the project templates provided by the installed plugins.

Pick **Maven Project** and continue to configure this project's details by clicking **Next**.

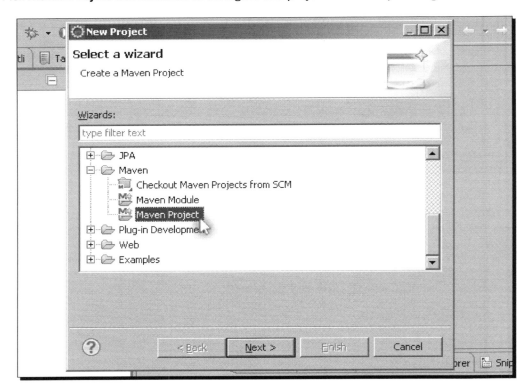

The **New Maven Project** wizard gathers the project information which it will use to set up the project structure and create its **POM** (**Project Object Model**).

In Maven, new projects can be created based on a template (or archetype). This is especially useful when a big part of the project's contents can be generated or when the directory structure is elaborated.

In our case, the projects are simple. Therefore, we will not use archetypes: tick the **Create a simple project** checkbox.

Eclipse project working sets allow further group projects in the workspace to reduce clutter when working in workspaces with a large number of projects. We will not use any working sets for this example.

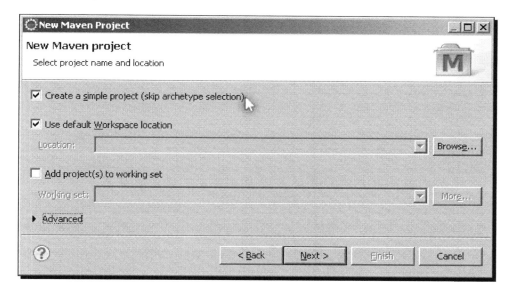

To continue with the project creation wizard, click **Next**. This gets us to the project identification.

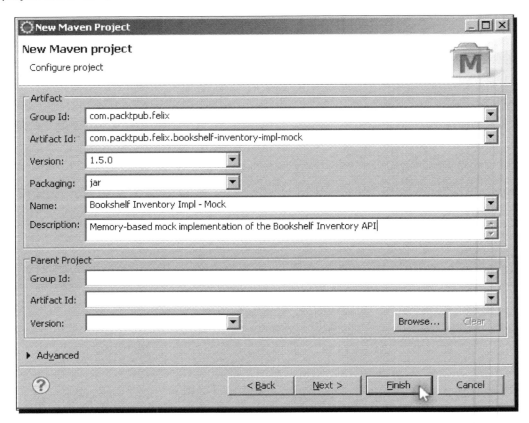

In this step, fill in the project information, as described in *Chapter 5*. Notice that we've left the packaging to its default value (jar). The bundle custom packaging is defined by the maven-bundle-plugin, which we have not declared yet in the project configuration. We'll edit it in the POM in the next step when adding dependencies and plugin declarations.

Maven allows us to optionally organize projects into structures, where child projects inherit common POM configuration from their parents. The Parent Project section of this form would be used to specify this project's parent. We will not set a parent for this project.

Click **Finish** to create the project.

What just happened?

This wizard has gathered the information necessary to construct a base Maven project for us. It contains the typical source structure and a POM that's based on the identification information we have provided.

This results in a project layout that looks like this:

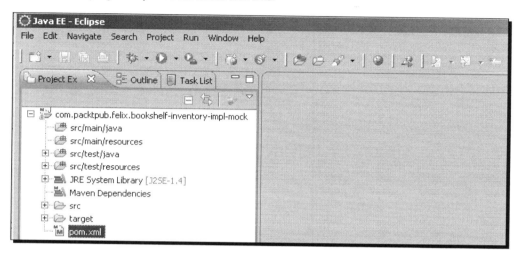

The m2clipse plugin keeps track of changes to the `pom.xml` file and updates the environment accordingly. For example, when we add our dependencies in the next step, they will be located by the Eclipse plugin and placed in the Maven Dependencies `classpath` container. Those are then made available to the environment when checking syntax, providing content assist, and so on. Also, when we set the `maven-compiler-plugin` constraints to the JVM version, the project assigned JRE System Library is updated.

The next step is to inspect the project POM and add the customizations for creating OSGi bundles.

Customizing the build process

As described in greater detail in *Chapter 5*, the Maven POM holds the project identification, as well as a wide range of description items. The POM that was generated by the m2clipse New Maven Project wizard is not yet complete from our project's point of view.

The m2clipse plugin provides a POM editor, which allows us to graphically edit the POM. When opened, by double-clicking on the `pom.xml` file, it displays a tabbed view showing the different parts of the POM, each part in a tab.

In our example, we'll just edit the POM in the XML format, in the last tab of the editor, and add the missing sections.

Time for action – completing the project

Open the POM and select the `pom.xml` tab. Add the missing POM sections, as described in *Chapter 5*, and save it. Saving the POM will trigger the m2clipse update of the project configuration.

Then create packages under the `src/main/java` source folder and add the Java sources in their respective packages.

The result should look like the following screenshot:

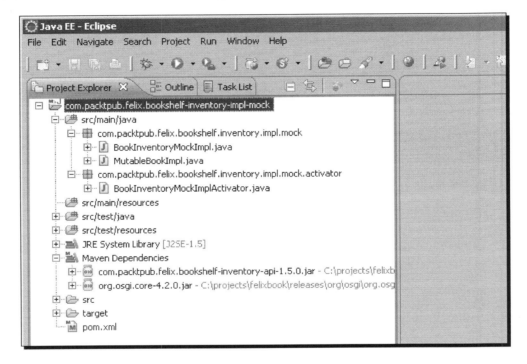

Notice that the **JRE System Library** was updated to reflect the **maven-compiler-plugin** settings and that the **Maven Dependencies** classpath container has the dependencies that are declared in the POM.

Importing a Maven project into Eclipse

Adding a Maven project, which already has its file structure and POM defined into Eclipse, is also easy. In this example, we'll add the `bookshelf-inventory-api` project into Eclipse, after having constructed it as described in *Chapter 5*.

To add the `bookshelf-inventory-api` project to Eclipse, start by launching the New Java project wizard.

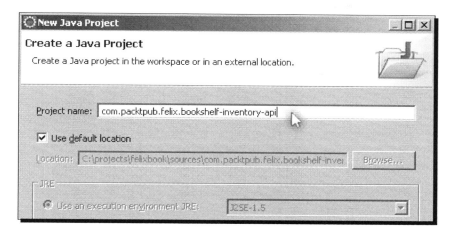

When you type in the name of the project (in this case, **com.packtpub.felix.bookshelf-inventory-api**), the wizard will detect an existing project and gray out most of the remaining options in this pane.

Click **Finish** to import this project. The result is a Java project containing the files in the directory structure.

However, this project is not yet configured to be managed by the m2clipse plugin. To enable this feature, right-click on the **project root** and select the **Maven -> Enable Dependency Management** option.

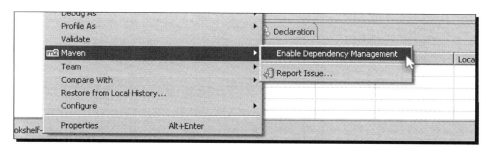

The project is now associated with the Eclipse m2clipse plugin. To make it refresh its configuration based on the existing pom.xml, right-click on the **project root** and select the **Maven -> Update Project Configuration**:

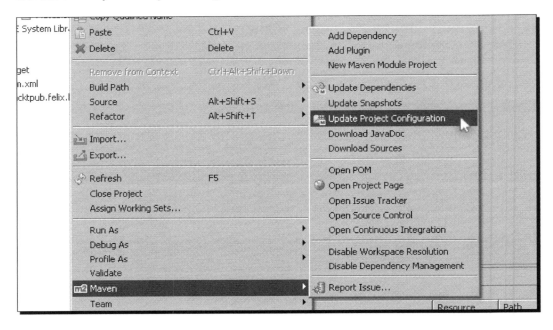

This will ask the m2 plugin to refresh the project's configuration, based on its POM.

Debugging with Eclipse

As a project's complexity grows with many bundles interacting with each other and their environment, logging as a means of debugging loses its efficiency. We turn towards remote debugging using the IDE.

In this section, we will see how to set up the application (in our case, standalone Felix) for remote debugging. Then we will see how to connect with the IDE as control console. The stepping in debug mode is not covered, but can be learned in the *Help* sections.

We'll look into the following:

◆ Using the **Java Platform Debugger Architecture** (**JPDA**) to connect to the Felix application using a Java IDE as a debugging tool

◆ Running Felix embedded in Eclipse

◆ Debugging the bundles on an embedded Felix

Remote debugging configuration

Remote debugging is much simpler than most people think. Basically, when starting the application, we ask the JVM to start listening on a port so that we can connect to it later. Then we connect using a Java IDE and control the JVM's execution flow.

This allows us to stop the processing and peek into variables and attributes, or inspect the execution flow by stepping through the different method calls.

Setting up the remote application

First we need to tell the JVM to start the Felix framework in the remote `debug` mode. This is done through a set of command-line parameters passed to the Java application.

Time for action – editing the Felix run script

If you had created a startup script for Felix, now it's the time to make it allow remote debugging. The following shows the updated startup script enabling remote debugging of the Felix framework:

```
java
  -Xrunjdwp:transport=dt_socket,address=8787,server=y,suspend=n
  -Xdebug
  -jar bin/felix.jar
```

We tell the JVM to start in the `debug` mode; the set of options added to the command line will enable debugging and instruct the JVM to listen to the port 8787 for debug clients to connect.

The `suspend` option controls whether the JVM should halt at start and wait for a client to connect before continuing, or whether it should just start while listening for an eventual client connection. In our case, we've set `suspend=n` because we're not interested in capturing the startup of the framework. You may need to change it to `y` if you'd like to debug bundle activation as part of the framework startup procedure.

Launching Felix with remote debugging turned on displays something like:

```
Listening for transport dt_socket at address: 8787


Welcome to Apache Felix Gogo


g!
```

The JVM is now running and waiting, listening to port `8787` for a remote debugger to connect. This won't take too long to happen; we're going to connect our client debugger next.

Configuring the IDE for remote debugging

In Eclipse, we will set up a remote debug profile that is configured to connect to the Felix framework we have started in the previous step.

Once created, the remote debug profile can be used every time we wish to connect to the remote framework. In many cases, we'll be able to connect and disconnect without disturbing the framework.

We will now set up a new remote debug profile in Eclipse. To do that, open the **Debug Configurations** panel through the **Run -> Debug Configurations...** menu item. This same configuration panel can also be reached through other means, for example, by right-clicking on the **project root**.

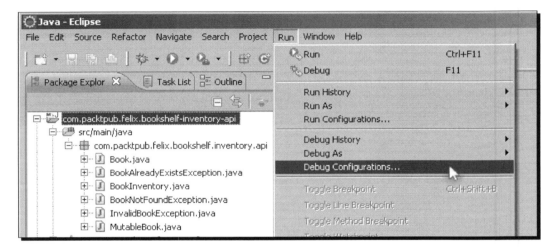

The **Debug Configurations** panel that appears holds the debug profiles available. They are organized by profile type. The one we're interested in is the **Remote Java Application** type.

In the debug configuration panel, find the **Remote Java Application** debug configuration type, right-click on it, and choose **New**.

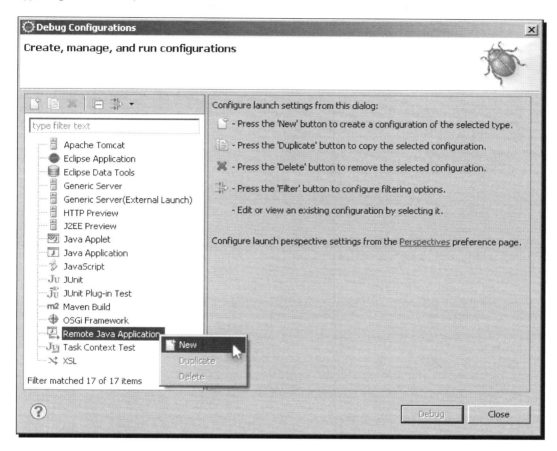

A new remote debug entry is created with default values. Most of the default values that are pre-filled do not need to be changed.

We will update the following items:

- ◆ The name of the profile. I've set it to **Felix (localhost on 8787)**
- ◆ The main targeted project for the debugging
- ◆ The port to use while connecting to the remote JVM

To update the debug target project, click **Browse** and select it. Here, we're targeting the **bookshelf-inventory-impl-mock** project. This debug configuration will be attached to it. Also update the **Port** to **8787**.

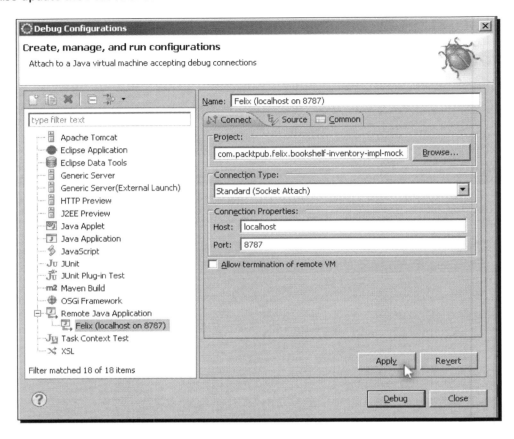

When you click on **Apply** to accept the changes, the profile is ready to be launched. At this point, you can make it connect right away by clicking **Debug**, or just close this configuration panel and start debugging later.

Connecting to Felix remotely

With the remote debugging configuration in place, we are ready to connect to the Felix application and stop the execution thread at bundle activation.

To prepare for this, if you haven't done so already, complete *Chapter 5* and *Chapter 6*. The result of which is the deployment, installation, and start of the inventory layer on the Felix framework. Then stop the `bookshelf-inventory-impl-mock` bundle, as we want to capture the call to the bundle activator while the bundle is starting.

Set a breakpoint

Let's set a breakpoint at the first expression of the `start()` method of
`BookshelfInventoryMockImplActivator`. Do that by double-clicking on
the side bar in the class source code editor.

```
BookInventoryMockImplActivator.java

    package com.packtpub.felix.bookshelf.inventory.impl.mock.activator;

import org.osgi.framework.BundleActivator;

    public class BookInventoryMockImplActivator implements BundleActivator
    {
        private ServiceRegistration reg = null;

        public void start(BundleContext context) throws Exception {
            System.out.println("\nStarting Book Inventory Mock Impl");
            this.reg = context.registerService(BookInventory.class.getName(),
                new BookInventoryMockImpl(), null);
        }

        public void stop(BundleContext context) throws Exception {
            System.out.println("\nStoping Book Inventory Mock Impl");
```

The debugger will now suspend the execution when it is connected to a remote JVM that
reaches this point.

Start the remote debugger

If this is the first time you've run it, the debug profile may not be listed in the quick-pick
debug drop-down list. In that case, you can start it by going to the **Debug configurations**
panel (see the preceding screenshot). Otherwise, it appears as follows:

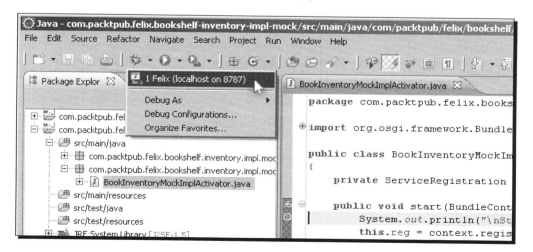

Select it to initiate the debugging and launch the connection to the remote server. The debugger is now connected to the remote JVM.

When you start the `bookshelf-inventory-impl-mock` bundle in Felix, the Eclipse debugger will capture the execution flow when it reaches the breakpoint.

If this is the first time you've run the debugger, you'll get a perspective switch suggestion. In Eclipse, perspectives provide different ways for representing the content and layout of the graphical interface.

The Debug perspective shows panels laid out for debugging, with additional functionality for stepping through the execution, viewing the call stack, inspecting variables, and so on.

Running embedded Felix

Sometimes, to quickly check something out or for quick develop-test cycles, it is useful to embed the target application framework directly in the IDE.

The OSGi Pax Runner, introduced and installed earlier in this appendix, provides a harness for many open source OSGi frameworks including Felix. In this section, we will look at how to use it to embed Felix into Eclipse.

Configuring embedded Felix

Embedding Felix will consist of launching it in an OSGi Framework container, which is set up as a run configuration in Eclipse. Open the **Run Configurations...** panel.

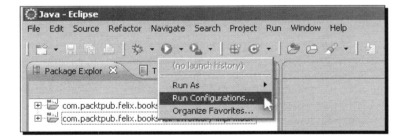

In the **Run Configurations...** panel, find the **OSGi Framework** configuration type and use it to create a new run profile.

The configuration entry is added with default values pre-filled. Change the configuration name to **Embedded Felix** and select the target framework in the **Framework** drop-down menu.

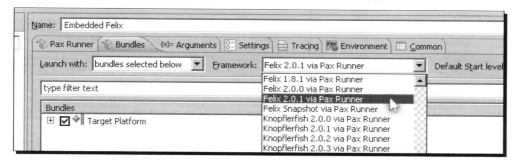

At the point of writing this appendix, the latest version of embedded Felix available is 2.0.1. The example will show snapshots using that entry. However, be sure to check for updates to the **Pax Runner** plugin that support the later version; the configuration steps should not be very different.

Next, in the following **Bundles** listing, deselect the root **Target Platform** (we will install the additional bundles ourselves).

This configuration can now be saved and run.

 The **Run** and **Debug** profiles are linked. This configuration will also appear under the Debug configurations.

Taking it for a ride

Let's give our newly embedded Felix a try. Running the **Felix (2.0.1)** profile that was set up a little earlier will start Felix and display its TUI in the Console window in Eclipse.

The console, as you see it here, is a bit different from the one provided by Felix 3.0. Version 2.0 of the Felix distribution was based on the Apache Felix Shell Service and the Shell TUI. For example, here you type **ps** for a list of the bundles. You can type **help** for the few commands available here and to learn how to use it.

From this point onwards, this is the same as with a shell-launched Felix application. The difference is that it's running inside Eclipse.

```
┌─────────────────────────────────────────────────────────────────┐
│ [] Problems  @ Javadoc  [] Declaration  [] Console ☒   C Progress │
│ Felix 2.0.1 (embedded) [OSGi Framework] C:\Programs\Dev(          │
│                                                                   │
│ Welcome to Felix                                                  │
│ =================                                                 │
│                                                                   │
│ -> ps                                                             │
│ START LEVEL 4                                                     │
│    ID    State           Level   Name                            │
│ [   0] [Active     ] [    0] System Bundle (2.0.1)                │
│ [   1] [Active     ] [    4] Apache Felix Bundle Repository (1.4.2)│
│ [   2] [Active     ] [    1] Apache Felix Shell Service (1.4.1)   │
│ [   3] [Active     ] [    1] Apache Felix Shell TUI (1.4.1)       │
│ ->                                                                │
└─────────────────────────────────────────────────────────────────┘
```

Adding OBR repositories

For the completeness of the example, let's install the `bookshelf-inventory-impl-mock` bundle.

The bundle repository service on this Felix framework is not yet configured. We will start by adding the OBR repositories we're using, namely, the default Felix repository and our local releases repository.

In this version of the console, OBRs are added using the command `obr add-url`:

   ◆ `obr add-url http://felix.apache.org/obr/releases.xml`.
   ◆ `obr add-url file:/C:/projects/felixbook/releases/repository.xml`.

Type those commands on the console in Eclipse.

Starting a test bundle

Now that the OBR service in the embedded Felix instance knows where to find our bundles, we can install the `Bookshelf Inventory Impl - Mock` bundle.

In this version of the console, bundles are installed and started from the OBR using the following command:

```
-> obr start "Bookshelf Inventory Impl - Mock"

Target resource(s):
-------------------
    Bookshelf Inventory Impl - Mock (1.5.0)
Required resource(s):
--------------------
    Bookshelf Inventory API (1.4.0)

Deploying...
Starting Book Inventory Mock Impl
done.
```

We now have our inventory implementation running in the embedded Felix. Let's look at how to use the embedded Felix that we have just set up for debugging bundles.

Debugging embedded

The embedded Felix framework can be debugged by launching its run configuration in the debug mode. To do that, just select it from the Debug Configurations or from a shortcut in the Debug drop-down menu.

The debugging process from this point on is the same as that described in the previous remote debugging sections.

Summary

Here, we looked at additional ways to improve productivity by using tools such as a build and dependency management, and an Integrated Development Environment extended with useful plugins. We also learned how to debug a Felix environment remotely and by embedding it into an IDE.

By now, you should know how to do the following:

♦ Configure Eclipse for use with Maven and with Felix

♦ Create a bundle Maven project in Eclipse

♦ Launch the Felix framework for remote debugging

♦ Set up Eclipse to remotely connect to it

♦ Set up Felix as an embedded framework in Eclipse using Pax Runner

♦ Launch the embedded framework either in the Run or in the Debug mode

B
Where to Go from Here?

I hope you've enjoyed reading this book and have learned enough of the basics to drive yourself to follow the fast-paced OSGi evolution. This appendix attempts to motivate you further by introducing some of the slightly more advanced topics you could follow through as the next steps.

One of the interesting aspects of the development of an OSGi service platform you should have understood is that you're not bound to a specific implementation provider: an OSGi-compliant bundle runs on an OSGi compliant service platform.

This appendix suggests a few other topics that should be at a close reach, with a good understanding of what's been learned here.

In this appendix, we will take a few brief overviews:

- ◆ On other admin consoles
- ◆ On declarative services
- ◆ On persistent storage
- ◆ On web services
- ◆ On **Java Management Extensions (JMX)**
- ◆ On other topics, a collection of other interesting leads to follow

Of course, those are not intended to be full introductions, but should give you enough keywords and concepts to follow on and research on your own.

On declarative services

We've briefly mentioned OSGi Declarative Services in *Chapter 1, Quick Intro to Felix and OSGi*, without going into the details. The provided functionality helps with the process of publishing, binding, and finding of services. It also handles service dependencies.

In this book, we've looked at iPOJO to assist us with this task. It's an alternative to Service Component Runtime of OSGi declarative services in that it provides similar functionality through different means.

Declarative services define the service components, their properties, and references to other services, using an XML descriptor kept in the bundle's OSGI-INF directory and referenced from a manifest header (instead of it being encoded completely into a header, as we saw with iPOJO).

Refer to the Felix Service Component Runtime bundle and its documentation at http://felix.apache.org/site/apache-felix-service-component-runtime.html.

Another available alternative to OSGi Declarative Services to do some research on is that proposed by Spring Dynamic Modules, which introduces Blueprint Service specification.

On persistent storage

A next good skill to learn would be how to add persistence to the data used by a service. For example, in the case study we implemented here, a persistent storage service would allow us to keep the Book data entries between platform restarts. It would also allow us to significantly improve search performance.

Generally, there are a few available choices for storage; the selection of the one to use depends a lot on the application's requirements.

For example, in scenarios where fast and frequent reads are needed with relatively infrequent writes that are allowed to be slower, then a good choice would be a **Java Naming and Directory Interface (JNDI)** service connection to a naming directory provider (LDAP, DNS, and so on). This choice is especially useful when this data needs to be read by distributed remote parties (for example, user authentication services).

In scenarios where complex searches and frequent updates are required, a relational database could be a better choice, using a **Java Database Connectivity (JDBC)** service connected to relational database (Oracle, MySQL, or HSQLDB, to name a few), or using a persistence framework (like Hibernate).

While looking at implementing persistence, you must also keep an eye on the potential need for transactionality of persistence operations. Transactional operations are a set of operations that are considered as a group, whereby the changes in the group are committed if all the operations in the group succeed, but they are all rolled back if one of them fails. A good place to start with this is by reading about the **Java Transaction API (JTA)**.

On web services

As you require your application to be open for sharing and information within a network of components, in a Web 2.0 fashion, you'll want to integrate technologies such as web services, REST-based information publishing, and so on.

A good place to start your investigation on how to integrate the web services functionality to your applications is to look at Apache's CXF distributed OSGi sub-project, which implements the OSGi Remote Services specification (*Chapter 13* of the OSGi 4.2 Compendium Specification), as well as the OSGi Remote Service Admin specification (*Chapter 12* of the OSGi 4.2 Enterprise Specification).

Apache CXF Distributed OSGi service provides access to your services through SOAP over HTTP (by means of a WSDL description), as well as through JAX-RS, among potential others. Using a bundle activator to expose a web service using CXF boils down to registering the service along with a set of dictionary properties.

Alternately, you may also want to look at using Spring Web Services or embedding Axis2 in your service platform to provide the web services' functionality.

On Java Management Extensions (JMX)

In a distributed environment, managing applications remotely and gathering performance statistics is an important factor in simplifying the overall system administration. **Java Management Extensions (JMX)** have become a standard in achieving those tasks.

The OSGi Service Platform Enterprise Specification specifies a JMX Management Model (section 124), which defines an API for controlling the framework as well as simple means to exposing bundles and services.

At the point of writing of this book, the **Managed OSGi** framework (**MOSGI**) Felix sub-project is not yet released. However, it is an interesting project to keep an eye on (or contribute to) its progress. It provides, through JMX, functionalities such as:

◆ Infrastructure management
◆ Deployment of probes for gateway monitoring
◆ Gathering of log entries and alarms

It also provides an extensible graphical management console.

There are also other available providers of JMX probes and monitoring agents; a quick Google search will point you in the right direction.

Additional topics

This section gathers a few additional topics that are interesting to look at in the context of OSGi development:

- For developing more advanced web applications, consider looking into the development of **Google Web-Toolkit (GWT)** applications on an OSGi service platform. With the knowledge base you've picked up here, you should be able to move onto that with little trouble.

- **Universal plug-and-play (UPnP)** is part of the OSGi specification base. UPnP specification-compliant services can interact with UPnP devices, control them, and potentially download and manage code on remote systems. Applications can range from interaction with a printer or TV to acquisition of images from a webcam, controlling lights, shades or heating in the home.

- If you're interested in mobile development, you can also check out the work that's been done on embedding the Apache Felix framework on Google Android. Bundles you develop on Felix can be transformed for the Android using a set of tools in a relatively straightforward manner (check `http://felix.apache.org/site/apache-felix-framework-and-google-android.html`).

All that we have seen is a very short list of the world of opportunities that lay before you.

Summary

The applications of OSGi are in continuous evolution. New and creative uses of the flexibility it allows are discussed and published frequently.

In this last appendix, we've looked at some additional paths you can follow in extending your knowledge in OSGi and some potential leads to enrich the functionality your application features.

C

Pop Quiz Answers

Chapter 1: Quick intro to Felix and OSGi

1	c	A bundle is a regular **Java archive** (**JAR**) augmented with additional OSGi-specific headers in its manifest. Refer to the sections *Anatomy of a bundle* and *The OSGi headers* for a review.
2	b	The OSGi headers are used to tell the framework about the bundle, its identification information, the packages it requires, and those that it provides. Refer to the section *The OSGi headers* for a review.
3	b	Setting the active start level to 3 makes the framework first stop the bundles on start level 4, then change the active start level. Refer to the section *Start levels* for a review.

Chapter 2: Setting up the Environment

1	b	A life-cycle defines a sequence of phases, the execution of which achieves purposes such as releasing a bundle or generating documentation for it.
2	c	The POM is an XML file associated with a project and used by Maven in making decisions on how to build it.

Chapter 3: Felix Gogo

1	b	The `lb` command is used to list the installed bundles in Gogo.
		Note: `ps` was used in previous versions, when the Felix Shell TUI was the default Felix Framework Distribution shell.
2	c	`stop 0` will request a stop of the system bundle leading to the framework shutdown. Note: `shutdown` was used in previous versions, when the Felix Shell TUI was the default Felix Framework Distribution shell.

Chapter 5: The Book Inventory Bundle

1	c	There is no need for OSGi-specific interfaces. Review *The Book bean interface* section.
2	b	Having configured the project `packaging`, `maven-bundle-plugin`, and the `distributionManagement` in the project POM, Maven will deploy the bundle and update the repository descriptor when you include the deploy target.
3	b	Implementing a `BundleActivator` (and declaring it in the bundle manifest) will give you access to the `BundleContext` during the start and stop of the bundle. The context can be used to register a service.

Chapter 6: Using the OSGi Bundle Repository

1	b	OSGi does not apply any constraints on the naming or storage structure of bundles. The OBR specification provides a service interface definition for querying bundle repositories and an XML file structure for repositories.
2	b	The OBR service is configured with access to a set of repositories, which it will inspect to find unfulfilled dependencies, and installs them.
3	c	Although answer b is not wrong, the same effect can be achieved in one operation using the `obr:deploy` command with the `-s` flag.
4	c	The Felix Maven Bundle Plugin attaches to the `deploy` phase goals and updates the repository XML file.
		Note: Answer b is not wrong, but it is not recommended because it is manual and thus error prone.

Chapter 7: The Bookshelf: First Stab

1	c	Review the section on bundle states in Chapter 1.
2	c	a and b; the activator's `start()` method is called when the bundle is starting and its `stop()` method is called when the bundle is stopping.

Chapter 11: How About a Graphical Interface?

1	b	The service locator pattern consists of requesting one or more instances of a service through a registrar component.
2	d	Although option c is the simplest one that is used in this book, all of the options accomplish the same effect.

Chapter 13: Improving the Graphics

1	a	A Web Container extends an Http Service with web application features. Refer to the beginning of this chapter.
2	b	JSPs, just like servlets, have access to a servlet context. In the context of OSGi, the context contains the `BundleContext` mapped to the `osgi-bundlecontext` attribute.

Index

Symbols

A

B

optional dependencies 228
web console, installing 231
web console, starting 231
productivity tools
about 276
build management system 276
IDE 276
Project Object Model. *See* **POM**
proxy configuration, property names
http.proxyAuth 269
http.proxyHost 269
http.proxyPort 269

R

refresh command 46, 47, 264
REGISTERED event 225
registerJsps() method 245
registerService method 95
regular expression (regex) 54
remaining pages, implementing
JSP imports 254
list book by category, implementing 253, 254
remote debugging configuration
Felix run script, editing 289
IDE, configuring 290-292
remote application, setting up 289
Remote Shell Service 23
removeBook method 83
repos refresh command 148, 151
Require-Bundle header 17
resolve command 45

S

scope commands, OBR
bundles, updating 107
obr:deploy 106
obr:info 105
obr:javadoc 107
obr:list 104
obr:refresh 107
obr:repos 103, 104
obr:source 107
scripts
about 153
book population script, creating 153-155

searchBooks method 83
search command
about 152
syntax signatures 138
Security Layer, OSGi framework 11
service data
persistence, adding 300
Service layer, OSGi framework 11
Service Locator pattern, IoC
about 159
framework 159
service reference, in JSP
authentication pages, completing 249, 250
obtaining 247, 248
service, using 251
SessionBean class, writing 248, 249
services, Felix project
dependency manager 22
file install 22
Gogo 22
iPOJO 23
Maven bundle plugin 23
Maven SCR plugin 23
OSGi Bundle Repository Service 23
Remote Shell Service 23
Shell Service 23
Shell TUI 23
Web Console Service 23
SessionBean class 248
set command 57
shared service registry 14, 15
Shell Service 23
Shell TUI 23
Smart Home market 9
source command 153
start() method 110
start command 45, 46
startedBook() method 118
start levels, OSGi framework
about 18
active start level 18, 19
implementing 20, 21
Start Level Service 18
stop command 45
storeBook method 83

Thank you for buying
OSGi and Apache Felix 3.0 Beginner's Guide

About Packt Publishing

Packt, pronounced 'packed', published its first book "*Mastering phpMyAdmin for Effective MySQL Management*" in April 2004 and subsequently continued to specialize in publishing highly focused books on specific technologies and solutions.

Our books and publications share the experiences of your fellow IT professionals in adapting and customizing today's systems, applications, and frameworks. Our solution based books give you the knowledge and power to customize the software and technologies you're using to get the job done. Packt books are more specific and less general than the IT books you have seen in the past. Our unique business model allows us to bring you more focused information, giving you more of what you need to know, and less of what you don't.

Packt is a modern, yet unique publishing company, which focuses on producing quality, cutting-edge books for communities of developers, administrators, and newbie's alike. For more information, please visit our website: www.packtpub.com.

About Packt Open Source

In 2010, Packt launched two new brands, Packt Open Source and Packt Enterprise, in order to continue its focus on specialization. This book is part of the Packt Open Source brand, home to books published on software built around Open Source licences, and offering information to anybody from advanced developers to budding web designers. The Open Source brand also runs Packt's Open Source Royalty Scheme, by which Packt gives a royalty to each Open Source project about whose software a book is sold.

Writing for Packt

We welcome all inquiries from people who are interested in authoring. Book proposals should be sent to author@packtpub.com. If your book idea is still at an early stage and you would like to discuss it first before writing a formal book proposal, contact us; one of our commissioning editors will get in touch with you.

We're not just looking for published authors; if you have strong technical skills but no writing experience, our experienced editors can help you develop a writing career, or simply get some additional reward for your expertise.

Apache OfBiz Cookbook

ISBN: 978-1-84719-918-8   Paperback: 300 pages

Over 60 simple but incredibly effective recipes for taking control of OFBiz

1. Optimize your OFBiz experience and save hours of frustration with this timesaving collection of practical recipes covering a wide range of OFBiz topics.

2. Get answers to the most commonly asked OFBiz questions in an easy-to-digest reference style of presentation.

3. Discover insights into OFBiz design, implementation, and best practices by exploring real-life solutions.

Apache MyFaces Trinidad 1.2: A Practical Guide

ISBN: 978-1-847196-08-8   Paperback: 292 pages

Develop JSF web applications with Trinidad and Seam

1. Develop rich client web applications using the most powerful integration of modern web technologies

2. Covers working with Seam security, internationalization using Seam, and more

3. Get well-versed in developing key areas of web applications

4. A step-by-step approach that will help you strengthen your understanding of all the major concepts

Please check **www.PacktPub.com** for information on our titles

Apache CXF Web Service Development

ISBN: 978-1-847195-40-1   Paperback: 336 pages

Develop and deploy SOAP and RESTful Web Services

1. Design and develop web services using contract-first and code-first approaches

2. Publish web services using various CXF frontends such as JAX-WS and Simple frontend

3. Invoke services by configuring CXF transports

4. Create custom interceptors by implementing advanced features such as CXF Interceptors, CXF Invokers, and CXF Features

5. The first practical guide on Apache CXF with real-world examples

Apache JMeter

ISBN: 978-1-847192-95-0   Paperback: 140 pages

A practical beginner's guide to automated testing and performance measurement for your websites

1. Test your website and measure its performance

2. Master the JMeter environment and learn all its features

3. Build test plan for measuring the performance

4. Step-by-step instructions and careful explanations

Please check **www.PacktPub.com** for information on our titles